ONS 聯合國

FS

NACIONES UNIDAS

НЫЕ НАЦИИ

DICTIONARY OF WORLD STAMPS

PHILATELIC ATLAS OF THE WORLD

KENNETH C LOGAN

HAMLYN

Designed and produced by
Autumn Publishing Limited,
10 Eastgate Square,
Chichester, West Sussex

Published by the Hamlyn Publishing Group Limited,
Bridge House, 69 London Road,
Twickenham, Middlesex, England.

First published 1986

Printed in Italy by G. Canale & C. S.p.A. Turin

ISBN 0-600-50309-7

CONTENTS

ABOUT THE AUTHOR

Kenneth Logan was born at Lausanne, Switzerland. After completing his education in that country, he came to London in 1936 and was articled as an apprentice in cartography with the London Geographical Institute, George Philip & Son Ltd. During the Second World War, having worked at the Ordnance Survey as a cartographer for some years, he served in the Army's Intelligence Corps, in Italy for a short time and then in Austria. Demobbed at the end of 1947, he worked for some years in the Colonial Office's Surveys Department, engaged on overseas mapping projects. In 1952 he transferred to the mapping branch of the War Office, later Ministry of Defence, during which time he travelled extensively in Western Europe. It was in that period that he became a keen philatelist and began work on the DICTIONARY OF WORLD STAMPS. With an ever-changing world, this book has taken several years to compile. Retired in 1982, he now lives in Selsey, Sussex.

INTRODUCTION

The history of postage stamps reflects in a remarkable way the history of the world for almost 150 years. Their pictorial display and inscriptions portray changes in the world political scene in an original and encyclopaedic form — changes in the sovereignty and status of many lands, from small islands to large countries, changes in territorial boundaries and country names. Some show the overthrow of governments and rulers, the rise of new ones, the forlorn hopes or the ambitions of others. War and peace, revolution and restoration, occupation, independence restored — all are reflected in the multitude of postage stamps issued since their introduction in 1840.

They also portray flashbacks to earlier historical events, to great men, and to achievements of the past. They portray in graphic form the ever-changing national and international political scene in the world from the early days of railways and steam packets to the age of jet planes and space travel.

The multiplicity of those changes, all of which are reflected in the large number of postage stamps issued, is not easy to illustrate graphically. But the maps on the following pages attempt to show the principal ones, by dividing the period since 1840 to the present into 'historical stages' during which the greatest amount of change took place.

HOW TO USE THE BOOK

The Dictionary section of the book lists in alphabetical order the inscriptions of stamp-issuing authorities and of countries and islands which issue stamps. Against each entry in the Dictionary, the map page to which it refers is shown in the left-hand column. Inscriptions which are in Greek or in Cyrillic (Bulgarian, Russian, Serbian) are transliterated in accordance with the British PCGN and American USBGN systems of transliteration. Names of countries are in accord with official British usage.

GREAT BRITAIN

The invention of the system of adhesive stamps for pre-paid postage in Great Britain in May 1840 is credited to Sir Rowland Hill (1795-1879). The advent of this Government-run facility for the conveyance of mail at a reasonable fee was soon to satisfy a universal need for communicating with absent family and friends, and to enhance the promotion of commerce and industry. This facility, begun in Great Britain and Colonies, soon spread abroad and countries in Europe and the rest of the world also introduced a similar system.

This expansion in international communication led to the need for founding a co-ordinating body concerned solely with postal matters and the international General Postal Union was formed in 1874, later re-named Universal Postal Union (UPU). Because Great Britain was the first country to introduce that system, it is the only state not to inscribe the country name on its postage stamps. The only way of identifying British stamps is by the effigy of the reigning Sovereign.

Early free franking marks.

Sir Rowland Hill (1795-1879) was credited with the invention of adhesive postage stamps in May 1840.

The Bath-London Mail Coach. The postmaster leans out of the window to pass up a bag of mail which is picked up without the mailcoach having to make a stop. Circa 1840.

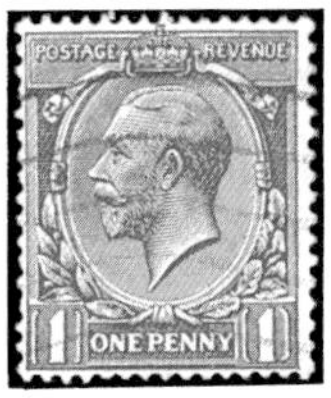

The above map shows the principal Mail Coach routes out of London. The Mail Coach service from London ended in 1846 when it was replaced by rail.

EUROPE Pre-1871

GERMANY — *United and forming the Second Reich, May 1871. States and local authorities issuing stamps pre-1871.*

Baden (Grand Duchy)
Bayern (Bavaria, Kingdom)
Bergedorf (town issues)
Braunschweig (Brunswick, Duchy)
Bremen (Hanseatic town)
Hamburg (Hanseatic town)
Hannover (Kingdom)
Heligoland (British and German issues)
Lübeck (Hanseatic town)
Mecklenburg-Schwerin (Grand Duchy)
Mecklenburg-Strelitz (Grand Duchy)
Norddeutscher Post bezirk (North German Confederation Postal Administration)
Oldenburg (Grand Duchy)
Preussen (Prussia, Kingdom)
Sachsen (Saxony, Kingdom)
Schleswig (Duchy)
Schleswig-Holstein (Duchies)
Thurn & Taxis (Principality)
Württemberg (Kingdom)

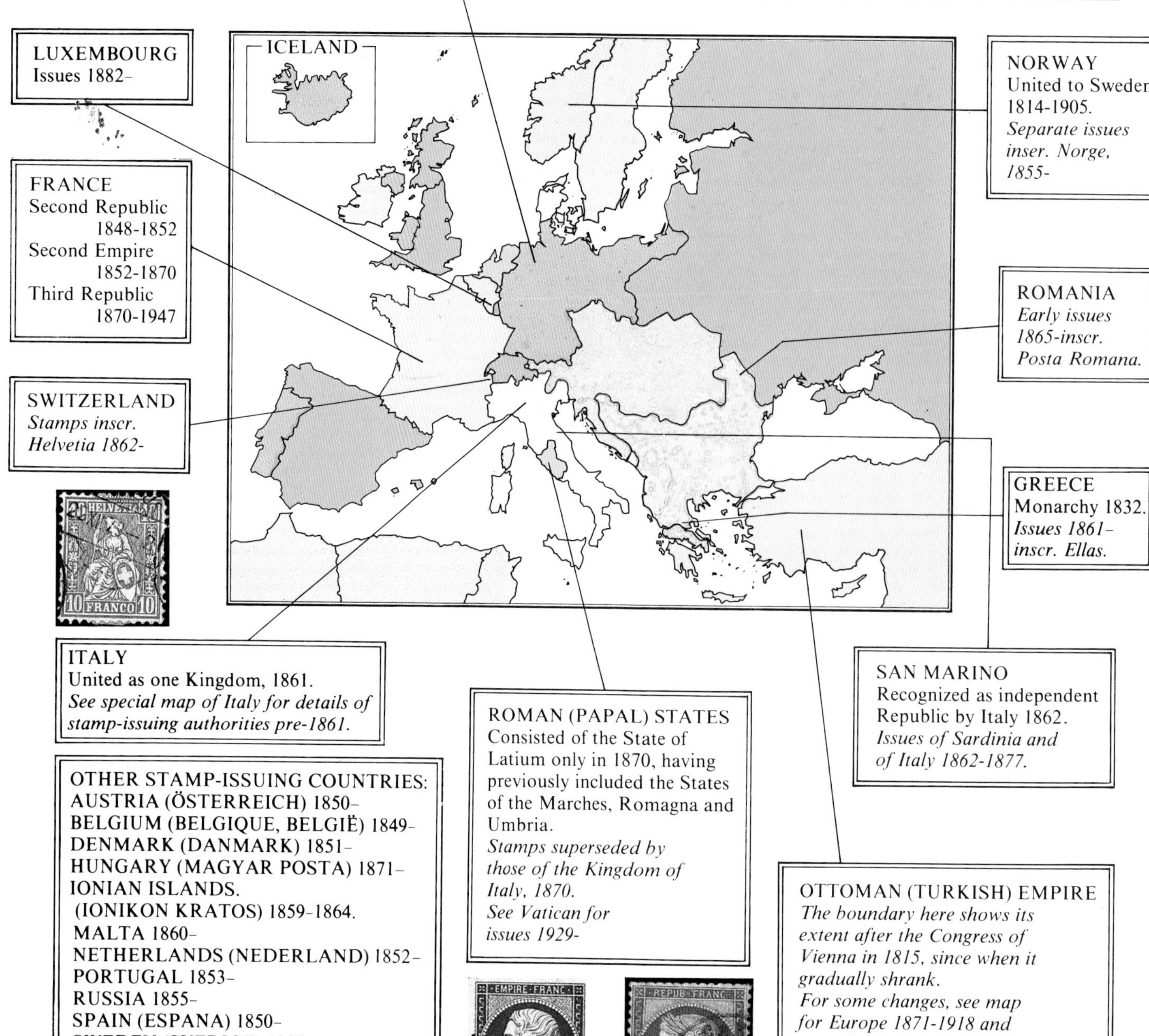

LUXEMBOURG
Issues 1882–

FRANCE
Second Republic 1848-1852
Second Empire 1852-1870
Third Republic 1870-1947

SWITZERLAND
Stamps inscr. Helvetia 1862-

NORWAY
United to Sweden 1814-1905.
Separate issues inscr. Norge, 1855-

ROMANIA
Early issues 1865-inscr. Posta Romana.

GREECE
Monarchy 1832.
Issues 1861– inscr. Ellas.

ITALY
United as one Kingdom, 1861.
See special map of Italy for details of stamp-issuing authorities pre-1861.

ROMAN (PAPAL) STATES
Consisted of the State of Latium only in 1870, having previously included the States of the Marches, Romagna and Umbria.
Stamps superseded by those of the Kingdom of Italy, 1870.
See Vatican for issues 1929-

SAN MARINO
Recognized as independent Republic by Italy 1862.
Issues of Sardinia and of Italy 1862-1877.

OTTOMAN (TURKISH) EMPIRE
The boundary here shows its extent after the Congress of Vienna in 1815, since when it gradually shrank.
For some changes, see map for Europe 1871-1918 and special map of the Empire.

OTHER STAMP-ISSUING COUNTRIES:
AUSTRIA (ÖSTERREICH) 1850–
BELGIUM (BELGIQUE, BELGIË) 1849–
DENMARK (DANMARK) 1851–
HUNGARY (MAGYAR POSTA) 1871–
IONIAN ISLANDS.
(IONIKON KRATOS) 1859-1864.
MALTA 1860–
NETHERLANDS (NEDERLAND) 1852–
PORTUGAL 1853–
RUSSIA 1855–
SPAIN (ESPANA) 1850–
SWEDEN (SVERIGE) 1855–

EUROPE 1871-1918

GERMANY
United in May 1871, as the Second Reich.
Stamps inscr. Reichspost 1872-

FINLAND
Grand Duchy under Russian rule till Dec. 1917, when it became an independent Republic.
Republic issues 1917-, inscr. Suomi.

ROMANIA
With the union of Moldavia and Wallachia 1858/61, became a Principality in the Ottoman Empire, and an independent Kingdom in 1881.

NORWAY
United to Sweden 1814, independent Kingdom 1905.

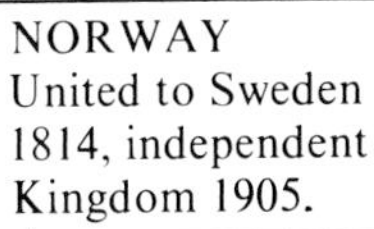

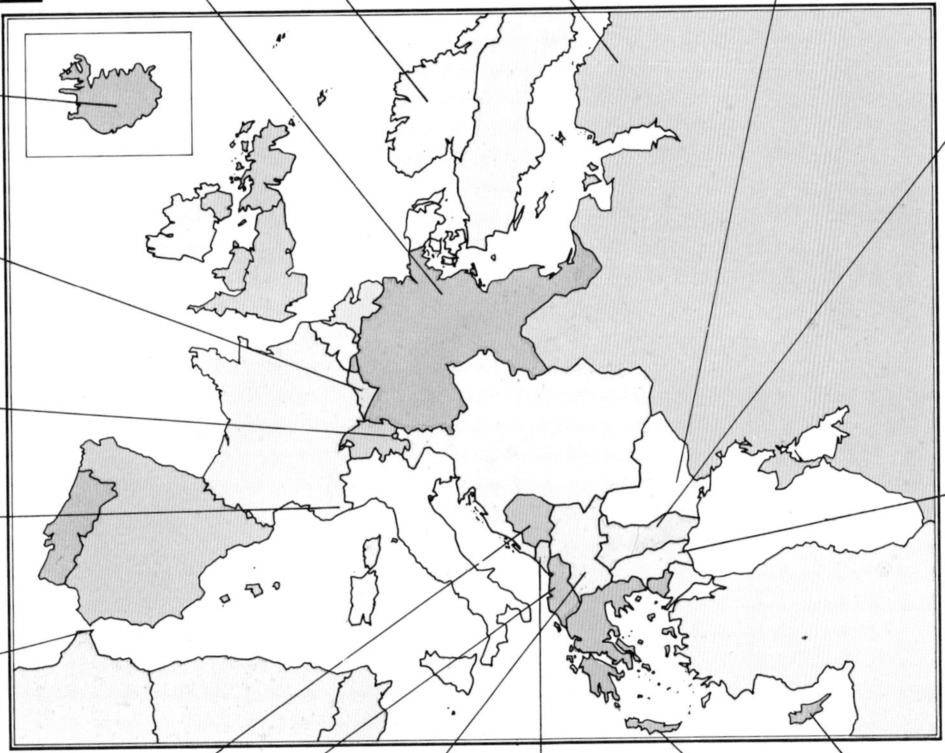

ICELAND
Under Danish rule till 1944.
Separate issues inscr. Island 1873-

ALSACE-LORRAINE
(France)
Annexed to Germany 1871-1918.

LIECHTENSTEIN
Issues 1912-

MONACO
Issues 1885-

GIBRALTAR
British Territory 1713, now a British Dependent Territory.
Issues 1886–

BULGARIA
Principality under Turkish rule 1878, enlarged 1885 by the union of Eastern Roumelia, Kingdom in 1908.
Issues 1879-

EASTERN ROUMELIA
Autonomous Province of the Ottoman Empire 1878, became part of Bulgaria 1885 and named South Bulgaria.
Issues inscr. Roumélie Orientale or R.O. 1880-1884.

CYPRUS
British in 1878, previously in the Ottoman Empire
Issues 1880-

BOSNIA-HERZEGOVINA
Previsously Turkish, occupied by Austria-Hungary in 1878, to which it was annexed 1908.
Austrian PO issues 1879-1918.

ALBANIA
Independent from the Ottoman Empire 1912/13, Principality 1914 (Kingdom 1928).
Issues 1913-

SERBIA
Principality in the Ottoman Empire 1817 1817, independent Kingdom 1882. Part of the Kingdom of the Serbs, Croats and Slovenes, 1918.
Principality and Kingdom issues 1874-1914.

MONTENEGRO
Principality 1852 under Turkish rule, independent 1878, Kingdom 1910, united to Serbia 1918 as part of the Kingdom of Yugoslavia.
Principality and Kingdom issues 1874-1914.

CRETE
Autonomous under Turkish rule until 1898, annexed to Greece 1913.
Greek issues 1900-1910.
Austrian issues 1903-1914.
British issues 1898-1899.
French issues 1902-1903.
Italian issues 1900-1911.
(La Canea)
Russian issues 1899.

EUROPE 1919–1945

(Boundaries are as in 1937. See also special maps of Europe: Local Sovereignty changes 1871–1954 on pages 16–17, and Plebiscites on pages 18–19.)

ICELAND
Under Danish rule 1814–1918, autonomous State in union with Denmark 1918–1944, independent Republic May 1944.
Republic issues inscr. Island 1944–

DANZIG
Free City 1920–1939, became Polish city of Gdansk 1945.
Free City issues 1920–1939. Polish PO issues 1925–1939.

ESTONIA, LATVIA, LITHUANIA
Formerly part of Russia, independent Republics 1918, under Russian administration 1940, German occupation 1941–1944. Annexed to the USSR end of 1944 and Republics of the USSR since then.

POLAND
Independent Republic 1918, divided between Germany and the USSR and occupied by these 1939–1941. Restored as an independent Republic 1944.
Republic issues 1918–1939, and 1944–, inscr. Poczta Polska or Polska.

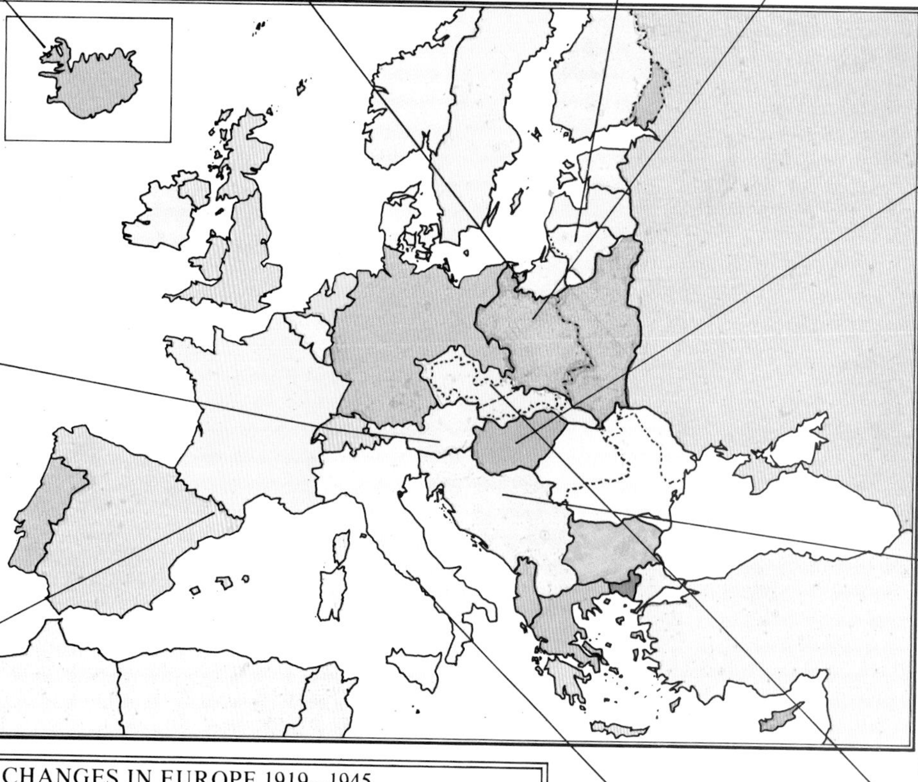

HUNGARY
Republic Nov. 1918, after political upheavals became a Regency 1920–1944. Republic 1945/46.
Issues inscr. Magyar Posta, or Magyarorszag.

AUSTRIA
Republic Nov. 1918.
Issues 1918–1938.
Annexed to Germany 1938–1945.
German stamps used during that period
Independence restored May 1945.
Republic issues, inscr. Österreich 1945–

YUGOSLAVIA
Kindom of the Serbs, Croats and Slovenes established 1918 by the union of Serbia, Croatia, Slovenia, Bosnia–Herzegovina and Montenegro. Name of State changed to Yugoslavia in 1929.
Issues with various inscr., some in Cyrillic 1918–

ANDORRA
Spanish PO issues 1928–
French PO issues 1931–

MAIN TERRITORIAL CHANGES IN EUROPE 1919–1945

1. Eastern Karelia – Finnish administration 1940–1947. To USSR 1947.
2. Memel – to Lithuania 1923–1939. To Germany 1939–1944. To USSR 1944.
3. Danzig – Free City 1920–1939. To Poland (Gdansk) 1945.
4. A,B – Poland – German – Soviet division line 1939–1941.
5. Sudetenland – To Germany 1938–1945. Return to Czechoslovakia 1945.
6. Bohemia and Moravia – German 'Protectorate' 1939–1945. Return to Czechoslovakia 1945.
7. Slovakia – 'Autonomous' State under German rule 1939–1945. Return to Czechoslovakia 1945.
8. Austria Annexed to Germany 1938–1945.
9. Southern Czechoslovakia – To Hungary 1938–1945. Return to Czechoslovakia 1945.
10. Carpatho–Ukraine – To Hungary 1939–1945. To USSR 1945.
11. Transylvania – To Romania 1918/20.
12. South Galicia – To Romania 1918/20.
13. Bessarabia – To Rumania 1918/20. To USSR 1940–1941 (part of the Soviet Moldavskaya SSR 1947).
14. Dobrogea strip – To Bulgaria 1940.
15. Thracia – To Greece 1919/20.

VATICAN CITY
Sovereign State 1929.
Issues inscr. Poste Vaticane 1929–

CZECHOSLOVAKIA
Republic 1918/19. Region of Sudetenland annexed to Germany 1938–1945. Bohemia and Moravia occupied by Germany as a 'Protectorate' 1939–1945.
Issues inscr. Böhmen und Mähren, and Čechy a Morava 1939–1945.
Slovakia an 'independent State' under German rule.
Issues inscr. Slovensko 1939–1945.
Republic restored 1945.

EUROPE from 1945

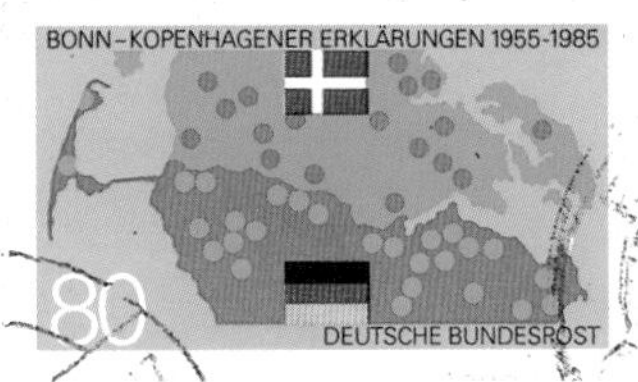

FEDERAL REPUBLIC OF GERMANY
Issues inscr. Bundesrepublik Deutschland 1949–

GERMAN DEMOCRATIC REPUBLIC
Issues inscr. Deutsche Demokratische Republik (DDR) 1949–

EASTERN KARELIA
Finnish administration 1940–1947. To USSR 1947.
Finnish issues 1940–1947.

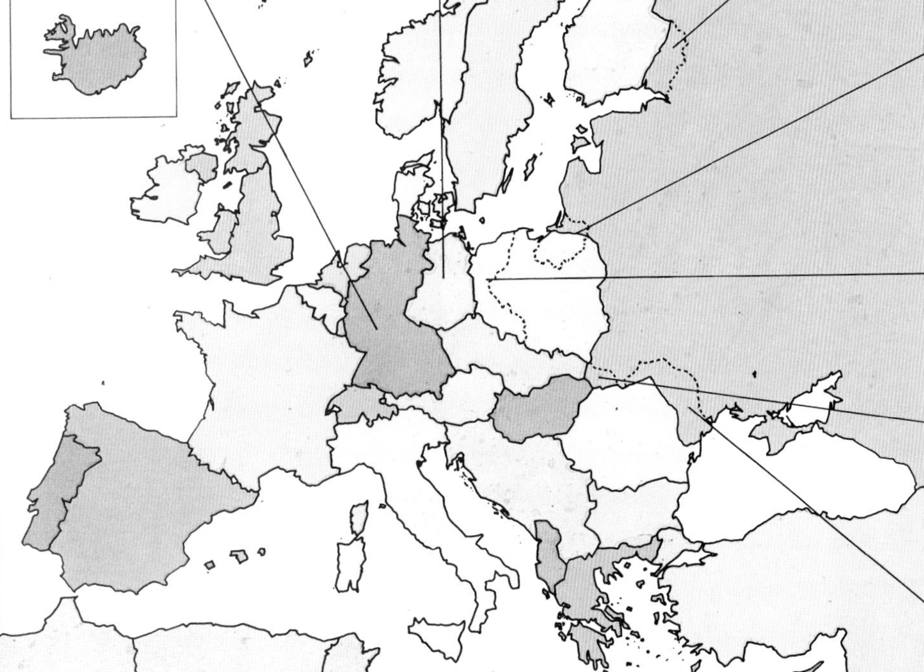

EAST PRUSSIA
Partitioned between Poland and the USSR 1945.

POLAND
Former eastern part of Germany (Pomerania and Silesia) annexed to Poland 1945.

CARPATHO-UKRAINE
to USSR 1945.

BESSARABIA
To USSR 1947 and part of the Moldavskaya SSR.

LOCAL SOVEREIGNTY CHANGES 1871-1954

Those local sovereignty changes are shown which have had an effect on philately and for which some clarification of political events might be useful. They exclude both the "Plebiscite" areas depicted on pages 18-19 and the more important changes shown on the other maps of Europe. Boundaries here are depicted as after 1945.

HELIGOLAND, HELGOLAND
Danish possession till 1814, British Colony 1814 to 1890.
In Aug. 1890, given to Germany in exchange for the Island of Zanzibar and other African territories. *Hamburg Postal Agency issues 1859-1867. British issues 1867-1890. Germany Reichspost issues 1890-* Used as British RAF bombing target after WWII, island returned to Germany (FRG) 1 Mar. 1952.

SUDETENLAND (Czechoslovakia)
Territory annexed to Germany Oct. 1938, restored to Czech sovereignty 1945.
General German stamp issues used 1938-1945.
Local issues made by certain towns 1938, the German names of which are: Asch, Aussig, Karlsbad, Konstantinsbad, Niklasdorf, Reichenberg-Maffersdorf, and Rumburg.

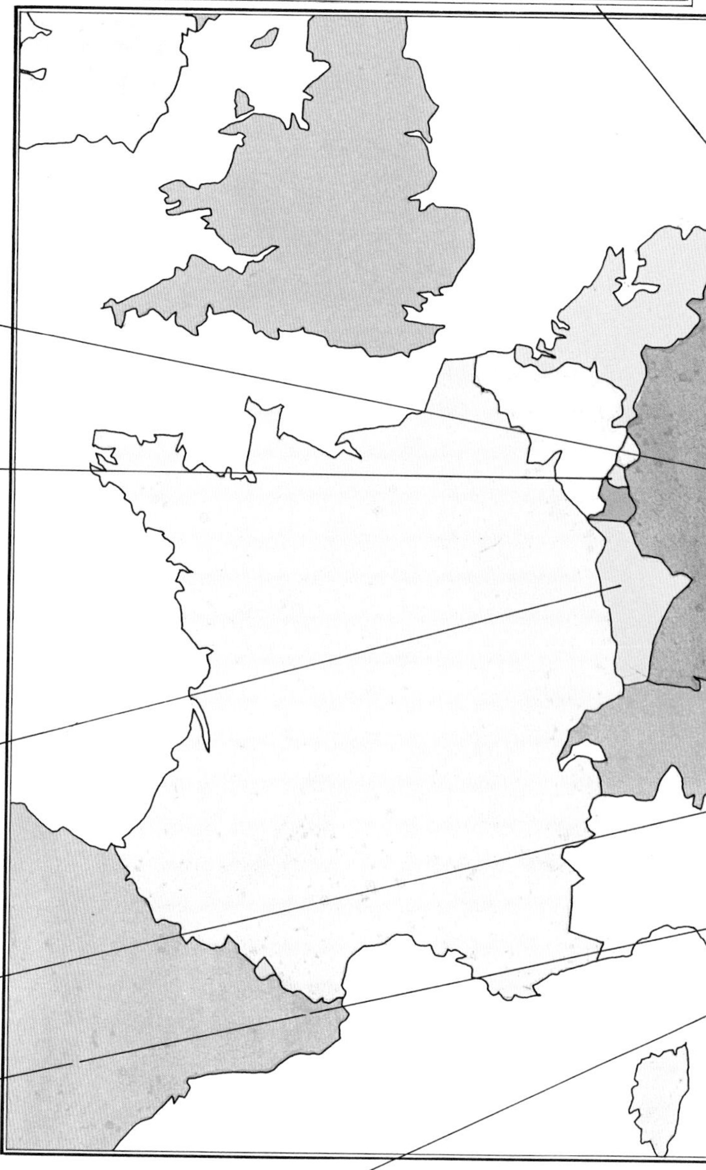

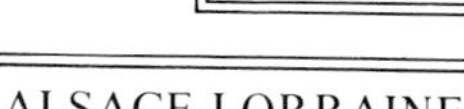

EUPEN, and MALMÉDY
Territory annexed to Belgium 1920.
Belgian occupation of Germany issues 1920-1921.

ALSACE-LORRAINE
To France up to 1871, annexed to Germany 1871-1918, and 1940-1945.
Return to French sovereignty 1945.
German issues (Norddeutscher Postbezirk) 1871.
German issues 1940-1941 (inscr. Elsass, and Lothringen; special issue inscr. Saverne 1944).

VENETIA TRIDENTINA
Formerly part of Austria (Südtirol = South Tyrol), ceded to Italy 1919/20.
Italian issues 1918 (some inscr. Trentino).

TRIESTE
To Austria up to 1918, to Italy 1919/20.
Italian issues 1918-1919 (some inscr. Venezia Giulia).
Yugoslav occupation provisional issues 1945 (some inscr. Trst, Istra, etc).
Free Territory under Allied Military Govt. 1947-1954.
Zone A issues 1947-1954 (inscr. AMG FTT = Allied Mil. Govt. Free Territory of Trieste).
Zone B issues, Yugoslav Military Govt. 1948-1954 (inscr. STT VUJA or ST Trsta VUJA).
City to Italy 1954.

VENEZIA GIULIA & ISTRIA
To Italy 1919/20, formerly in Austria (Julische Venetien).
Italian issues for areas acquired from Austria 1918-1919 (some inscr. Trieste).
Allied Military Govt. issues 1945-1947 (inscr. AMG VG).
Yugoslav occupation provisional issues 1945 (some inscr. Istra, Trst, etc).
Yugoslav Military Govt. issues 1945-1947 (some inscr. Istria, and VUJA = Vojna Uprava Jugoslovenske Armije).
Province of Istria ceded to Yugoslavia 1947.
Yugoslav issues 1948-1954 (inscr. STT VUJA, or ST Trsta VUJA).

DANZIG, GDANSK
Formerly part of Germany, an independent Free City Jan.1920-Sep.1939. *Free City issues 1920-1939, some inscr. Freie Stadt Danzig. Issues of Polish PO in Danzig 1925-1939.*
To Germany 1 Sep. 1939-1945.
Part of Poland from 1945, city named GDANSK.

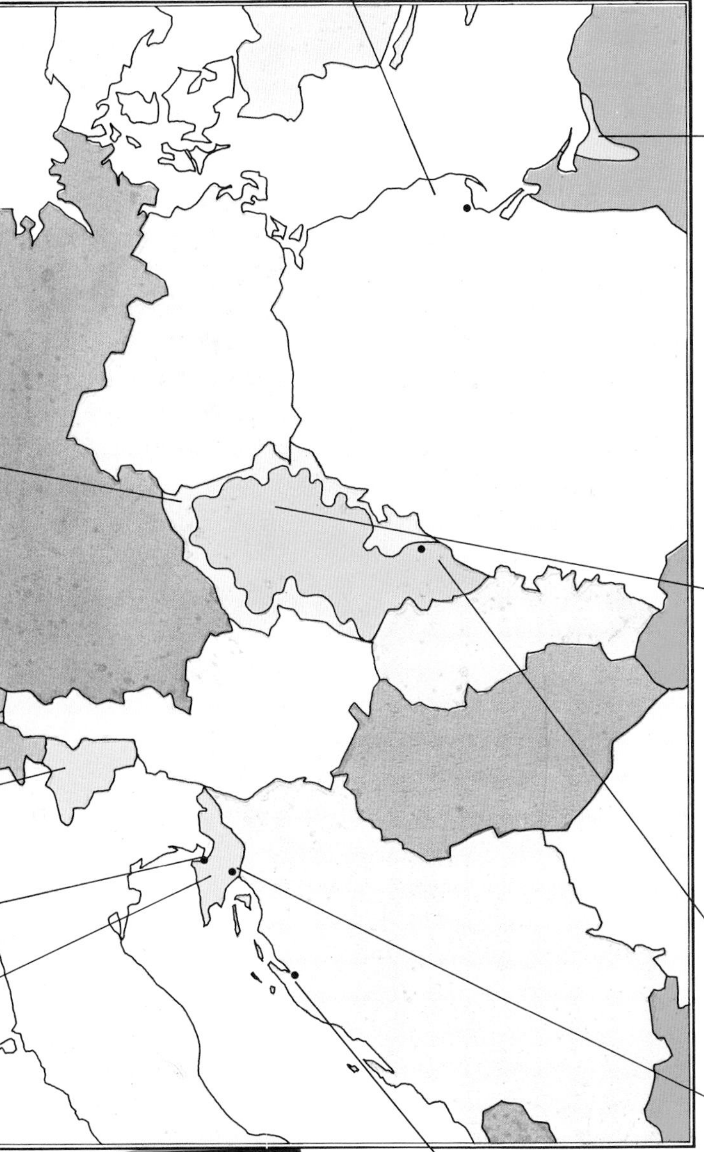

MEMEL
Formerly part of Germany (East Prussia), came under international control 1919-1923, with French administration.
French Mandate issues 1920-1922, (opr. on French and German stamps, inscr. Memel or Memelgebiet).
Incorporated into Lithuania 1923 and named KLAIPEDA.
Lithuanian issues (Klaipeda) 1923-1925. (Lithuanian definitives used 1925-1939). Local German issues 1939, inscr. Memelland.
Part of Germany again, Mar. 1939.
Incorporated into the USSR 1945 in the new LITOVSKAYA SSR (formerly Lithuania).

BÖHMEN und MÄHREN (Bohemia and Moravia)
Part of Czechoslovakia 1919-1939, German 'Protectorate' 1939-1945.
German issues 1939-1945 (with German inscr. Böhmen und Mähren, and Czech inscr. Čechy a Morava).
Local German issue for prison camp of THERESIENSTADT, 1943 (Czech town of Terezin).
Return to Czech sovereignty 1945.

MÄHRISCH-OSTRAU
(Moravska-Ostrava in Moravia, Czechoslavakia).
German occupation Mar. 1939.
Local German issue 1939 with political slogan inscr. 'Wir sind frei' = 'We are free'.

ZARA, ZADAR
Formerly Austrian, to Italy 1919-1920 and 1943-1947.
German occupation issues 1943-1944.
Ceded to Yugoslavia 1947, town named ZADAR.

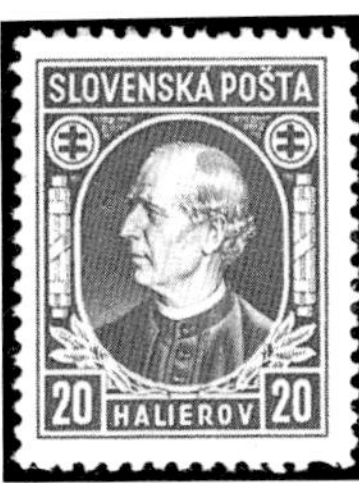

FIUME, RIJEKA
Formerly Austrian.
Allied occupation issues 1918-1919.
Free City 1919-1924.
Free City issues 1919-1924.
Annexed to Italy 1924.
Italian issues 1924.
Italian occupation issues 1941 (opr. Fiume, and Kupa).
Yugoslav occupation issues 1945.
City ceded to Yugoslavia Feb. 1947, and named RIJEKA.

PLEBISCITES 1920-1955

SAAR, SARRE, SAARGEBIET
French administration 1919-1935.
Plebiscite 1934/35, united to Germany 1935-1945.
Issues under French administration 1920-1935.
Plebiscite issues 1934.
French occupation issues 1945-1947.
Economic attachment to France 1947-1956.
Special issues 1947-1956.
Plebiscite 1955.
Plebiscite issues 1955.
Incorporation into Germany, FRG, 1.1.1957.
German issues inscr. SAARLAND 1957-1959.
(Issues of FRG Bundespost 1959-)

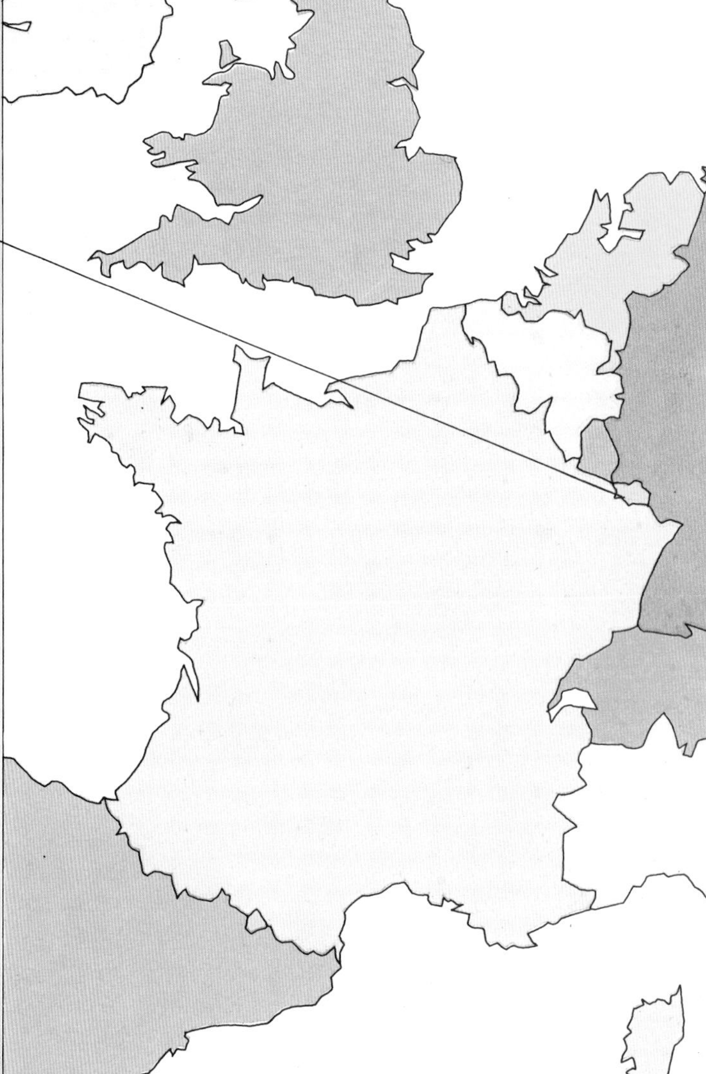

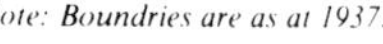
Note: Boundries are as at 1937.

Sarre

SCHLESWIG, SLESVIG
(NORTH SCHLESWIG)
Plebiscite March 1920, the northern part becoming Danish, the southern part German.
Plebiscite issues 1920.

MARIENWERDER (East Prussia)
Plebiscite July 1920, territory remained part of Germany.
Plebiscite issues 1920.
To Poland 1945, town named KWIDZYN.

ALLENSTEIN, OLSZTYN
Plebiscite July 1920, territory remained part of Germany (East Prussia).
Plebiscite issues 1920.
Town now part of Poland, named OLSZTYN.

OBERSCHLESIEN, HAUTE SILESIE, GORNY SLASK (UPPER SILESIA)
Plebiscite March 1921, the western part remained part of Germany, the eastern sector annexed to Poland.
Plebiscite and International Commission issues 1920-1922.

KÄRNTEN (CARINTHIA, Yugosl.KORUŠKA)
Plebiscite Oct. 1920, when southern Carinthia remained part of Austria.
Plebiscite issues 1920:
Austrian, some opr. KÄRNTEN ABSTIMMUNG
Yugoslav (Slovenia), opr. KGCA.

ITALY up to 1920

Italy was united as one Kingdom in 1861 and stamp issues of the Kingdom began in 1862, with the exception of the Roman (Papal) States (1870). Before that date, the following component States and Duchies issued their own stamps:
NAPLES (Kingdom, later Province). MODENA (Duchy, later Provisional Govt.) PARMA later Provisional Govt). ROMAGNA. ROMAN (Papal or Church) States. SARDINIA (Kingdom). SICILY (Kingdom. With Naples, formed the Kingdom of the Two Sicilies). TUSCANY (Grand Duchy, later Provisional Govt).

LOMBARDY–VENETIA
Austrian Italy, consisted of (1) Lombardy, and (2) Venetia, incorporated in Italy 1859 and 1866 respectively.
Issues 1850–1864 with German inscr. K.K. Poststempel.

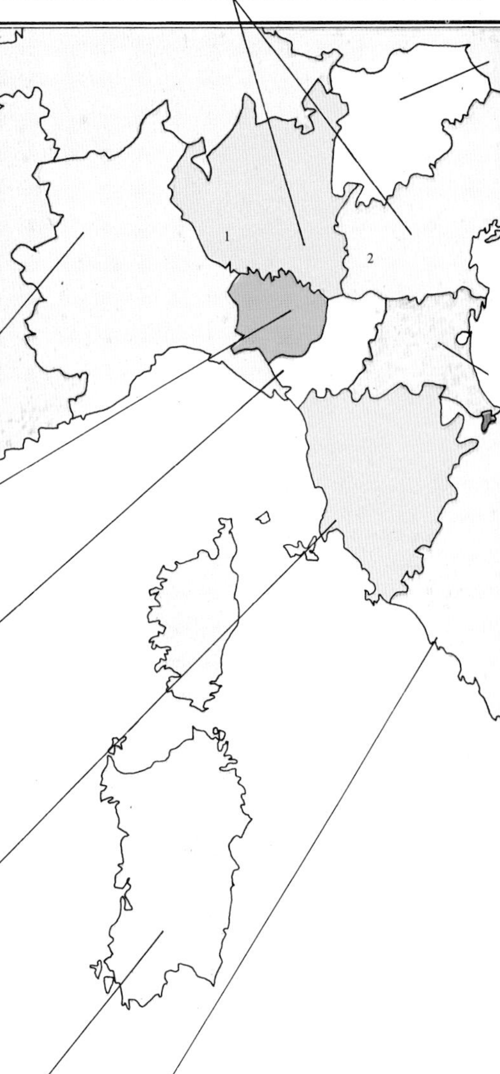

PIEMONTE
Part of the Kingdom of Sardinia up to 1861.

PARMA
Duchy issues 1852–1859.
Provisional Govt. issues 1859–1860.
Superseded by issues of Sardinia 1860, and by those of Italy in 1862.

MODENA
Duchy issues 1852–1859.
Province issues 1859–1860.
Superseded 1860 by stamps of Sardinia, and by those of Italy in 1862.

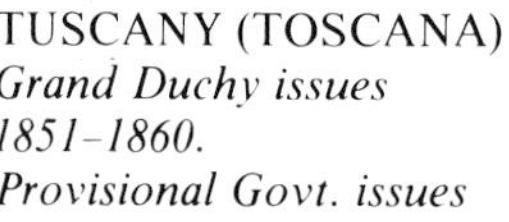

TUSCANY (TOSCANA)
Grand Duchy issues 1851–1860.
Provisional Govt. issues 1860–1861.
Superseded in 1862 by stamps of Italy.

SARDINIA
The Kingdom consisted of Sardinia and Piemonte (also Savoy up to 1860).
Kingdom issues 1851–1862.
Superseded by Italy issues in 1862.

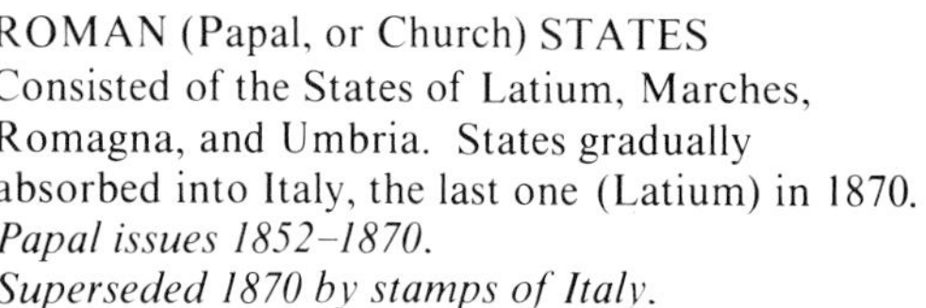

ROMAN (Papal, or Church) STATES
Consisted of the States of Latium, Marches, Romagna, and Umbria. States gradually absorbed into Italy, the last one (Latium) in 1870.
Papal issues 1852–1870.
Superseded 1870 by stamps of Italy.

SOUTH TYROL
(Venetia–Tridentina)–Part of Austria (Südtirol) till 1919/20, when annexed to Italy.

SAN MARINO
Independent Republic 1862.
Issues of Sardinia, and later of Italy, with various inscr. 1862 – 1877.
Independent issues 1877

ISTRIA and part of VENETIA GIULIA– Part of Austria (Julische Venetien) until 1919/20, when annexed to Italy.
Italian issues 1918–1919.
(some inscr. Trieste).

FIUME
Free City 1920–1924.
Allied occupation issues 1918–1919.
Free City issues 1919–1924.
(To Yugoslavia 1947 and named Rijeka).

ROMAGNA
A Roman (Papal) State till 1860.
Issues of the Roman (Papal) States 1852–1859.
Separate provisional issues 1859–1860.
Superseded 1860 by stamps of Sardinia, and by issues of Italy in 1862.

ZARA
Annexed to Italy 1919/20. (To Yugoslavia 1947, town named Zadar).

SICILY
Together with the Kingdom of Naples, formed the Kingdom of the Two Sicilies. Absorbed in the Kingdom of Italy, 1861.
Issues of Naples (Kingdom, later Province) 1858–1862.
Issues of Sicily 1859–1862.
Superseded 1862 by Italy issues.

OTTOMAN EMPIRE UP TO 1915 (WITH THE LEVANT)

The furthest extent of the Empire shown here is as it was after the Congress of Vienna in 1815. The next main changes took place in 1878 following the Russo-Turkish war of 1877-78, as a result of which Romania, Serbia and Montenegro became independent. Bulgaria remained a Principality tributary to Turkey but lost Macedonia and Eastern Roumelia, which became autonomous. Russia retained Bessarabia, Cyprus was ceded to Great Britain and Austria was given administrative authority over Bosnia and Herzegovina. The period 1908-1913 marked the next important stages in the shrinking Empire, with numerous political upheavals and the two Balkan Wars of 1912 and 1913. These events changed the map of the Balkans considerably until, in 1915, the boundaries of the Ottoman Empire in Europe were virtually the same as those of modern Turkey. The Levant region was lost to Turkey after the World War of 1914-1918.
The numerous changes are reflected in the postage stamps issued by the various authorities during these decades.

OTTOMAN EMPIRE
Turkish issues 1863-1921 (some with French inscr. "Empire Ottoman" or "Postes Ottomanes").
POs of other countries also issued stamps:
Austria, France, Germany, Great Britain, Italy, Romania, Russia.

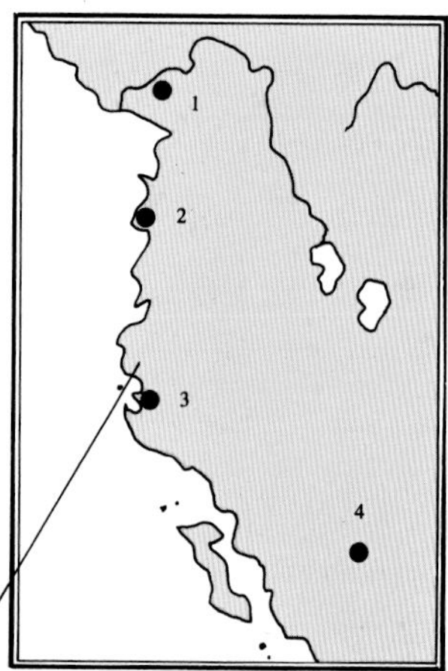

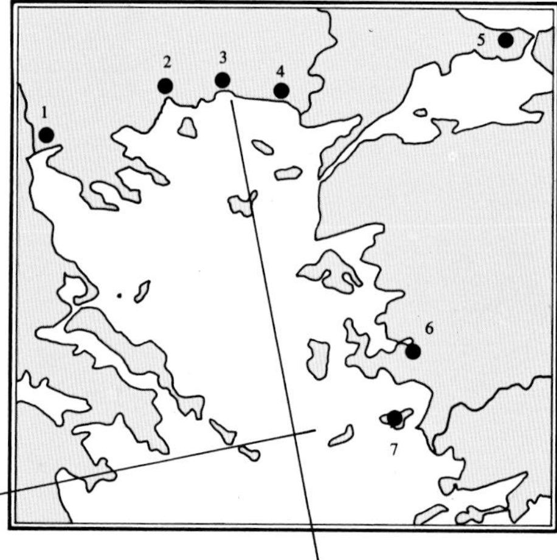

ALBANIA
Independent from Turkish rule 1912/13, Principality 1914. (Kingdom 1928).
Italian POs at:
1. *Scutari di Albania (Shkodra).*
2. *Durazzo (Durrës).*
3. *Valona (Vlora).*
4. *Janina (Ioannina, now Greece).*

AEGEAN (DODECANESE) ISLANDS
Formerly Turkish, occupied by Italy 1912, ceded to Italy by Turkey 1920. (restored to Greece 1947).
Italian issues 1912-1944.

FOREIGN POs at:
1. *Salonica (Thessaloniki) - Italian PO.*
2. *Cavalle (Kavalla) - French PO.*
3. *Dédéagh (Alexandroupolis) - French PO.*
4. *Port-Lagos (Porto Lago) - French PO.*
5. *Constantinople (Istanbul) - German and Italian POs.*
6. *Smyrna (Izmir) - German and Italian POs.*
7. *Vathy (Vathi, on island of Samos) - French PO (to Greece 1913).*

BOSNIA-HERZEGOVINA
Austrian occupation 1878, annexed to Austria 1908. (Part of Yugoslavia 1918).
Austrian PO issues 1879-1918.

SERBIA
Independent Kingdom 1882, formerly Principality in the Ottoman Empire.
Principality and Kingdom issues 1866-1918.

ROMANIA
Tributary Principality in the Ottoman Empire by the union of Moldavia and Wallachia, 1858/61. Independent Kingdom 1881.

THRACE (Thraki, Greece)
Region part of Bulgaria 1913 (annexed to Greece 1919/20).
Issues of temporary autonomous Govt. of Western Thrace 1913. (Greek occupation issues 1920).

MONTENEGRO
Independent 1878, Kingdom 1910. (United to Serbia 1918 as part of Yugoslavia).
Principality and Kingdom issues 1874-1914.

BULGARIA and EASTERN ROUMELIA
United 1885, Principality in the Ottoman Empire, independent Kingdom 1908.

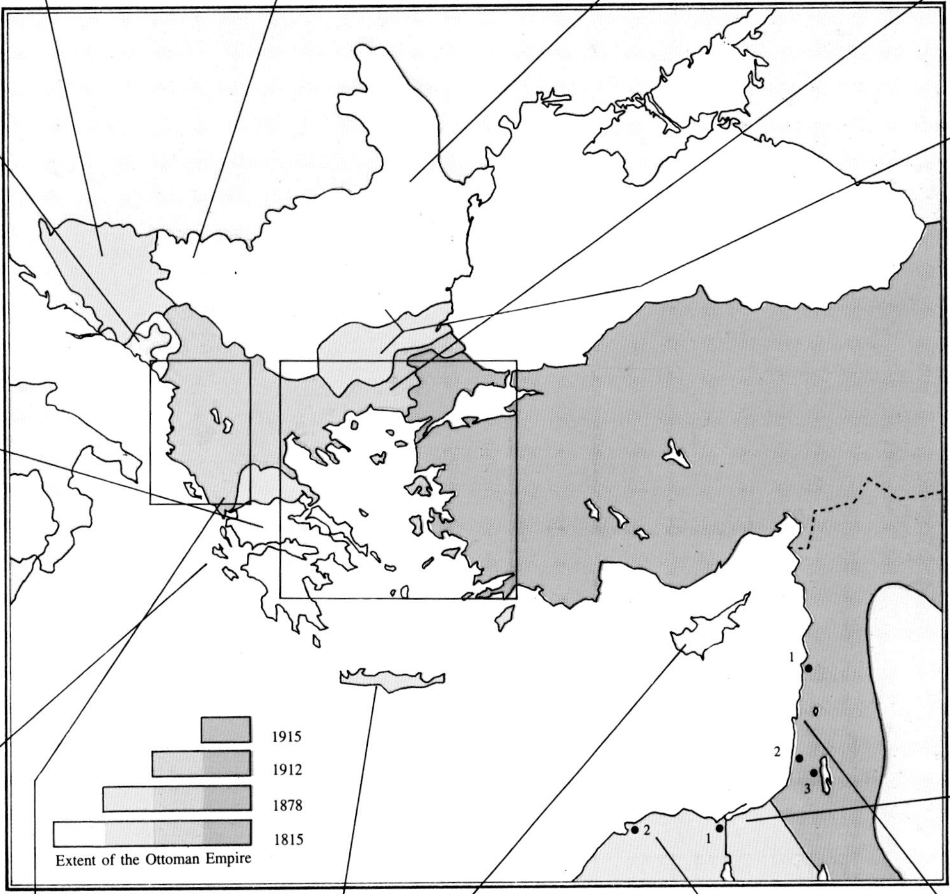

GREECE
Monarchy 1832.
Issues 1861-, inscr. Ellas.

IONIAN ISLANDS
Republic under British protection 1815-1863, ceded to Greece 1864.
British issues 1859-1864.

SUEZ CANAL
Opened in 1869
Issues of Suez Canal Company (Canal Maritime de Suez) 1868.

1915
1912
1878
1815
Extent of the Ottoman Empire

THESSALY
(Thessalia, Greece)
Formerly under Turkish rule, to Greece 1881.
Turkish occupation issues (Greek-Turkish war) 1898.

CYPRUS
In the Ottoman Empire till 1878, when it became British.
British issues 1880-1960.

EGYPT
Vice regency within the Ottoman Empire, occupied by the British 1882.
Issues of French POs at:
1. Port Said and
2. Alexandria 1899-1930.

SYRIA and PALESTINE
1. Beirut - German PO.
2. Jaffa (Tel Aviv-Yafo) - German PO.
3. Jerusalem - German and Italian POs.

CRETE
Under Turkish rule until 1898, joint administration by France, Great Britain, Italy and Russia 1898-1913, annexed to Greece 1913.
Issues by POs of Austria, France, Great Britain, Greece, Italy and Russia.

UNITED STATES OF AMERICA UP TO 1865

The USA Congress established new postal rates of 5c and 10c in 1845, as a result of which the Postmaster of New York issued his own adhesive stamps. Other Postmasters in other cities did likewise and used either handstamps or adhesive "Provisional" stamps. These are listed below. They were superseded in 1847 by the first "Definitives" issued by the Federal Government.

Postmaster's Provisional issues 1845 – 1847:

Alexandria	(Va.)	New Haven	(Ct.)
Annapolis	(Md.)	New York	(N.Y.)
Boscawen	(N.H.)	Providence	(R.I.)
Brattleboro	(Vt.)	St. Louis	(Miss.)
Lockport	(N.Y.)	Tuscumbia	(Ala.)
Millbury	(Mass.)		

U.S.A. – General issues 1847 –
(inscr. US Post Office
or US Postage)

"PONY EXPRESS"
Inaugurated by the US Government in 1860, this horse-ridden mail system ran from St. Joseph (Missouri) to the Pacific coast near San Francisco, and was superseded by the telegraph some 2 years later. Mail took some 10 days to convey (but it took only just over 7½ days to transmit President Abraham Lincoln's Inaugural Address across the continent).

The above map includes the present-day boundaries of the Westernmost states

CONFEDERATE STATES OF AMERICA
(Civil War 1861–1865)

Following the establishment of a Southern Congress early in 1861 in opposition to that of the Federal Union in Washington, a state of civil war existed in May 1861 between The Union and the seceding Confederate States. As a result, Postmasters in some 100 towns in the South issued "Provisional" stamps of their own for a short period, notably the cities of Mobile (Alabama) and New Orleans (Louisiana). Other cities known to have issued "Provisionals" are listed below. These were superseded by regular issues of the Confederate States later in 1861.

Postmaster's Provisional issues 1861 (selection):

Athens	(Georgia)	Lynchburg	(Va.)
Baton Rouge	(Louisiana)	Macon	(Georgia)
Beaumont	(Texas)	Madison	(Florida)
Bridgeville	(Alabama)	Marion	(Va.)
Charleston	(S. Carolina)	Memphis	(Tennessee)
Danville	(Va.)	Mobile	(Alabama)
Emory	(Va.)	Nashville	(Tennessee)
Frederickburg	(Va.)	New Orleans	(Louisana)
Goliad	(Texas)	New Smyrna	(Florida)
Gonzales	(Texas)	Petersburg	(Va.)
Greenville	(Alabama)	Pittsylvania	(Va.)
Greenwood	(Va.)	Pleasant Shade	(Va.)
Grove Hill	(Alabama)	Rheatown	(Tennessee)
Helena	(Texas)	Salem	(Va.)
Independence	(Texas)	Spartanburg	(S.Carolina)
Jetersville	(Va.)	Tellico Plains	(Tennessee)
Knoxville	(Tennessee)	Uniontown	(Tennessee)
Lenoir	(N.Carolina)	Unionville	(S. Carolina)
Livingston	(Alabama)	Victoria	(Texas)

General issues 1861–1864.

UNITED STATES OF AMERICA FROM 1865

ALASKA
Formerly under Russian administration, became a possession of the USA in 1867, and admitted as the 49th. State of the USA in 1959.

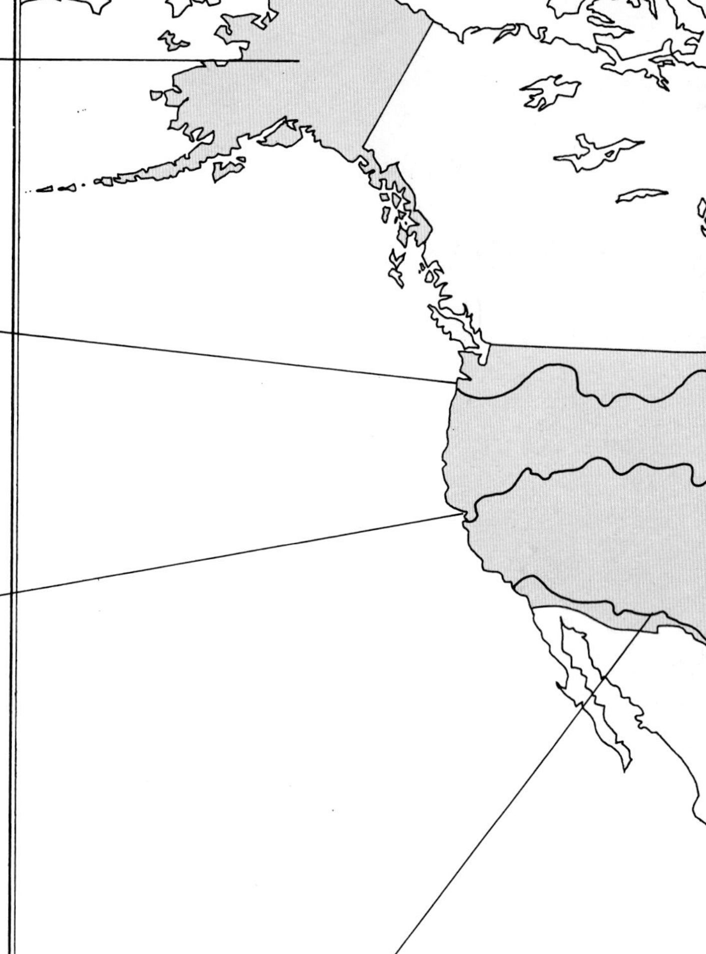

NORTH PACIFIC RAILROAD
The "Great Northern" was built from the western end of Lake Superior, Minnesota, through North Dakota, Montana, and through the Rocky Mountains into Idaho, Washington State and ending at Portland near the Pacific coast, Oregon, where the old "Oregon Trail" ends. Completed in 1883.

UNION - CENTRAL PACIFIC RAILROAD
The first American transcontinental railroad. The Union Pacific was built from Chicago westwards, and the Central Pacific from the Pacific coast eastwards through the Sierra Nevada mountain range - both lines joining at Promontary Point, Utah, in May 1869.

HAWAII
Possession of the USA 1898, the 50th. State of the USA in 1959.

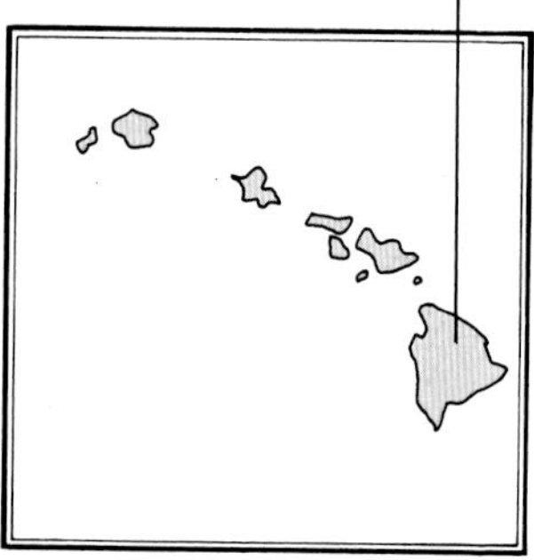

SOUTHERN PACIFIC RAILROAD
Starting from New Orleans, Louisiana, the Southern Pacific was built across Texas and westward through New Mexico, Arizona and up to Los Angeles, California. The line was completed in 1883.

U.S.A. *General stamp issues 1847 - (inscr. US Post Office or US Postage).*
See also: Canal Zone, Cuba, Guam, Hawaii, Philippines, Puerto Rico and USA POs in China *(inscr. Shanghai).*

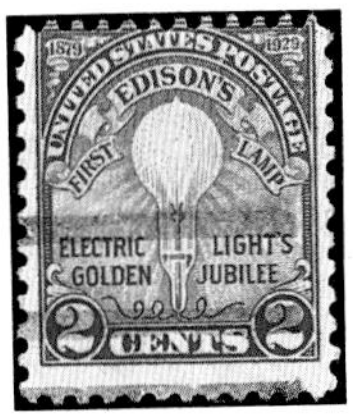

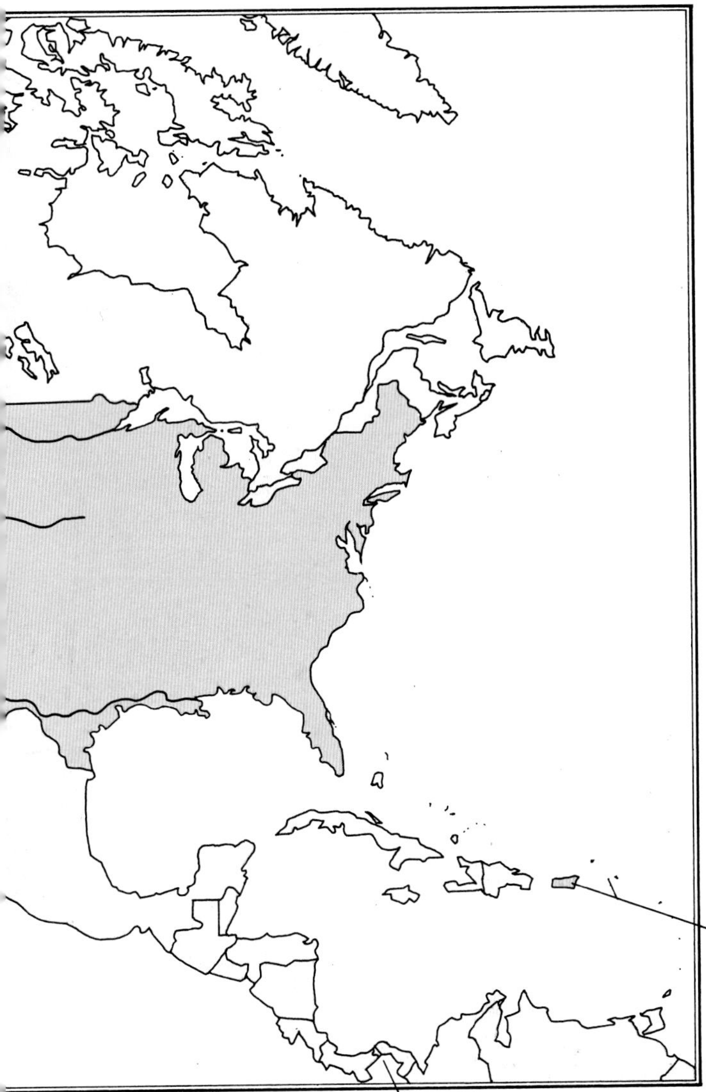

PUERTO RICO
Previously a Spanish Colony, USA territory since 1898.
VIRGIN ISLANDS, USA - USA territory since 1917, previously the Danish West Indies.

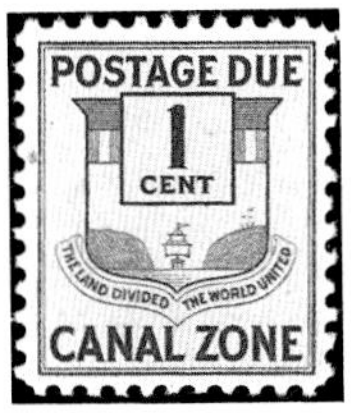

CANAL ZONE
Territory leased by Panama to the USA, 1903 - 1979. Canal opened 1914.

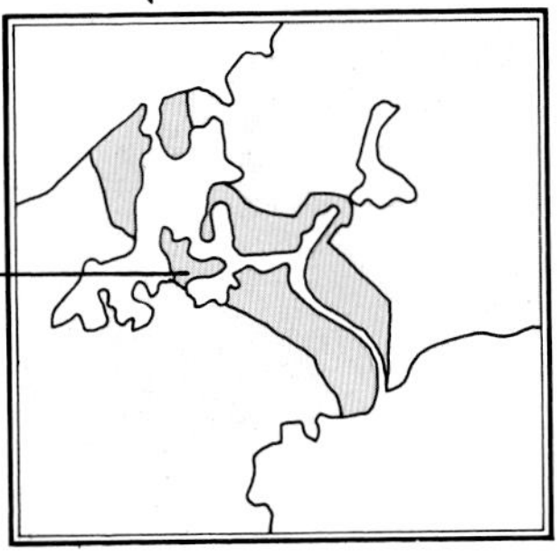

CANADA

General issues 1851–
BRITISH COLUMBIA and VANCOUVER ISLAND issues 1860–1865 (part of Dominion of Canada 1871).
VANCOUVER ISLAND issues 1865.
(Joined to British Columbia 1866)
NEW BRUNSWICK – issues 1851–1868.
NEWFOUNDLAND – issues 1857– 1949.
(early issues inscr. ST. JOHN'S NEWFOUNDLAND)
(Joined to Canada 1 April 1949)
NOVA SCOTIA – issues 1851–1868.
PRINCE EDWARD ISLAND – issues 1861–1873.
(Province of Dominion of Canada July 1873)

The Dominion of Canada was formed 1 July 1867 by the union of Canada, New Brunswick and Nova Scotia.

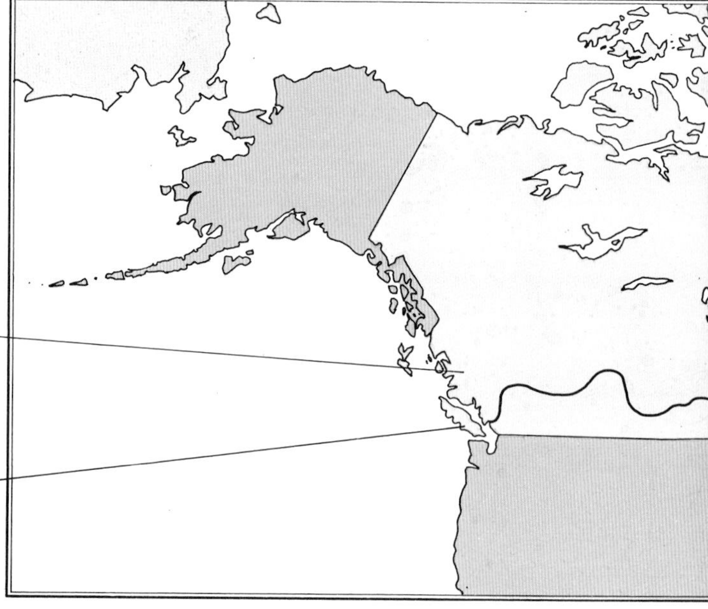

BRITISH COLUMBIA
to Canada 1871.

CANADIAN PACIFIC RAILWAY
Begun in 1881 and completed in 1885, the first through train from Montreal, Quebec, to Port Moody in British Columbia travelled in June 1886, taking over 5½ days for the journey.

CANADA
5 CENTS 5

CANADA 5
PLAINS OF ABRAHAM · PLAINES D'ABRAHAM

NOVA SCOTIA
TWELVE & ½ CENTS

NEW BRUNSWICK POSTAGE
5 CENTS 5

NEWFOUNDLAND
POSTAGE
2 TWO CENTS 2

DOMINION OF CANADA July 1867.

NEWFOUNDLAND
to Canada April 1949.

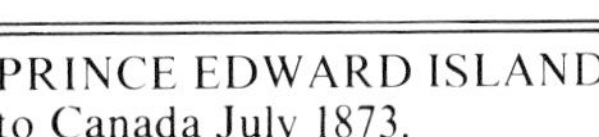
PRINCE EDWARD ISLAND
to Canada July 1873.

NEWFOUNDLAND
POSTAGE
20 TWENTY CENTS 20

CANADA
10 CENTS 10

1497 NEWFOUNDLAND 1947
POSTAGE
5c CABOT IN THE "MATTHEW" OFF CAPE BONAVISTA 1497 5c

CANADA POSTAGE

CANADA POSTAGE
1 ONE CENT 1

CANADA
1c

1909 1959
CANADA POSTES POSTAGE

$1
CANADA

15c
CANADA

CANADA
5c

Canada 6
Alex Mackenzie from Canada by land 22d July 1793

CANADA
7 cents

CANADA
6

CENTRAL AMERICA AND CARIBBEAN

MEXICO
Formerly Spanish, Empire 1822–1823, Republic 1824–1864, Empire 1864–1867, Republic 1867.
Republic issues 1856–1864.
Empire issues 1864–1867.
Republic issues 1867–
Also some local, provisional and Civil War issues at various times.

BAHAMAS
British possession 1783, independent Commonwealth State July 1973.
Issues 1859–

BERMUDA
British Colony 1684, now a British Dependent Territory.
Issues 1865–

CUBA
Spanish till 1898, USA rule 1899–1902, autonomous Republic subject to USA control 1902–1934, independent Republic 1934.
Spanish issues 1855–1898.
USA admin. issues 1899–1902.
Republic issues 1902–

GUATEMALA
Formerly Spanish, independent Republic 1844
Issues 1871–

TURKS and CAICOS ISLANDS
British Colony, now a Dependent Territory. At different times associated with the Bahamas and Jamaica
Issues of Turks Islands 1867–1900.
Issues of Turks and Caicos Islands. 1900–

EL SALVADOR
Formerly Spanish Colony, independent 1821, Republic 1839.
Issues 1867–

NICARAGUA
Formerly Spanish, independent 1821, Republic 1839.
Issues 1862–

CAYMAN ISLANDS
British Colony, now Dependent Territory.
Issues 1901–

JAMAICA
British Colony 1655, self-govt. 1944, independent Commonwealth State Aug. 1962.
Issues 1860–

BELIZE
British Colony of British Honduras 1862, re-named Belize 1973, independent Commonwealth State Sep. 1981.
Issues of British Honduras 1866–1973.
Issues of Belize 1973–

HAITI
Formerly French Colony, independent State 1804.
Issues 1881, inscr. République d'Haïti.

PUERTO RICO
Spanish possession till 1898, USA sovereignty since then.
Issues of Cuba used 1855–1873.
Spanish occupation issues 1873–1898.
USA issues, opr. 1899–1900.

COSTA RICA
Formerly Spanish, independent 1821, Republic 1839.
Issues 1863–

HONDURAS
Formerly Spanish, independent 1821, Republic 1839.
Issues 1866–

PANAMA
A State of Colombia till 1903, independent Republic 1903. Canal Zone leased to the USA 1903.
Colombian State issues 1878–1903.
Republic issues 1903–
Issues of USA Canal Zone 1904–

DOMINICAN REPUBLIC
Independent Republic 1865.
Issues 1865–

The entire region has been a scene of ever-changing events for centuries and its history during the past 150 years or so has been no exception: revolutions, changes of sovereignty and federations. Brief details of two noteworthy Federations are given here:

1. LEEWARD ISLANDS FEDERATION (1871-1956): The British islands in this group were federated as one Colony in 1871, consisting of Presidencies: Antigua, St. Christopher (St. Kitts)-Nevis, Anguilla, Montserrat, Dominica (until end of 1939), the British Virgin Islands. The Federation was dissolved in 1956. *It issued its own stamps, inscr. Leeward Islands, 1890–1956, while at the same time the constituent islands also issued their own (details in the boxes for each island).*

2. WEST INDIES FEDERATION (or BRITISH CARIBBEAN FEDERATION): Formed in 1958, dissolved in 1962 when Trinidad and Jamaica seceded. It consisted of: Barbados, Jamaica, Leeward Islands (except British Virgin Islands), Trinidad and Tobago, and the British Windward Islands.

WINDWARD ISLANDS: Geographically they consist of: Dominica (Brit.) (part of the Leewards till end 1939, under administration of the Windwards 1940-1959), Martinique (Fr.), St. Lucia (Brit.), St. Vincent (Brit.), the Grenadines (Brit., divided between St. Vincent and Grenada), Grenada (Brit.).

ANGUILLA
Part of the British island group of St.Kitts (St.Christopher)-Nevis till 1967, since when it came under British administration. *Issues 1967–*

ANTIGUA and BARBUDA
British possessions, Antigua a Crown Colony in 1956. The two islands are an independent Commonwealth State since Nov. 1981. *Issues of Antigua 1862–1981. Issues of Barbuda 1922–1981. Issues of Antigua and Barbuda 1981–*

U.S. VIRGIN ISLANDS
Formerly the Danish West Indies (Dansk-Vestindien), USA territory by purchase, Jan 1917.
Issues of Danish West Indies 1855–1917 (USA stamps current 1917–).

BRITISH VIRGIN ISLANDS
Formerly a British Colony, now a British Dependent Territory.
Issues 1866–
Leeward Islands issues also used till 1956.

MONTSERRAT
British Colony, now a British Dependent Territory.
Issues 1876–
General issues of Leeward Islands used also till 1956.

ST. KITTS (or ST. CHRISTOPHER), NEVIS, ANGUILLA
British Colony. Anguilla left the association 1967. Now the independent Commonwealth State of St. Kitts-Nevis since 1983.
Stamp issues are complex. See Dictionary for details.

GUADELOUPE
Former French Colony, an Overseas Département of France 1946.
Issues 1884-1947. (French stamps used 1947–).

MARTINIQUE
Former French Colony, an Overseas Département of France 1946.
Issues 1886–1947 (French stamps used 1947–).

DOMINICA
British Colony and part of the Leewards till end 1939, under administration of the Windward Islands 1940. An independent State in the Commonwealth, Nov. 1978 and known as Commonwealth of Dominica.
Issues 1874–

ST. LUCIA
British since 1814, independent Commonwealth State Feb. 1979.
Issues 1860–

BARBADOS
British possession 1627, independent Commonwealth State Nov. 1966.
Issues 1852–

TRINIDAD and TOBAGO
British possessions, islands came under one administration in 1889, and an independent Commonwealth State, Aug. 1962.
Issues of Trinidad 1847-1913.
Issues of Tobago 1879–1896 (stamps of Trinidad used 1896–1913).
Issues of Trinidad and Tobago 1913–

NETHERLANDS ANTILLES
Dutch possessions. Autonomous as part of the Kingdom of the Netherlands, Dec. 1954.
Issues inscr. Curaçao 1873–1948.
Issues inscr. Nederlandse Antillen 1948–

GRENADA
British Colony till Feb. 1974, when it became independent in the Commonwealth. Includes some islands of the Grenadines.
Issues 1861–
Issues of Grenada Grenadines 1973–

ST. VINCENT and the GRENADINES
Former British Colony, now independent in the Commonwealth, Oct. 1979.
Issues of St. Vincent 1861–
Issues of Grenadines of St. Vincent 1973–

SOUTH AMERICA

The status of the boundaries shown here is as they are at present. Following a stormy history, especially during the 19th. century, several changes of international frontiers took place since around 1810/30, the most recent about 1942 (Peru).
Dates of political events are sometimes at variance due to there being a time lapse in some cases between the date when a revolution began and when a regular from of civil rule was established or recognized.

GUYANA
Former Colony of British Guiana, independence May 1966 and renamed Guyana, Republic in the British Commonwealth Feb. 1970.
Issues of British Guiana 1850–1966.
Issues of Guyana 1966–

COLOMBIA
Formerly Spanish, independent 1819, formed successively Greater Colombia (with Ecuador and Venezuela) till 1830, then New Granada, the Granada Confederation and the United States of Colombia in 1861.
Issues of Granada Confederation 1859–1860
Issues of U.S. of New Granada 1861.
Issues of U.S. of Colombia 1862–1886
Republic issues 1886–
(See Dictionary for issues of the States of Colombia).

VENEZUELA
Spanish possession till 1811/19, and part of Greater Colombia 1819–1830, independent Republic 1830.
Issues 1859–

ECUADOR
Formerly Spanish, later part of Greater Colombia, independent Republic 1830. Includes the Pacific islands of Galapagos (a Province of Ecuador in 1973).
Issues 1865–
Separate issues of Galapagos Islands. 1957–1959.

PERU
Previously Spanish, independent 1821, . Republican Government 1828.
Issues 1858–
(Some local issues made in period 1881–1885.)

CHILE
Formerly Spanish, independent Republic 1818/21. Northern part of the country annexed following the 1879–1883 war against Peru and Bolivia.
Issues 1853–
Issues of Tierra del Fuego 1891
(southermost part of the country).

BOLIVIA
Formerly Spanish, independent Republic 1825.
Issues 1866–

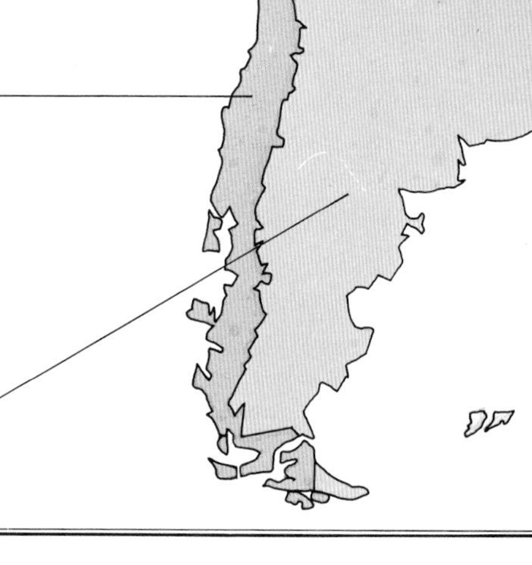

ARGENTINA
Former Spanish possession, independent 1816, became a Confederation and later a Republic. The region of Patagonia became part of Argentina in 1881.
Issues 1858–
(Some local issues were made in 1858: Buenos Aires, Cordoba, and Corrientes.)

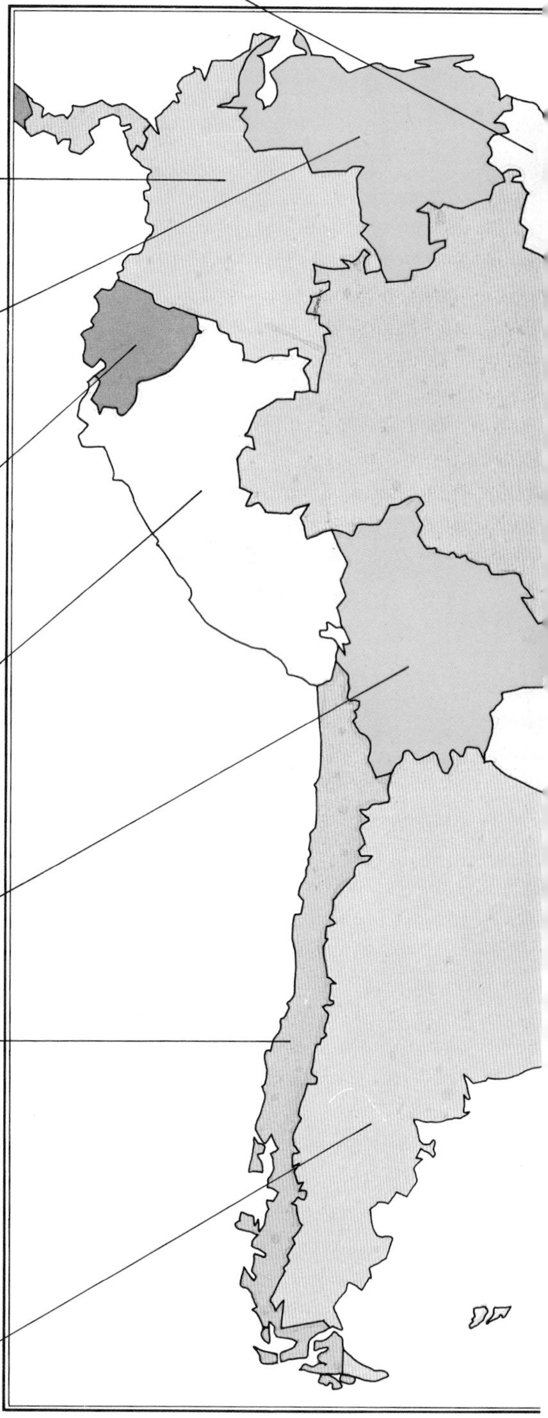

SURINAM (SURINAME)
Former Colony of Dutch Guiana, autonomous as part of the Kingdom of the Netherlands, Dec. 1954, though still a part of the Netherlands West Indies. Independent Nov. 1975.
Issues 1873–

FRENCH GUIANA (GUYANE FRANÇAISE)
Former French Colony, an Overseas Département of France 1946.
Issues 1886–1947.
(Stamps of France current 1947–)
Issues of Inini 1932–1946.
Inini had an autonomous administration 1932–1946, when it returned to the administration of Guyane.

BRAZIL
Portuguese possession till 1815, Empire 1822–1889, Republic since then.
Empire issues 1843–1889.
Republic issues 1890–

PARAGUAY
Former Spanish possession, independent Republic following a revolt begun in 1811.
Issues 1870–

URUGUAY
Former Spanish possession, known also as Banda Oriental, independent Republic 1825.
Issues 1856–

AFRICA UP TO 1915/1919

Few parts of the world have seen as many changes during the past 100 years as in Africa: colonial gains, combinations and federation of territories, changes of boundaries and sovereignty, independence of colonies, changes in civil administration and territorial names. All these are reflected in the vast number of postage stamps issued.
Boundaries on this map are generally as they were in the period 1912/1919, until when many changes had already occurred where territories which are now States had undemarcated frontiers (Allied Boundary Commissions were still surveying frontiers in the field after 1919).
SEE DICTIONARY FOR DETAILS OF STAMP ISSUES AND OTHER INFORMATION

FRENCH WEST AFRICA (AFRIQUE OCCIDENTALE FRANÇAISE = A.O.F)
Formed in 1895 with administrative seat at Dakar, it eventually comprised the French Colonies of: Ivory Coast (Côte d'Ivoire), Dahomey (now Bénin), French Guinea (Guinée), Upper Volta (Haute-Volta, now Burkina), Mauritania (Mauritanie), Niger, Sénégal, and French Sudan (Soudan Français). The Federation lasted till 1958.

MOROCCO AGENCIES
5 CENTIMOS

TUNISIE POSTES
50
RF

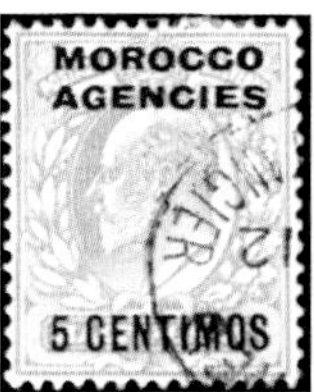

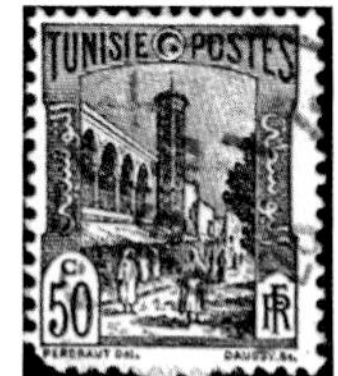

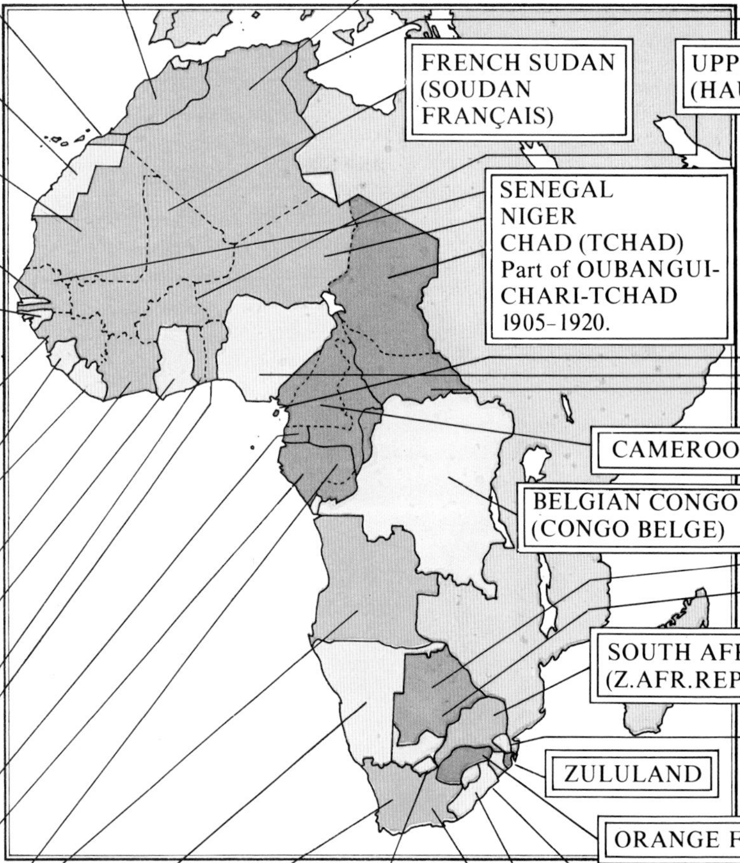
SPANISH MOROCCO (MARRUECOS)
MOROCCO (MAROC)
ALGERIA (ALGÉRIE)
TUNISIA (TUNISIE)
RIO DE ORO
FRENCH SUDAN (SOUDAN FRANÇAIS)
UPPER VOLTA (HAUTE-VOLTA)
MAURITANIA (MAURITANIE)
FERNANDO POO
SENEGAL
NIGER
CHAD (TCHAD)
Part of OUBANGUI-CHARI-TCHAD 1905–1920.
NIGERIA (Including LAGOS, NORTH and SOUTH NIGERIA
THE GAMBIA
PORTUGUESE GUINEA (GUINÉ PORTUGESA)
OUBANGUI-CHARI-TCHAD
FRENCH GUINEA (GUINÉE)
SIERRA LEONE
LIBERIA
CAMEROON (KAMERUN)
BELGIAN CONGO (CONGO BELGE)
BECHUANALAND (Including STELLALAND)
MAFEKING
IVORY COAST (CÔTE D'IVOIRE)
GOLD COAST
TOGO
DAHOMEY/BÉNIN
SOUTH AFRICAN REPUBLIC (Z.AFR.REPUBLIEK)/TRANSVAAL
SWAZILAND PROTECTORATE
ZULULAND
SPANISH GUINEA/RIO MUNI
GABON
ORANGE FREE STATE
NATAL
SOUTH WEST AFRICA (DEUTSCH S.W.-AFRIKA)
GRIQUALAND WEST
BASUTOLAND
CAPE OF GOOD HOPE
ANGOLA

FRENCH CONGO (CONGO FRANÇAIS)
Formed by the union of the Territories of Congo and Gabon.

UNION OF SOUTH AFRICA
Union 1910 of the Provinces of Cape of Good Hope, Natal (incl. Zululand), Orange Free State, and Transvaal.

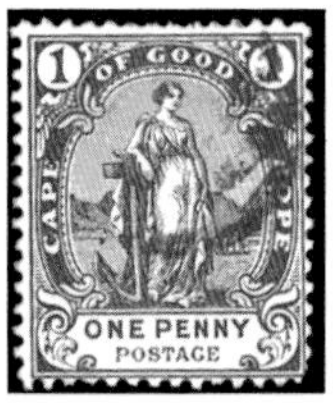
ONE PENNY
POSTAGE

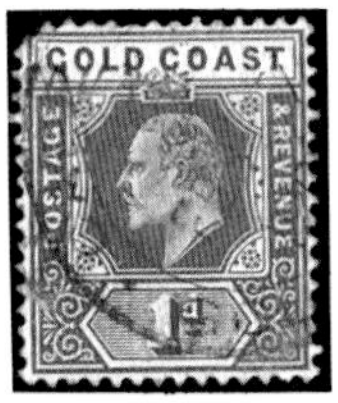
GOLD COAST

FRENCH EQUATORIAL AFRICA (AFRIQUE EQUATORIALE FRANÇAISE = A.E.F.)
Formed 1910 by the federation of the territories of Middle Congo (Moyen Congo), Oubangui-Chari-Tchad and Gabon (then French Congo). The Federation lasted till 1958.

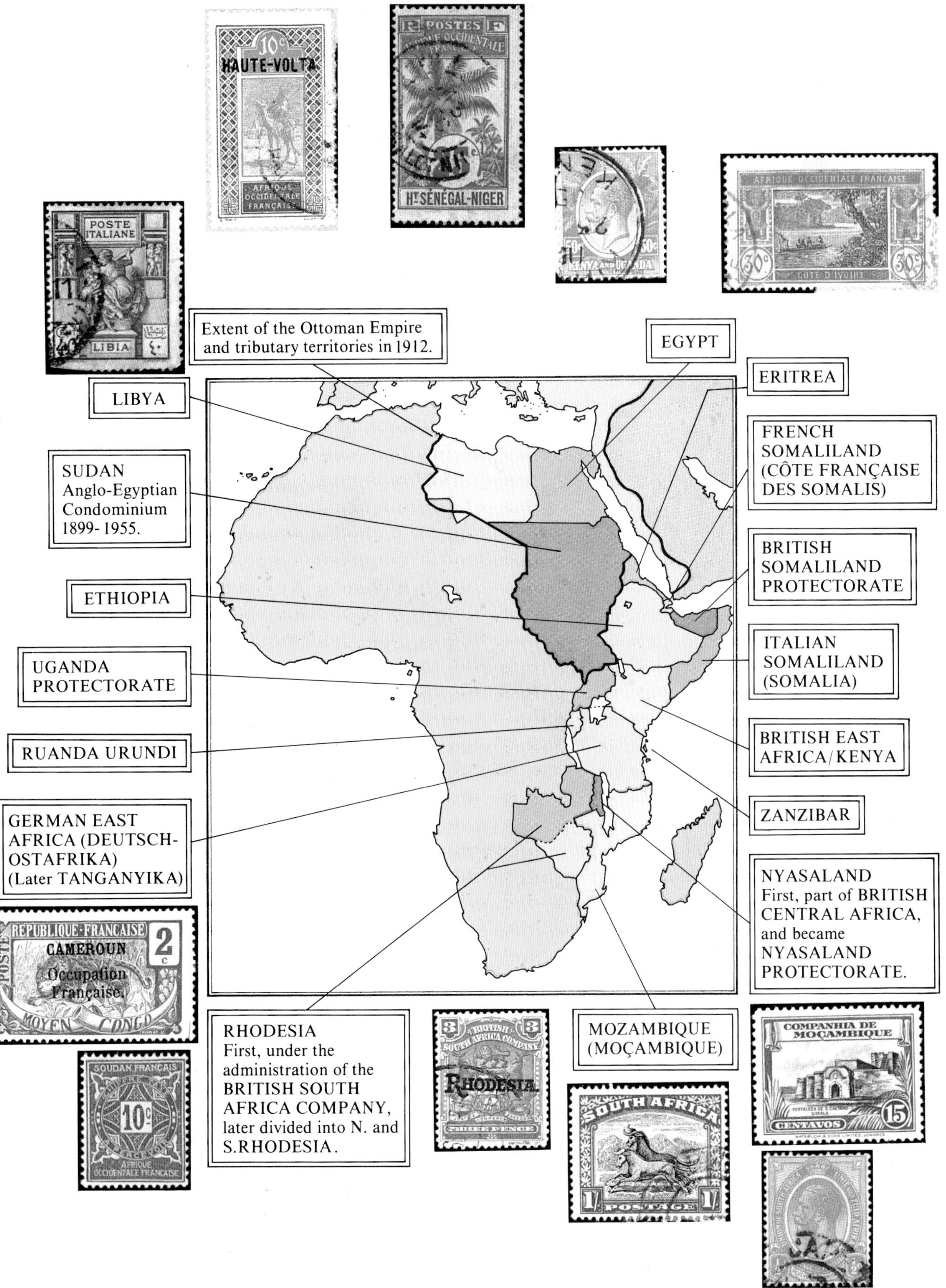
POSTE ITALIANE
LIBIA
10c
HAUTE-VOLTA
AFRIQUE OCCIDENTALE FRANÇAISE
POSTES
AFRIQUE OCCIDENTALE FRANÇAISE
Ht SÉNÉGAL-NIGER
KENYA AND UGANDA
AFRIQUE OCCIDENTALE FRANÇAISE
CÔTE D'IVOIRE
Extent of the Ottoman Empire and tributary territories in 1912.
EGYPT
ERITREA
LIBYA
FRENCH SOMALILAND (CÔTE FRANÇAISE DES SOMALIS)
SUDAN Anglo-Egyptian Condominium 1899-1955.
BRITISH SOMALILAND PROTECTORATE
ETHIOPIA
ITALIAN SOMALILAND (SOMALIA)
UGANDA PROTECTORATE
BRITISH EAST AFRICA/KENYA
RUANDA URUNDI
ZANZIBAR
GERMAN EAST AFRICA (DEUTSCH-OSTAFRIKA) (Later TANGANYIKA)
NYASALAND First, part of BRITISH CENTRAL AFRICA, and became NYASALAND PROTECTORATE.
REPUBLIQUE FRANCAISE
CAMEROUN Occupation Française.
MOYEN CONGO
RHODESIA First, under the administration of the BRITISH SOUTH AFRICA COMPANY, later divided into N. and S.RHODESIA.
BRITISH SOUTH AFRICA COMPANY
RHODESIA
MOZAMBIQUE (MOÇAMBIQUE)
COMPANHIA DE MOÇAMBIQUE
CENTAVOS
SOUDAN FRANÇAIS
10c
AFRIQUE OCCIDENTALE FRANÇAISE
SOUTH AFRICA
POSTAGE

AFRICA FROM 1919

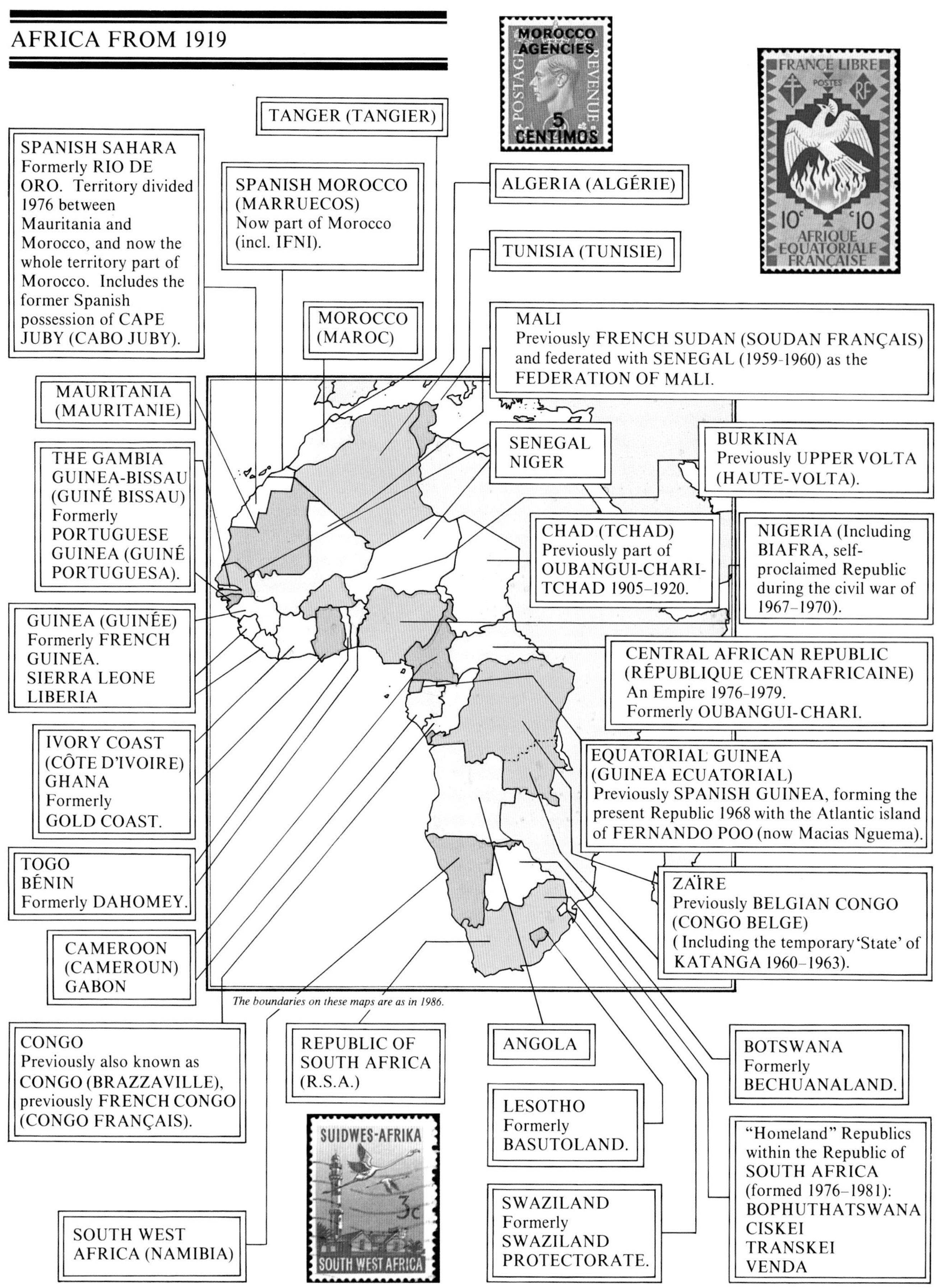

The boundaries on these maps are as in 1986.

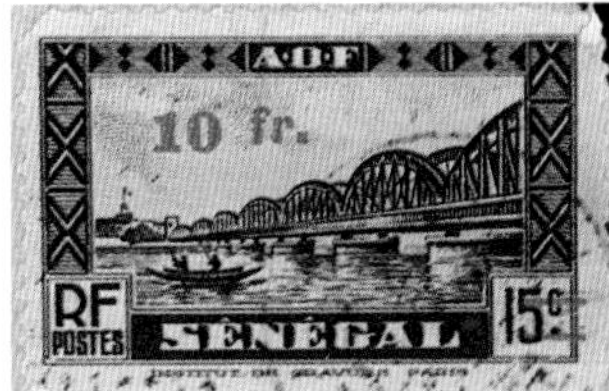

LIBYA
Including the territories of CYRENAICA, FEZZAN, and TRIPOLITANIA.

EGYPT
Later part of the UNITED ARAB REPUBLIC (U.A.R.).

ITALIAN EAST AFRICA (AFRICA ORIENTALE ITALIANA)
Comprising ERITREA, ETHIOPIA and ITALIAN SOMALILAND (period 1936–1942).

SUDAN
Anglo-Egyptian Condominium 1899–1955.

DJIBOUTI
Formerly named AFARS et ISSAS, and previously FRENCH SOMALILAND (CÔTE FRANÇAISE DES SOMALIS).

UGANDA
Formerly the UGANDA PROTECTORATE.

ETHIOPIA (including ERITREA)

KENYA

SOMALIA
Comprising the former ITALIAN SOMALILAND (SOMALIA) and BRITISH SOMALILAND PROTECTORATE, and including the territory of JUBALAND (OLTRE GIUBA) ceded by Kenya.

RWANDA
The northern part of the former RUANDA-URUNDI.

BURUNDI
Formerly part of RUANDA-URUNDI.

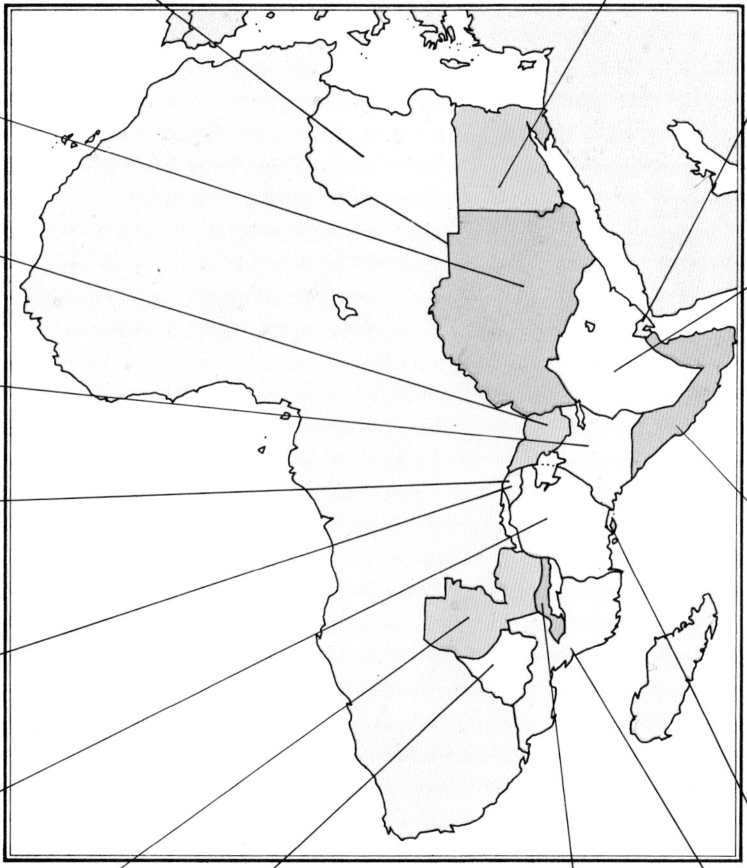

TANZANIA
Formerly TANGANYIKA.

ZANZIBAR
United with Tanganyika 1963 to form the Republic of TANZANIA.

ZAMBIA
Formerly NORTHERN RHODESIA.

ZIMBABWE
Formerly RHODESIA, and SOUTHERN RHODESIA.

MALAWI
Formerly NYASALAND PROTECTORATE.

MOZAMBIQUE (MOÇAMBIQUE)

ASIA UP TO 1923

The Far-eastern parts of Asia have been the scene of many conflicts and wars during the past 100 years. The Russo-Japanese war of 1904–1905 resulted in the southern part of the strategic island of Sakhalin being annexed to Japan. Korea was annexed to Japan in 1910 and has been a theatre of war again in 1950–1953, resulting in the new separate States of Korea and Korea (North). The State of Manchuria (Manchukuo) was formed in 1932 under the aegis of Japan, and after many changes was annexed to China. The Sino-Japanese war began in 1937, when large parts of China were occupied by Japan. Since 1953 the boundaries in the region have remained virtually as they are now, Taiwan being a separate State following the war of 1939–1945.
Following the Russian Revolution of 1917, many regions of southern and eastern Russia formed their own 'States', but these were all annexed to the USSR by 1923. All these changes are reflected in the multitude of postage stamps issued.

Demarcation line between Europe and Asia (Urals).

U.S.S.R.
Following the Russian Revolution of 1917, the federation of all component 'Republics' was proclaimed Dec. 1922.
Issues 1923–

R.S.F.S.R.
(Russian Soviet Federal Socialist Republic) —Established 1917 following the Russian Revolution.
Issues 1917–1923. (Superseded 1923 by USSR issues.)

UKRAINE
Formed a separate (temporary) Republic after the Russian Revolution.
Issues 1918-1923. (Superseded by USSR stamps.)

TRANSCAUCASIAN FEDERATION (E.S.F.S.R.)
Federation established in the wake of the Russian Revolution of Armenia, Azerbaidzhan and Georgia.
Issues 1923. (Superseded 1924 by USSR stamps.)

NEPAL
Independent Kingdom in the Himalayas.
Issues 1881–

AFGHANISTAN
After a stormy history, became a limited Monarchy, the country consisting of autonomous 'States' in the mid-19th. century (Kabul, Kandahar, Herat) — a period marked by some British intervention. Kingdom 1926, Republic 1973.
Issues 1870–

TIBET
Previously under Chinese rule, antonomous Theocracy 1912 (re-occupied by China 1950).
Issues 1912–1950.
Issues of Chinese POs in Tibet 1911.

TANNU TUVA (TOUVA)
Part of Outer Mongolia, Russian occupation 1914–1919.

MONGOLIA
Under Chinese rule, as Outer Mongolia, independent 1921.

USSR in ASIA
Several stamp issues were made in Siberia following the Russian Revolution of 1917 by various authorities in temporary power which opposed the Bolshevik regime, in the period 1919–1922. (See Dictionary for some details, under Russia).

TRANS-SIBERIAN RAILWAY
The section St. Petersburg (Leningrad) to Moscow was built in 1861, and the vast eastward stretch to Vladivostok in the Far East was finally completed in the period 1908–1916, the shorter section across Manchuria (Russian-occupied 1900–1905) built in 1901. On some maps of the period the railway is annotated as the *"Postal Route"*. It is some 5,800 miles long, taking over 7 days for the journey.
The great branch from the 'Trans-Siberian' to the Caspian Sea via Kazakhstan, Uzbekistan and Turkmenistan was completed 1881—1884. The new "Baikal-Amur-Magistral" (BAM) line has been under constuction for many years and is yet to be completed.

SAKHALIN ISLAND
Formerly Russian, the southern half was annexed to Japan 1905 (reverting to the USSR 1945, its sovereignty still unsettled).

MANCHURIA
Formerly part of China, Russian occupation 1900-1905.

JAPAN
An Empire for several centuries.
Issues 1871–
Issues of Japanese POs in China 1900–1922.
Issues of Japanese POs in Korea 1900–1901.

KOREA
Autonomous under Chinese rule till 1895, Japanese Protectorate 1905 and annexed to Japan 1910.
Empire issues 1884–1905.
(Japanese postal administration 1905.)

FORMOSA (TAIWAN)
To China up to 1895, part of Japan 1895–1945.

YUNNANFOU
French PO active 1900–1922. Now the town of Kunming, Yunnan Province of China.
French issues 1903–1922 (early issues inscr. Yunnansen).

HONG KONG
British Colony leased from China till 1997, now British Dependent Territory.
Issues 1862–

CHINA
Empire till 1912, when it became a Republic.
Empire issues 1878–1912.
Republic issues 1912–1949.
(See Dictionary for issues of Regions and Provinces, and for issues of foreign POs in China: British, French, German, Italian, Japanese, Russian, USA.)

BHUTAN
Independent Kingdom in the Himalayas.

MACAO (MACAU)
Portuguese Colony since 1554.
Issues 1884–

ASIA FROM 1923

TANNU TUVA (TOUVA)
Independent Republic 1928–1944, now part of the USSR as the Tuvin A.S.S.R.
Issues 1926–1944.

U.S.S.R
The boundaries of USSR in Asia were finally established in 1944 with the annexation of the former Republic of Tannu Tuva (Touva), now the Tuvin A.S.S.R.

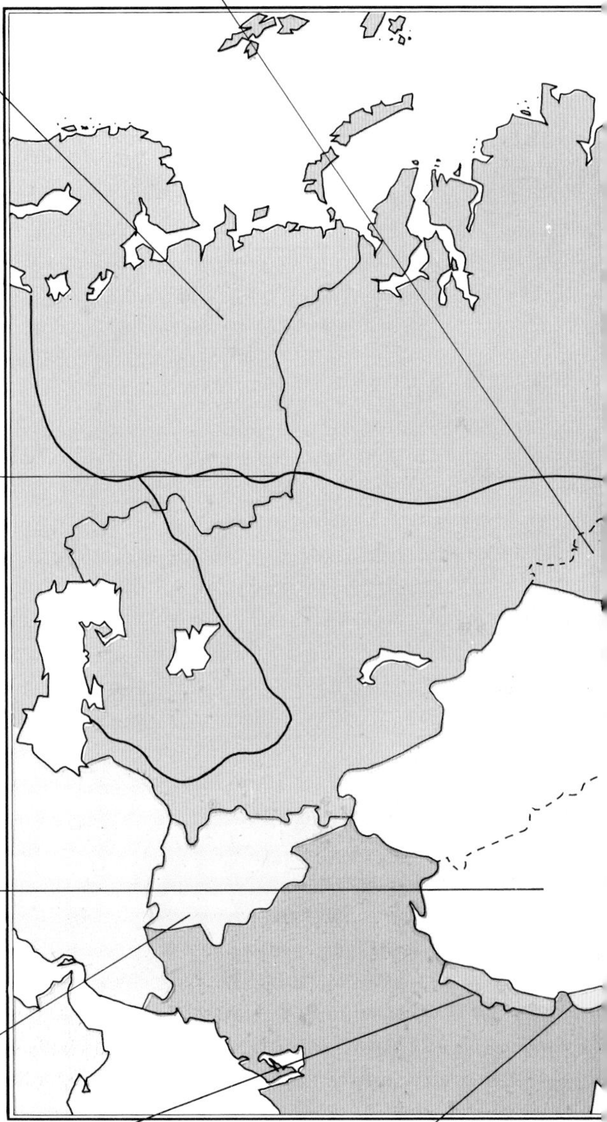

Demarcation line between Europe and Asia (Urals).

TIBET
Formerly autonomous, occupied by China 1950.
Issues 1912–1950.

AFGHANISTAN

NEPAL

BHUTAN
Independent Kingdom.
Issues 1962–

MONGOLIA
Independent 1921, Republic in 1924 and named Mongolian People's Republic.
Issues 1924–

MANCHURIA
Japanese Protectorate 1932 and Empire 1934–1945 (Manchukuo), Russian occupation 1945–1946, now part of China as the Province of Heilungkiang.
Issues under Chinese rule 1927–1929.
Issues of 'independent' Republic 1932–1934.
Empire issues (Manchukuo) 1934–1945.
Chinese administration issues 1946–1948.

SAKHALIN ISLAND

KOREA (NORTH)
Area of Korea north at Lat. 38°N. occupied by the USSR 1945, and formed into the separate Democratic People's Republic of Korea, established 1948 (though disputed outside the country).
Issues 1946– (See Dictionary for details).

JAPAN
Issues 1871–
(See Dictionary for Japanese occupation issues of neighbouring States during the 1941–1945 period).

KOREA (SOUTH)
The Republic of Korea (South Korea) came into being following the 1950–1953 war with (North) Korea.
Issues 1946– (See Dictionary for details).

PORT ARTHUR (now Lushun) and **DAIREN** (now Talien) — Towns under Chinese administration 1945, Port Arthur a joint Sino-Soviet naval base and Dairen a Free Port.

MACAO (MACAU)
Former Portuguese Colony, Overseas Province of Portugal 1961–1974 when it became a Territory administered by Portugal.
Issues 1884–

CHINA
Republic issues 1912–1949.
People's Republic issues 1949–
(See Dictionary for details on Japanese occupation issue).

HONG KONG
Hong Kong and Territories leased by China to Great Britain till 1997, at present a British Dependent Territory.
Issues 1862–

TAIWAN
Formerly known as Formosa, part of Japan 1895–1945, when it reverted to China, independent 1950 and known as the 'Republic of China', or China (Taiwan).
Issues of Chinese Nationalist Govt. and of Republic of China 1945–

INDIA AND SOUTH EAST ASIA UP TO 1947

The main characteristic of the history of this region during this period is its diverse European spheres of influence: British India and Ceylon, British influence in the Malayan Peninsula and Singapore; French Indochina, and the Netherlands Indies; the smaller French and Portuguese Settlements in India. All these have left their mark on philately.
See Dictionary for details on stamp issues.

INDIA
British Empire of India up to 1947.
(See box below for details on stamp-issuing States of India.)

FRENCH TERRITORIES IN INDIA (ÉTABLISSEMENTS FRANÇAIS DANS L'INDE)
Included the Territories of:
(1) CHANDERNAGOR
(2) YANAON
(3) PONDICHÉRY
(4) KARIKAL
(5) MAHÉ

SIAM/THAILAND
Kingdom of Siam, re-named Thailand 1939.

BURMA
Part of British India up to 1937 when it became autonomous under British rule.

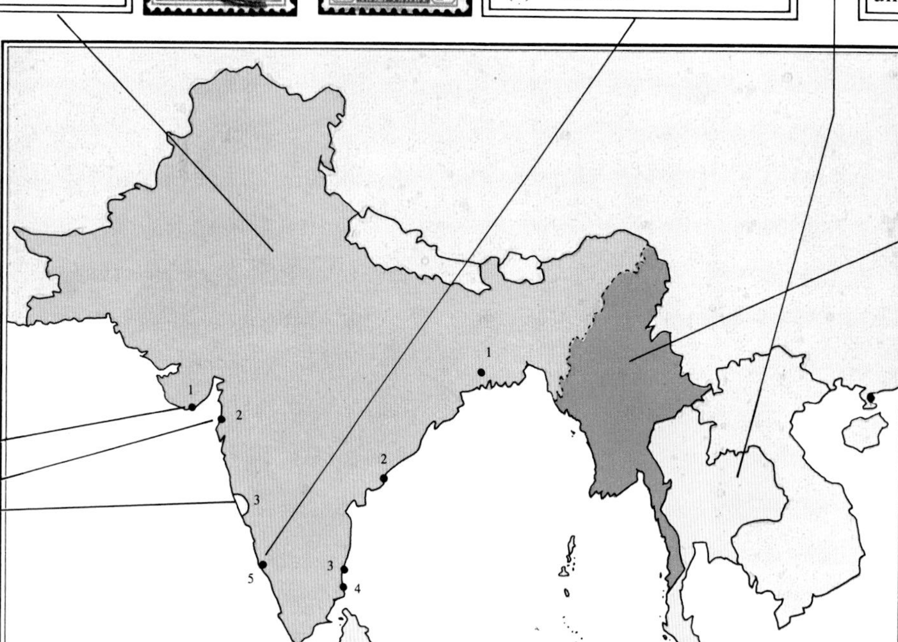

PORTUGUESE INDIA (INDIA PORTUGUESA, later ESTADO DA INDIA)
Included the Territories of:
(1) DIU
(2) DAMAO
(3) GOA

SINGAPORE
British Colony since the 1820's.

CEYLON
British Colony 1802/18.

MALAYA
Consisted successively of:
The STRAITS SETTLEMENTS (Crown Colony which included, among other territories, Labuan (off North Borneo), Malacca, Penang, Singapore).
The FEDERATED MALAY STATES (which included NEGRI SEMBILAN, PAHANG, PERAK, SELANGOR).
The following States also issued stamps: KEDAH, KELANTAN, PERLIS, TRENGGANU, JOHORE.
(Sultanates tributary to Siam till 1909.)

INDIA
The following States issued their own stamps (either opr. stamps of INDIA or separate local issues):
ALWAR, BAHAWALPUR, BAMRA, BARWANI, BHOPAL, BHOR, BIJAWAR, BUNDI, BUSSAHIR, CHAMBA, CHARKHARI, COCHIN, DHAR, DUTTIA (DATIA), FARIDKOT, GWALIOR, HOLKAR, HYDERABAD, INDORE, JAIPUR, JAMMU AND KASHMIR, JASDAN, JHALAWAR, JIND, KISHANGARH, LAS BELA, MORVI, NABHA, NANDGAON, NAWANAGAR, ORCHA, PATIALA (PUTTIALLA), POONCH, RAJASTHAN, RAJPIPLA, SIRMOOR (SIRMUR), SORUTH (SAURASHTRA), TRAVANCORE (later TRAVANCORE-COCHIN), WADHWAN.

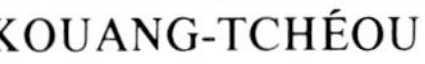

KOUANG-TCHÉOU
Small territory in south China, leased to France 1898, under administration of French Indochina, returned to China 1943.

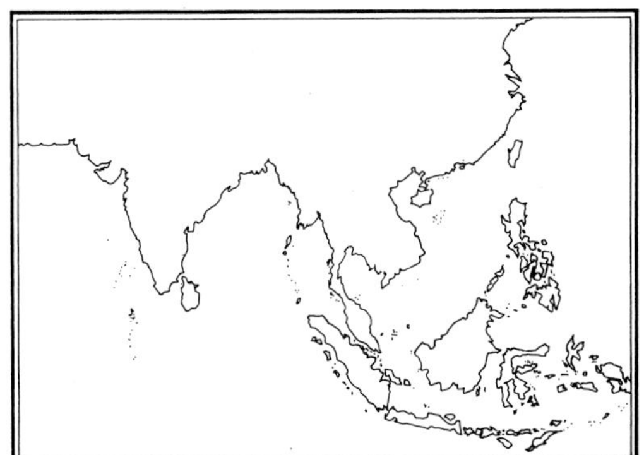

ANNAM et TONKIN
French Protectorate 1883, under administration of French Indochina 1887.

LAOS
Formerly an independent Kingdom, French Protectorate 1893 and part of French Indochina.

PHILIPPINES
Previously Spanish, USA Territory 1898, independent Republic 1946.

LABUAN
British territory off the coast of North Borneo, part of the Straits Settlements (Malaya) 1906, attached to North Borneo 1946.

FRENCH INDOCHINA

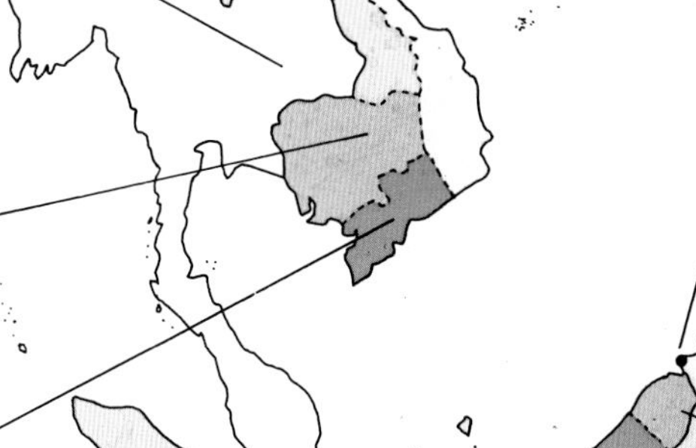

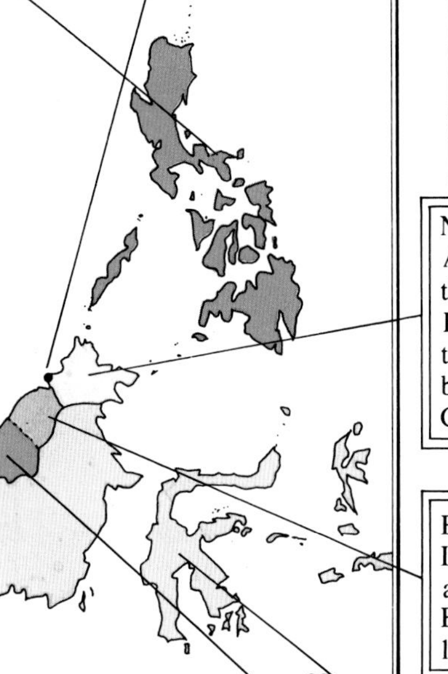

CAMBODIA (CAMBODGE)
Formerly an independent Kingdom, French Protectorate 1863 and later part of French Indochina.

COCHINCHINA (COCHINCHINE)
Part of French Indochina 1887/1888, later part of Vietnam 1946/1949.

NORTH BORNEO
Administration of the British North Borneo Company till 1946, when it became a Crown Colony.

BRUNEI
Independent Sultante and State under British protection 1888.

CELEBES

NETHERLANDS INDIES (NEDERLANDSCH-INDIË)
Colony of the Netherlands 1816-1941 (Japanese occupation 1941-1945). Republic proclaimed Aug. 1945.

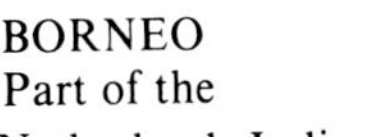

BORNEO
Part of the Netherlands Indies.

TIMOR
Eastern part of the island of Timor, Portuguese Colony.

SARAWAK
Independent State under British protection, Crown Colony 1946-1963.

FRENCH INDOCHINA (INDOCHINE)
Formed 1882-1888, uniting the French Colonies and Protectorates of Cochinchina, Cambodia, Annam et Tonkin, Laos (1893) and the Territory of Kouang-Tchéou (southern China). Under Japanese occupation 1941-1945.

INDIA AND SOUTH EAST ASIA FROM 1947

This region has undergone great upheavals during the past half century: World War of 1939-1945, when a large part of it was occupied by Japan; the wars in Indochina (now Vietnam), first involving France, then the USA; the troubles in Indonesia (the former Netherlands Indies). The most important political events of the post-1945 period were the attainment of independence by India, Burma, Pakistan, Sri Lanka (Ceylon), Bangladesh; the successive political changes in the Malayan Peninsula and Indochina and Vietnam.

See Dictionary for details on stamp issues.

BURMA
Part of British India up to 1937, autonomous under British rule 1937–1947 when it became an independent Republic outside the British Commonwealth (Union of Burma). (Japanese occupation 1942–1945.)

PAKISTAN
Part of British India, Dominion 1947, Republic 1956. East Pakistan became the Republic of Bangladesh in 1971.

BANGLADESH
Formerly East Pakistan (1947–1971), became an independent Republic in 1971 and member of the British Commonwealth in 1972.

THAILAND
Kingdom, reverted to the name of SIAM for a time 1945–1949.

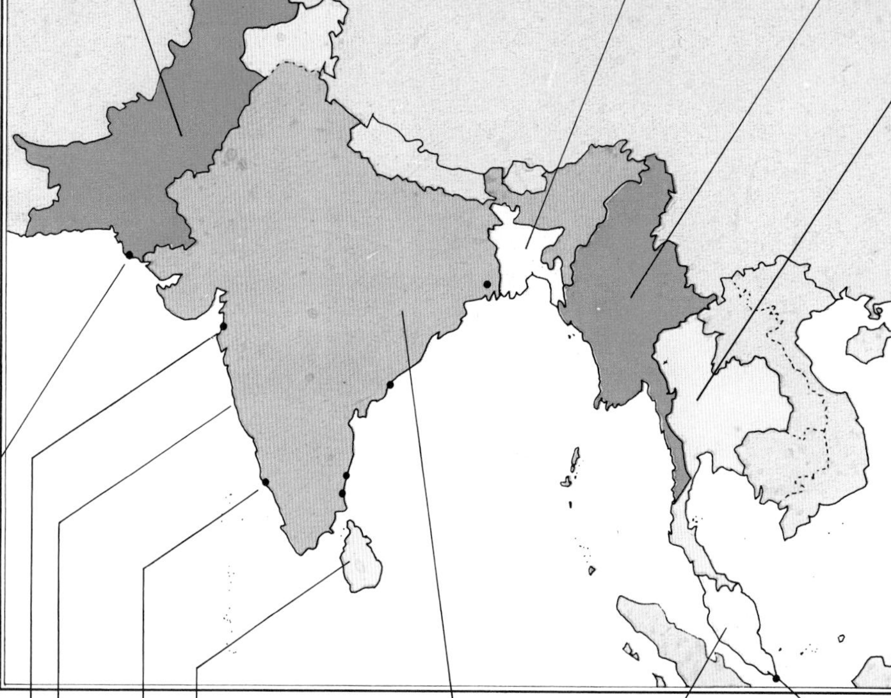

PORTUGUESE INDIA (INDIA PORTUGUESA)
The possessions of DIU, DAMAO and GOA became part of India in 1961.

INDIA
British Empire of India till 1947 when it became a Dominion, and Republic in the British Commonwealth in 1950.

SINGAPORE
Autonomous 1959, a State in the Federation of Malaysia 1963, but seceded from it in 1965 to become a separate State in the British Commonwealth.

FRENCH TERRITORIES IN INDIA (ÉTABLISSEMENTS FRANÇAIS DANS L'INDE)
Comprising CHANDERNAGOR, YANAON, PRONDICHÉRY, KARIKAL, AND MAHÉ, French PO's activities ended in 1954 and taken over by India.

SRI LANKA
Former British Colony of Ceylon, independent State in the British Commonwealth Feb. 1948, Republic in 1972 and re-named Sri Lanka.

MALAYSIA
Federation formed Sep. 1963 from the former States of the Federation of Malaya and including the State of Singapore, the Colonies of North Borneo (now Sabah) and Sarawak. State is part of the British Commonwealth (Singapore seceded from the Federation in Aug. 1965).

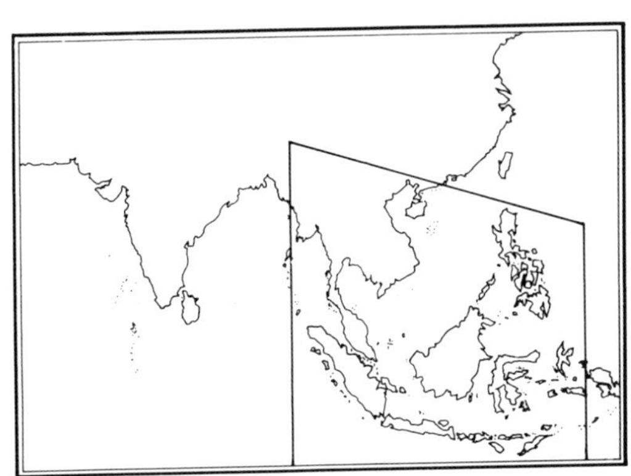

VIETNAM
Formerly French Indochina excepting the component States of CAMBODIA and LAOS which became independent States 1946–1949. Following years of conflict and the war involving the USA, became divided into North and South Vietnam in 1954, and after further upheavals became united as one State of Vietnam 1975/1978.

LAOS
Formerly part of French Indochina, independent Kingdom 1953, Republic in 1975.

ANNAM et TONKIN
Now incorporated in Vietnam.

PHILIPPINES

LABUAN
NORTH BORNEO (now SABAH)
SARAWAK
Territories part of the Federation of MALAYSIA, Sept. 1963.

BRUNEI
Sultanate, independent State, Dec. 1983.

SULAWESI
Formerly named CELEBES, part of Indonesia.

CAMBODIA (CAMBODGE)
Independent Kingdom 1953, Republic 1970/1971 and country named Khmer Republic (also unofficially, Kampuchea). Present situation unclear and conflicting.

COCHINCHINA
Part of Vietnam 1946–1949.

INDONESIA
Formerly the NETHERLANDS INDIES, independent State 1949.

TIMOR
Eastern part of the island on Overseas Territory of Portugal, became a Province of Indonesia in 1976 and renamed Loro Sae.

KALIMANTAN
Formerly named BORNEO, part of Indonesia.

ARABIA AND MIDDLE EAST UP TO 1919

With the exception of Persia (now Iran), the Nejd (central part of the Arabian Peninsula), and the small territories of Kuwait, Qatar, Muscat and Aden, practically the whole of this region was part of the Ottoman Empire. Its collapse during the period 1914—1919 led to many far-reaching changes, some of which are noted in the following pages.

SYRIA
Province in the Ottoman Empire.

Region of Mesopotamia.

TURKEY
Issues of the Ottoman Empire 1863–1921 (some with French inscr. "Empire Ottoman" or "Postes Ottomanes").

LEVANT REGION
See page 23 for details of foreign POs in Syria and Palestine.

CYPRUS
Formerly Turkish, British possession 1878.
Issues 1880–

LEBANON
Autonomous within the Ottoman Empire 1861.
Issues of French POs in the Levant inscr. BEYROUTH 1905.

PALESTINE
Turkish Province.

HEJAZ
Under Ottoman rule till 1916, when it became an independent Kingdom.
Issues 1916–1925.

NEJD
Sultanate.

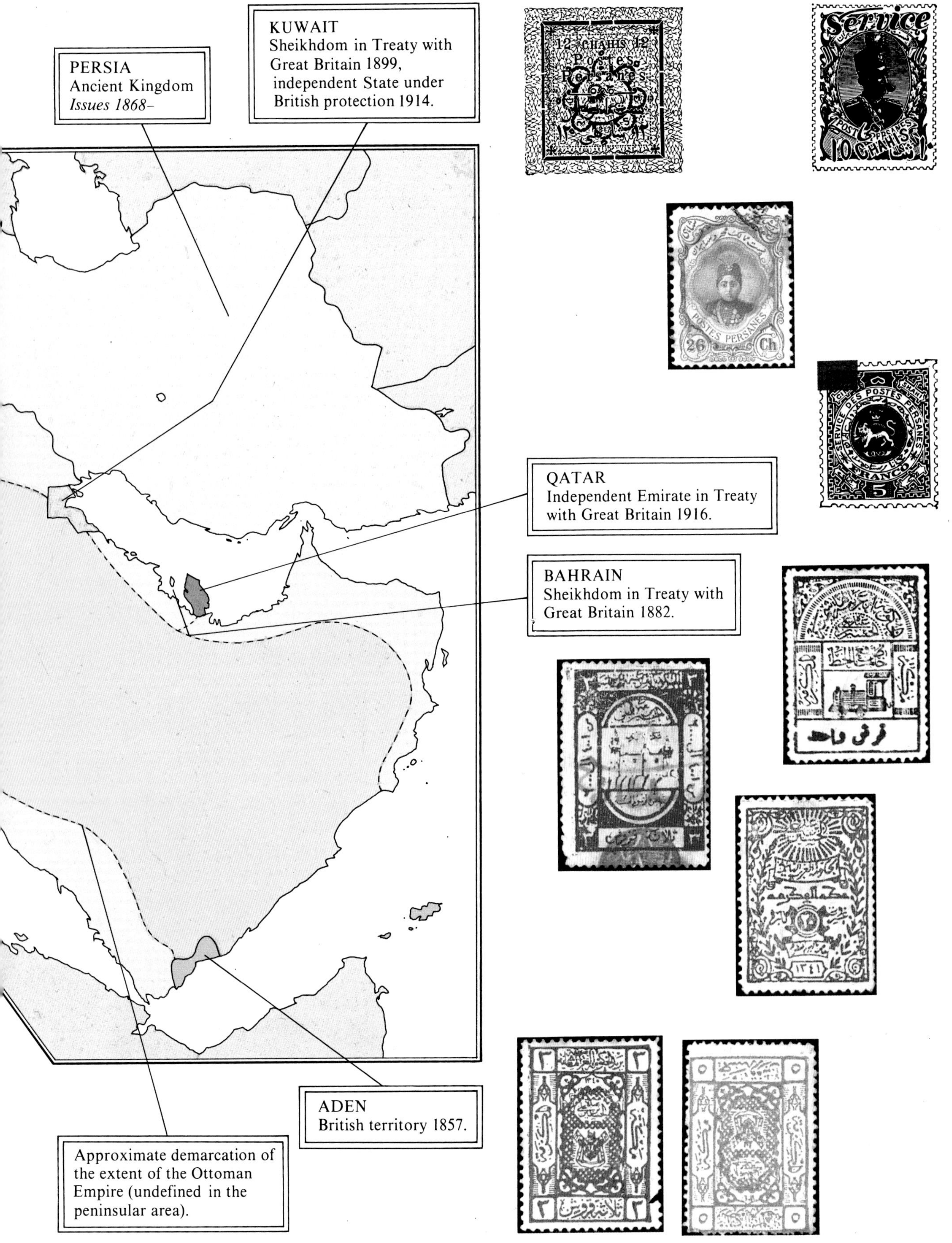
PERSIA
Ancient Kingdom
Issues 1868–
KUWAIT
Sheikhdom in Treaty with
Great Britain 1899,
independent State under
British protection 1914.
QATAR
Independent Emirate in Treaty
with Great Britain 1916.
BAHRAIN
Sheikhdom in Treaty with
Great Britain 1882.
ADEN
British territory 1857.
Approximate demarcation of
the extent of the Ottoman
Empire (undefined in the
peninsular area).
12 CHAHIS 12
Postes Persanes
Service
POSTES PERSANES
10 CHAHIS
POSTES PERSANES
26 Ch
SERVICE DES POSTES PERSANES
FRANCO
5

ARABIA AND MIDDLE EAST 1919 – 1948

Great changes in the political scene took place in this region following the end of the Ottoman Empire after the 1914-1918 war. Former Turkish Provinces became States, first under Mandate to either France or Great Britain, then as sovereign States: Hejd (Hejaz) (later together with Nejd becoming Saudi Arabia), Iraq, Jordan, Lebanon, Palestine (now Israel), Syria. The stamp issues of those territories well depict those changes.

IRAQ
British Mandate 1920–1932, Kingdom 1921–1932, independent Kingdom 1932–1958.
British occupation and Mandate issues 1918–1923.
Kingdom issues 1923–1958.

TURKEY
Issues of the Ottoman Empire 1863–1921.
Issues of Turkish Nationalist Govt. at Angora (Ankara) 1920–1923.
Issues of Republic 1923–

SYRIA
French Mandate 1919–1942, independent Republic 1942.
French occupation issues 1919–1923.
Arab Kingdom issues (under French Mandate) 1920.
French Mandate issues 1923–1933.
Republic issues (under French Mandate) 1934–1942.
Independent Republic issues 1942–

SANDJAK D'ALEXANDRETTE
Town and administrative region ('Sanjak') detached from Syria 1938 (then under French Mandate) and annexed to Turkey 1939 (now the Turkish town of Iskenderun).
French issues (opr. on Syrian stamps) 1938.
Turkish issues inscr. HATAY 1939.
(Hatay is the present Turkish town of Antakya, ancient Antioch in Syria, formerly in the Sanjak.)

PALESTINE
British occupation 1918–1923 and Mandate 1923–1948.
British occupation and administration issues 1918–1944.
(See Dictionary for special issues of Jordanian occupation, and Egyptian occupation of Gaza.)

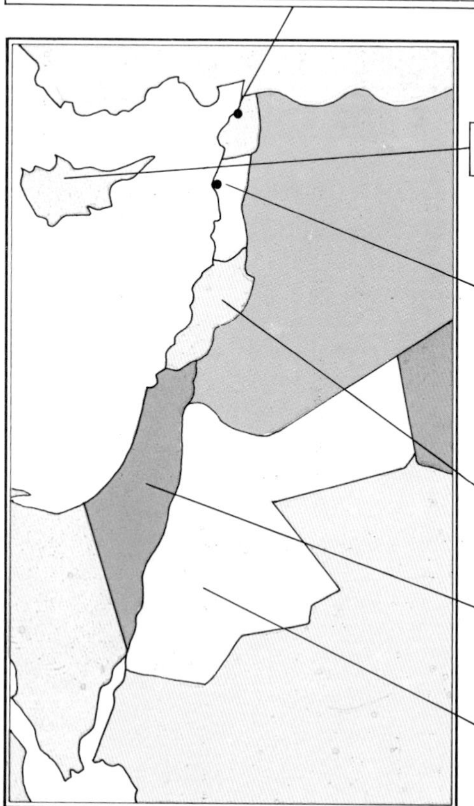

ALAOUITES/LATTAQUIÉ (Latakia)
French Mandate territory 1919–1937, when it was annexed to Syria. Name changed 1930 from Alaouites to Lattaquié (now the Syrian town of Al Ladhiqiyah).
Issues of Alaouites 1925–1930.
Issues of Lattaquié 1931–1935.

LEBANON
French Mandate 1922 and Republic under French Mandate 1926–1943, independent Republic 1944.
Issues 1924–1927.
Republic issues 1927–

PALESTINE

TRANSJORDAN
British Mandate 1920–1946, autonomous Emirate of Transjordan 1923, independent Hashemite Kingdom of Jordan 1946.
British Mandate issues 1920–1947.
Kingdom issues 1949–

IRAN
Named PERSIA until 1935.
Issues of Persia 1868–1935.
Issues of Iran 1935–

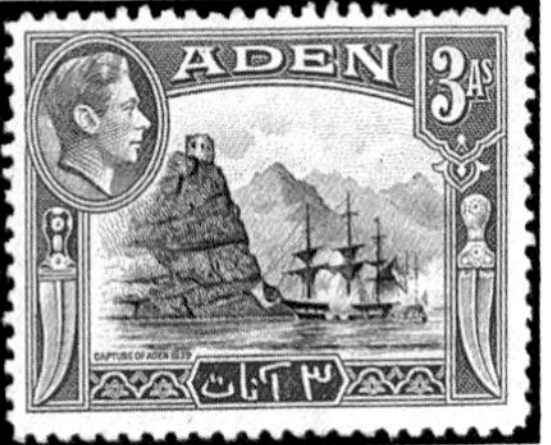

KUWAIT
Independent Sheikhdom under British protection 1914.
Sheikhdom issues 1923–1961.

MUSCAT
Independent Sultanate, first under the Postal administration of India, then of Great Britain.
Issues 1944–1948.

QATAR

BAHRAIN
Sheikhdom in Treaty with Great Britain 1882.
Issues 1933–1971.

SAUDI ARABIA
Kingdom formed 1926 by the union of the former Kingdom of Hejaz and the Sultanate of Nejd, first named Hejaz and Nejd, and Saudi Arabia in 1932.
Issues of Hejaz 1916–1925.
Issues of Nejd 1925.
Issues of Hejaz and Nejd 1926–1934.
Issues of Saudi Arabia 1934–

YEMEN
Kingdom issues 1926–1967.

ADEN
British possession administered by India to 1937, Crown Colony till 1963.
Issues 1937–1963.

ADEN PROTECTORATE STATES
Comprised the following:
KATHIRI STATE of SEIYUN.
QU'AITI STATE of SHIHR and MUKALLA, OR QU'AITI STATE in HADRAMAUT.
Issues 1942–1967.

ARABIA AND MIDDLE EAST FROM 1948

A significant political event in the region during this period was the creation of the independent State of Israel in May 1948. Many other changes also took place among the States of the Arabian Peninsula: new sovereign States came into being and various Federations were formed. As in other parts of the world, postage stamps portray the continuously-changing pattern of the political situation.

IRAQ
Became a Republic in 1958.
Republic issues 1959–

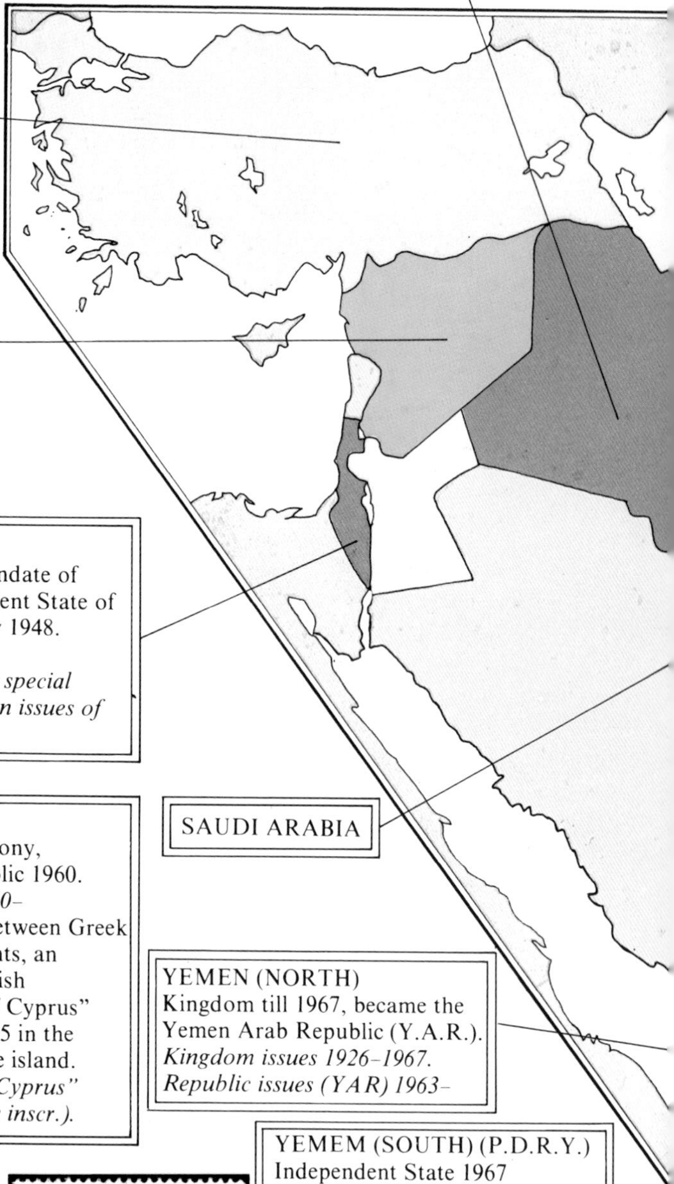

TURKEY

SYRIA
Independent Republic 1942. Merged with Egypt in 1958 to form the UNITED ARAB REPUBLIC (U.A.R.), dissolved end of 1961.
Independent Republic issues 1942–1958.
Issues as part of the U.A.R. 1958–1961.
Issues of Syrian Arab Republic 1961–

ISRAEL
Former British Mandate of Palestine, independent State of Israel founded May 1948.
Issues 1948–
(See Dictionary for special Egyptian occupation issues of GAZA.)

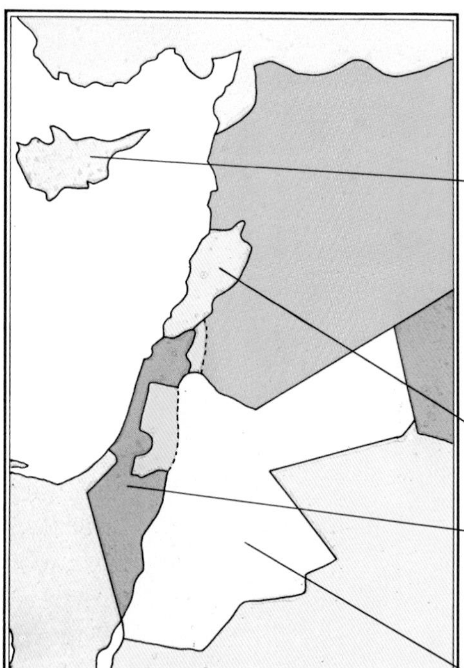

CYPRUS
Former British Colony, independent Republic 1960.
Republic issues 1960–
Following a split between Greek and Turkish elements, an autonomous "Turkish Federation State of Cyprus" was declared in 1975 in the northern part of the island.
Issues of "Turkish Cyprus" 1974– (with various inscr.).

SAUDI ARABIA

YEMEN (NORTH)
Kingdom till 1967, became the Yemen Arab Republic (Y.A.R.).
Kingdom issues 1926–1967.
Republic issues (YAR) 1963–

LEBANON

ISRAEL

JORDAN
Hashemite Kingdom 1946.
Kingdom issues 1949–
Issues of occupation of Palestine (Israel) 1948–1949.

YEMEM (SOUTH) (P.D.R.Y.)
Independent State 1967 consisting of the former British Colony of Aden and the Aden Protectorate States (which had formed the Federation of South Arabia 1963 – 1967). First known as South Yemen People's Republic, re-named PDRY 1970. The MAHRA STATE, being the Sultanate of Qishn and Socotra and formerly under British protection, became part of the PDRY 1967.
PDRY issues 1968–
Mahra State issues 1967.

IRAN
The Kingdom came to an end in 1979, replaced by a Republic.

KUWAIT
Sovereign State in 1961.
Independent State issues 1961–

BAHRAIN
Independent State in 1971.
Independent State issues 1971–

QATAR
Independent State in 1971.
Independent State issues 1971–

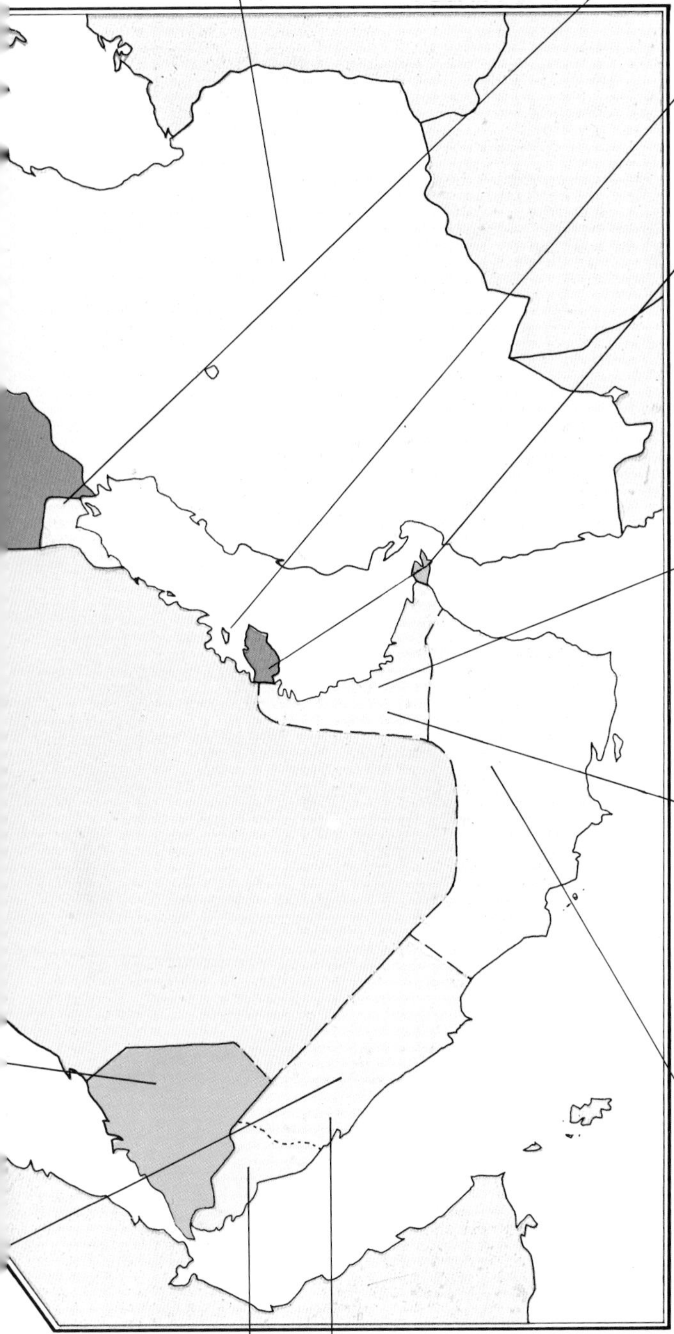

TRUCIAL STATES
Federation of Sheikhdoms in Treaty with Great Britain which comprised:

ABU DHABI
AJMAN
DUBAI
FUJAIRAH
RAS AL KHAIMAH
SHARJAH
UMM AL QAIWAIN

Issues of the Trucial States 1961–1963.
(The several States also issued their own stamps, see Dictionary for details.)

UNITED ARAB EMIRATES
A State, being a union of the same former Trucial States Sheikhdoms formed in 1971/72.
Issues of the U.A.E. 1973–

MUSCAT
Independent Sultanate, later becoming the Sultanate of MUSCAT and OMAN (1966–1971), and Sultanate of OMAN in 1971.
Issues of Muscat 1944–1948.
Issues of Muscat and Oman 1966–1970.
Issues of Oman 1971–

ADEN PROTECTORATE STATES Consisted of the States of: KATHIRI STATE OF SEYUN, QU'AITI STATE OF SHIHR AND MUKALLA (or QU'AITI STATE IN HADRAMAUT).
FEDERATION OF SOUTH ARABIA
Formed in 1963 and consisting of the British Crown Colony of Aden together with the former Aden Protectorate States, the territory became part of the new State of Yemen (South) in 1967.
Issues of Aden Protectorate States 1942–1967. (See Dictionary for issues of the separate States.)
Issues of Aden 1937–1963. Issues of Federation of South Arabia 1963–1966.

AUSTRALASIA UP TO 1914/1919

Formed as the Dominion of Australia Jan. 1901, itself a Federal Commonwealth, from the former Colonies of New South Wales, Queensland, South Australia, Tasmania (formerly Van Diemen's Land), Victoria, and Western Australia.
Issues of the component States of Australia, see separate boxes on this map.
General issues of Australia 1913–

NETHERLANDS NEW GUINEA (Nederlands Nieuw-Guinea)
Western part of the island of New Guinea and administratively part of the Netherlands Indies (Nederlandsch-Indië) until 1963, when it was ceded to Indonesia and re-named West Irian, now Irian Jaya.
Issues of Netherlands Indies 1864–1950.

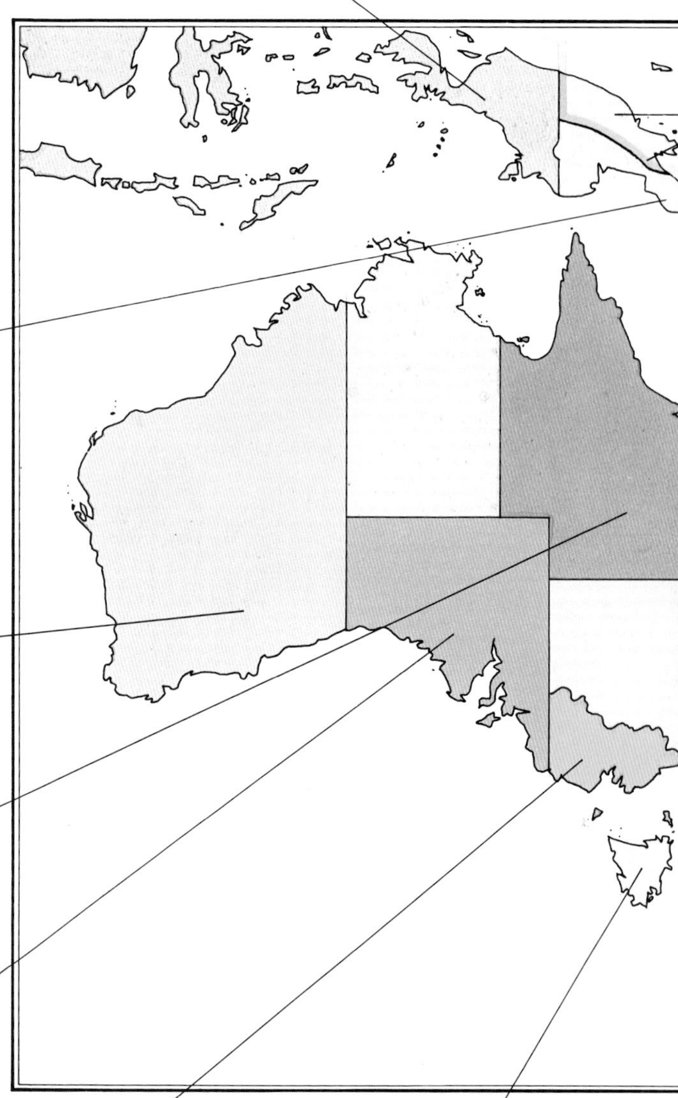

BRITISH NEW GUINEA (PAPUA)
Southwestern part of the island of New Guinea, British possession 1884, under the administration of Australia 1906. The whole eastern part of the island, including the former German possessions, was occupied by Allied Forces during the 1914–1918 war, becoming an Australian Mandate in 1920.
British issues (British New Guinea) 1901–1906.
Australian administration issues (Papua) 1906–1939.

WESTERN AUSTRALIA
British settlement 1829, a State of the Commonwealth of Australia 1901.
Issues 1854–1912.

QUEENSLAND
First a part of New South Wales, became a separate Colony 1859, and a State of the Commonwealth of Australia 1901.
Issues 1860–1911.

SOUTH AUSTRALIA
A British Province 1836, and a State of the Commonwealth of Australia 1901.
Issues 1855–1911.

VICTORIA
British Colony 1851, a State of the Commonwealth of Australia 1901.
Issues 1850–1912.

TASMANIA (formerly named VAN DIEMEN'S LAND)
British Colony 1825, a State of the Commonwealth of Australia 1901.
Issues 1853–1913.

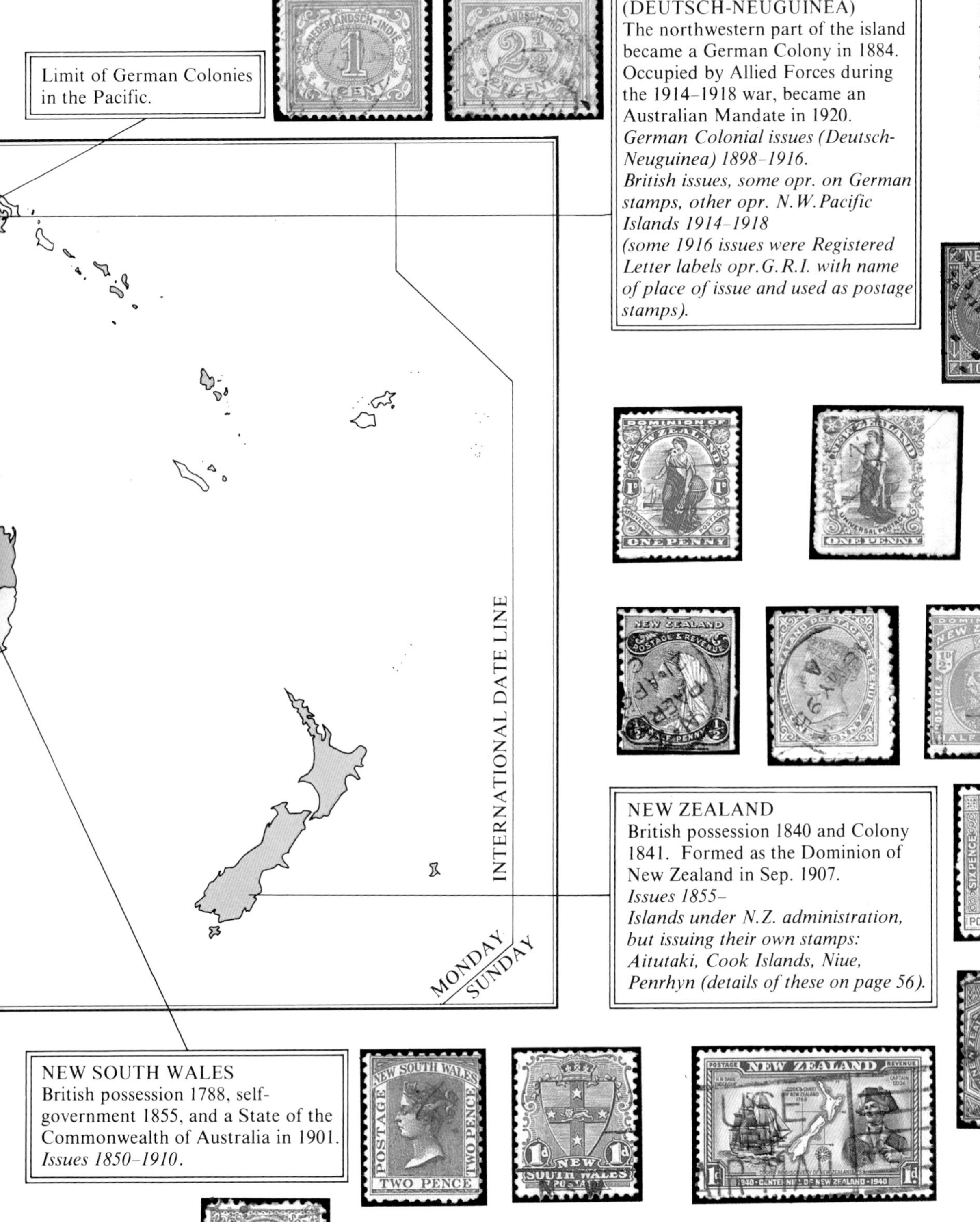

Limit of German Colonies in the Pacific.

GERMAN NEW GUINEA (DEUTSCH-NEUGUINEA)
The northwestern part of the island became a German Colony in 1884. Occupied by Allied Forces during the 1914–1918 war, became an Australian Mandate in 1920.
German Colonial issues (Deutsch-Neuguinea) 1898–1916.
British issues, some opr. on German stamps, other opr. N.W. Pacific Islands 1914–1918
(some 1916 issues were Registered Letter labels opr. G.R.I. with name of place of issue and used as postage stamps).

NEW ZEALAND
British possession 1840 and Colony 1841. Formed as the Dominion of New Zealand in Sep. 1907.
Issues 1855–
Islands under N.Z. administration, but issuing their own stamps: Aitutaki, Cook Islands, Niue, Penrhyn (details of these on page 56).

NEW SOUTH WALES
British possession 1788, self-government 1855, and a State of the Commonwealth of Australia in 1901.
Issues 1850–1910.

AUSTRALASIA FROM 1919

The most important political changes in this vast region were: The unification of the separate former British Colonies in Australia into one great Dominion in Jan. 1901, forming a Federal Commonwealth of the six component States (the Northern Territory having self-government in 1978, though constitutionally not a State).
This event was followed by the founding of the Dominion of New Zealand in 1907.
The end of the German Colonial Empire in the period 1914-1918 also caused a notable change in the region, affecting the former Colony of German New Guinea.
The last change was the cession of Netherlands New Guinea to Indonesia in 1963, that part of the island now named Irian Jaya.

NORTHERN TERRITORY
Territory of Australia administered by the State of South Australia till Jan. 1911, self-government July 1978, though not Constitutionally a State of Australia.

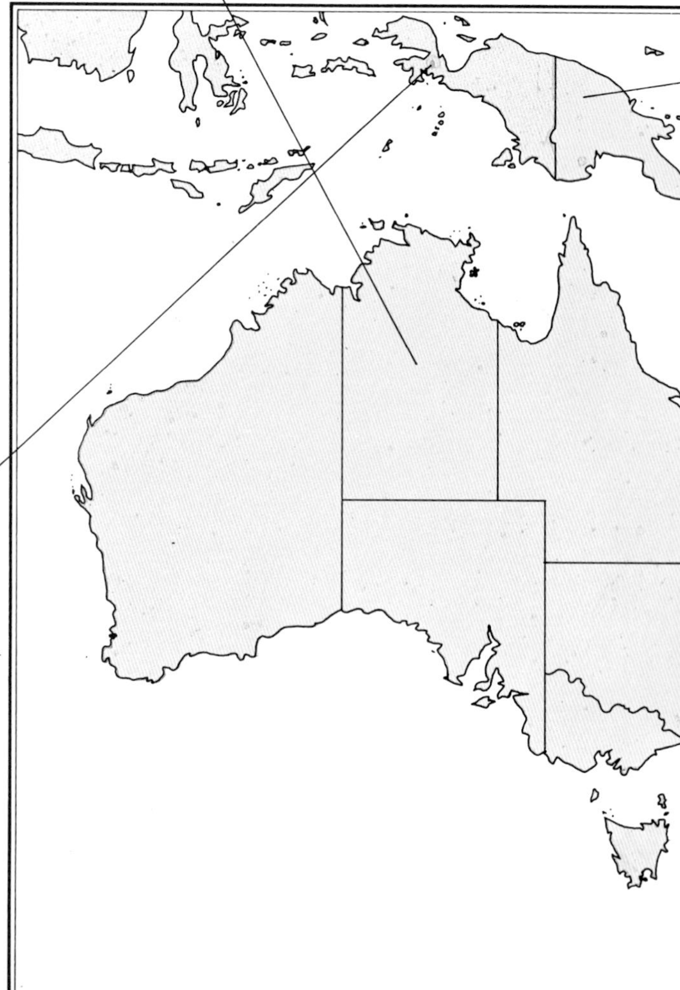

IRIAN JAYA
Formerly Netherlands New Guinea (Nederlands Nieuw-Guinea), under U.N. administration 1962–1963, and ceded to Indonesia 1963, first named West Irian, now Irian Jaya.
Issues of Netherlands New Guinea 1950–1962.
U.N. administration issues (U.N.T.E.A.) of West New Guinea 1962–1963.
Indonesian issues of West Irian (Irian Barat) 1963–1970.

AUSTRALIAN ISLANDS
Australian islands in the Indian Ocean: Sovereignty of the former British CHRISTMAS ISLAND (Indian Ocean) and the COCOS (KEELING) ISLANDS was transferred to Australia in 1958 and 1964 respectively *(details on page 62).*

AUSTRALIAN ANTARCTIC TERRITORY
(details on issues, see page 60–61).

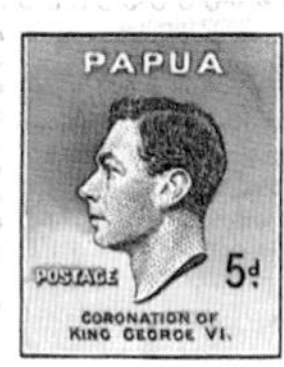

PAPUA NEW GUINEA
Consists of the former British New Guinea and former Colony of German New Guinea, became an Australian Mandate 1920. Autonomous rule under Australian Trusteeship in 1973, and an independent State in the British Commonwealth 1975.
Australian issues (Territory of New Guinea) 1925–1939.
Issues of Papua & New Guinea 1952 (Stamps of Australia current 1945–1952.)

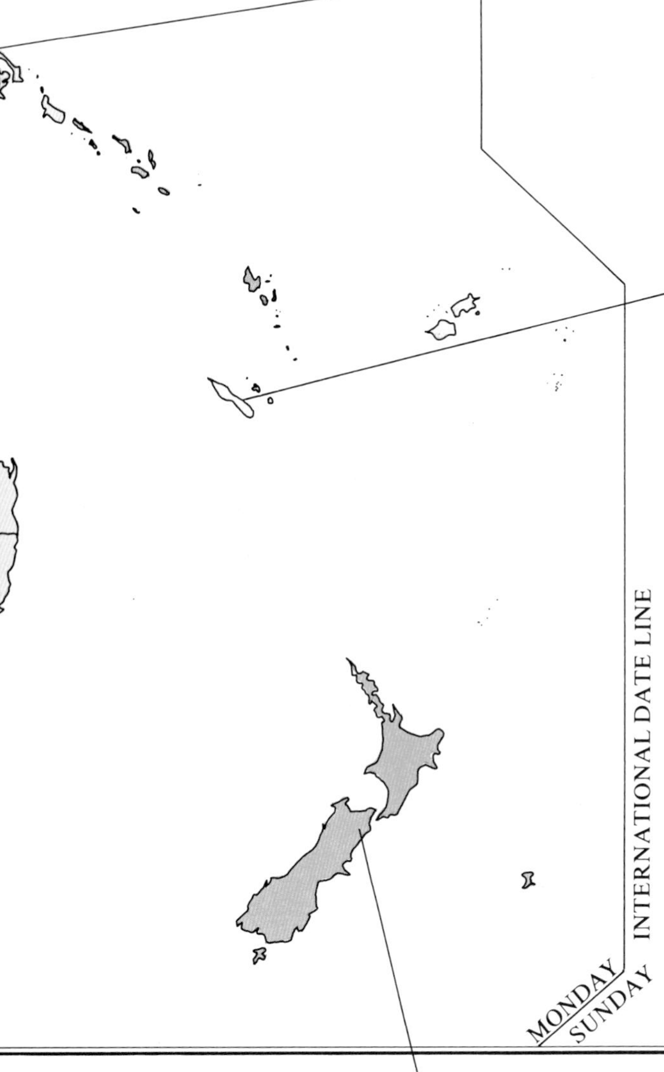

NORFOLK ISLAND
Island under the administration of Australia 1914–1960 and now a Dependent Territory of Australia.
Issues 1947–

NEW ZEALAND
Territories under New Zealand administration issuing their own stamps: Tokelau (or Union) Islands, and the Ross Dependency *(details on pages 59 and 60–61 respectively).*

PACIFIC ISLANDS UP TO 1914/19

The demarcation lines shown in the Pacific are not international boundaries. That on the left indicates the approximate extent of the German Colonies in the Pacific and that in the centre shows the approximate area of the French Oceanic Establishments (now French Polynesia).

MARSHALL ISLANDS
German Colony 1885, occupied by British and New Zealand Forces 1914, (Japanese Mandate 1920–1945).
German Colonial issues (Marschall- Inseln) 1897–1916.
British- N.Z.occupation issues 1914–1915.

MARIANA ISLANDS
Formerly Spanish, German Colony 1899, occupied by Japan 1914.
Spanish issues 1899.
German Colonial issues (Marianen) 1899–1916/19.

CAROLINE ISLANDS
German Colony 1899, occupied by Japan 1914.
German Colonial issues (Karolinen) 1899–1915/19.

GUAM
USA Territory 1898.
USA administration issues 1899.

NAURU ISLAND
Part of the Marshall Islands group, German Colony 1885–1914. (Under Allied Trusteeship 1916–1947 and administered by Australia.)

BRITISH SOLOMON ISLANDS
British Protectorate 1893/1899.
Issues 1907–1975.

MONDAY
SUNDAY

NEW CALEDONIA (NOUVELLE CALÉDONIE)
Island group, French possession 1853, with its Dependencies in 1887 including the islands WALLIS and FUTUNA.
Issues 1860–

NEW HERBRIDES/ NOUVELLES HÉBRIDES
Anglo-French Condominium established 1886/1906.
Issues (with both English and French inscr.) 1908–1980.

FIJI
British Colony 1874 (independent 1970).
Issues 1870–

TONGA
Group of islands forming an independent Kingdom, Protectorate of Great Britain May 1900.
Issues 1886–

NIUE
Island in the Cook Islands group.
Issues 1902 –

COOK ISLANDS
Group of islands under the administration of New Zealand 1901.
Issues 1892–

AITUTAKI
Island, part of the British Protectorate of the Cook Islands, under N.Z. administration 1901.
Issues 1903 – 1932.

PENRHYN ISLAND
(also named Tongareva)
Part of the Cook Islands group, British possession under the administration of New Zealand 1901.
Issues 1902–1932. 1973–

HAWAII
Formerly an independent Kingdom, possession of the USA in 1898 and USA Territory 1900.
Issues 1851–1899.
(Stamps of the USA used since 1899.)

GILBERT and ELLICE ISLANDS
British Protectorate 1892 and Colony Jan. 1916.
Issues 1911–1975.

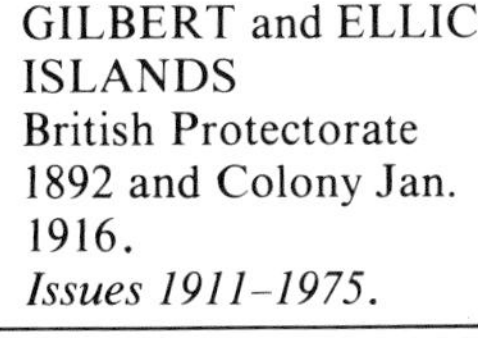

FRENCH POLYNESIA (ÉTABLISSEMENTS FRANÇAIS DE L'OCÉANIE)
French Colony 1880. Includes the island of TAHITI, which issued its own stamps.
Issues of Etabl. Français de l'Océanie 1892–1956. Separate issues of Tahiti 1882–1915.

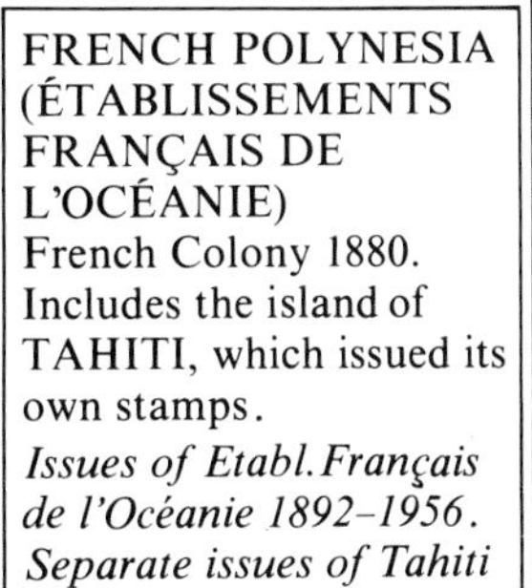

SAMOA
Island group and Kingdom, divided between Germany and the USA 1900, the western part to Germany and the eastern part to the USA. German Samoa occupied by N.Z. Forces 1914 and administered by New Zealand 1920–1961.
See Dictionary for stamp issues.

PITCAIRN ISLANDS
British Settlement 1887 (inhabited by the descendants of the "Bounty" mutineers since 1790).

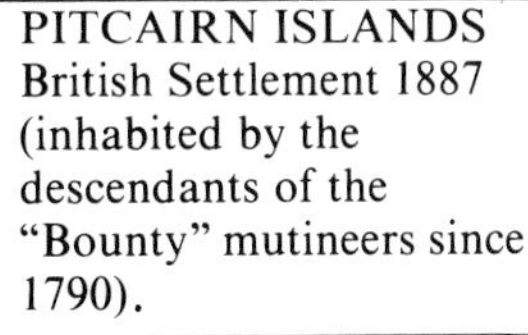

PACIFIC ISLANDS FROM 1919

The demarcation lines shown in the Pacific are not international boundaries. That on the left indicates the approximate extent of the US Trust Territory of the Pacific Islands and that in the centre shows the approximate area of French Polynesia.

MARSHALL ISLANDS
Former German Colony, under Japanese Mandate 1920–1945, and USA Mandate 1947 (U.N.Trust Territory).

HAWAII
USA possession 1898, became a State of the USA in 1959.

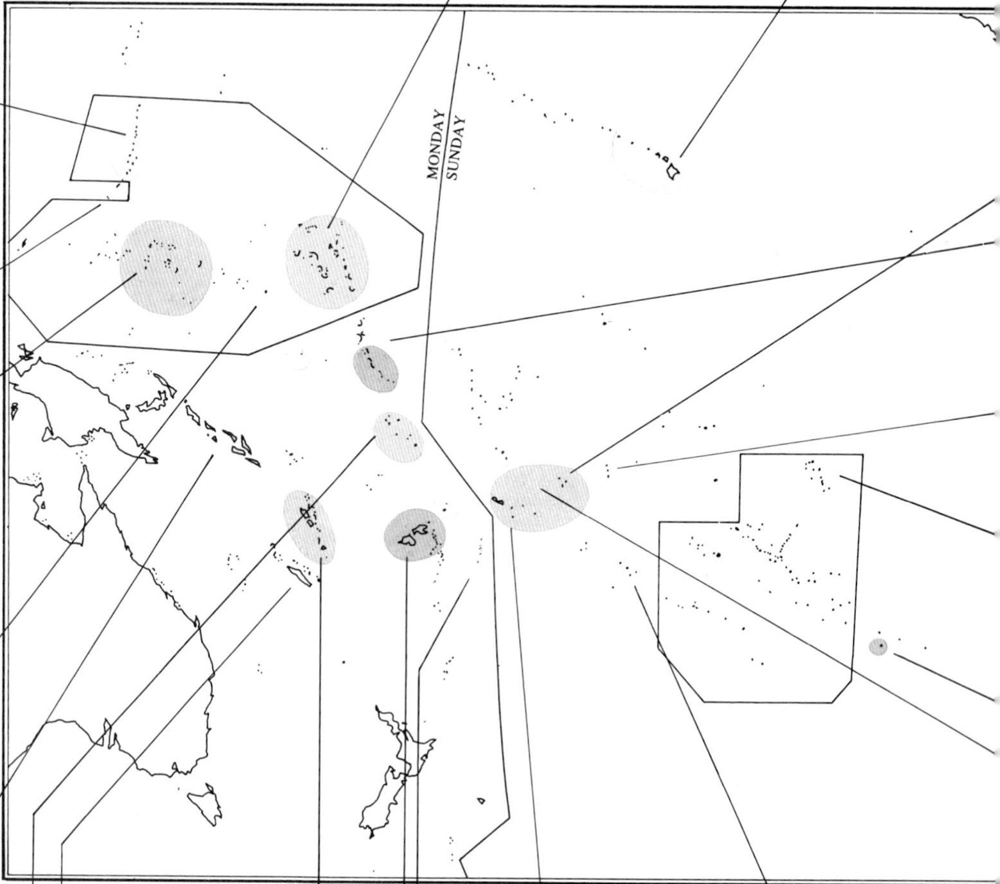

MARIANA ISLANDS
Formerly German Colony, occupied by Japan 1914, Japanese Mandate till 1945 and Trust Territory of the USA 1947.

GUAM
Former Spanish possession, USA Territory 1898.
USA administration issues 1899.
Local post service issues 1930.

CAROLINE ISLANDS
Former German Colony, occupied by Japan 1914 and Japanese Mandate till 1945, when it became a Trust Territory of the USA.

NAURU ISLAND
Former German Colony, under joint Trusteeship of Australia, Great Britain and New Zealand 1916-1947. Independent Republic Jan. 1968 and a special British Commonwealth Member.
British issues 1916–1968.
Republic issues 1968–

SOLOMON ISLANDS
Former British Protectorate 1893/99. Independent State in the British Commonwealth July 1978.
Issues of British Solomon Islands 1907–1975.
Issues of Solomon Islands 1975–

TUVALU
Formerly the Ellice Islands British Protectorate of the Gilbert and Ellice Islands. Separated from the Gilberts end 1975, and independent State in the British Commonwealth Oct. 1978, re-named TUVALU.
Issues of Gilbert and Ellice Islands 1911–1975.
Issues of Tuvalu 1976–

NEW CALEDONIA
(NOUVELLE CALÉDONIE)
Overseas Territory of France (T.O.M.) with its Dependencies, 1958. (Includes Wallis and Futuna, a separate "T.O.M." 1961).
Issues 1860–

VANUATU
Former Anglo-French Condominium of the New Hebrides/Nouvelles Hébrides. End of Condominium 1980 and independent Republic in the British Commonwealth, re-named VANUATU.
Issues of New Hebrides 1908–1980.
Issues of Vanuatu 1980–

FIJI
Formerly British Colony (1874), independent State in the British Commonwealth Oct.1970.
Issues 1870–

WALLIS and FUTUNA
Dependency of the French Territory of New Caledonia (Nouvelle Calédonie), and separate Overseas Territory of France (T.O.M.) 1961.
Issues 1920–

TONGA
Autonomous Kingdom in the British Commonwealth June 1970.
Issues 1886–

AITUTAKI
Island, part of the Cook Islands administration 1972, but still issuing its own stamps.
Issues 1903–1932
1972–

COOK ISLANDS
Formerly under the administration of New Zealand, internal self-govt.1965 and Associate State of New Zealand.
Issues 1892–

NIUE
Island in the Cook Islands group, Associated State of New Zealand 1974 with internal self-govt.
Issues 1902–

PENRHYN ISLAND
(also named TONGAREVA) In the Cook Islands Group.
Issues 1902–1932.
1973–

The aftermath of each of the two wars of 1914-1918 and 1939-1945 saw numerous changes in the sovereignty and political status of the many small islands and island groups. Among these were the changes in the former German Colonies in the Pacific, and the allocation of Mandated or Trust Territories to Australia, Japan, New Zealand and the USA. Many changes in the political status of former British and French island possessions also took place since 1945, all of which are reflected in the postage stamps issued.

TOKELAU (or Union) ISLAND
Group of small islands, formerly part of the Gilbert and Ellice Islands and part of New Zealand Jan. 1949.
Issues 1948–

KIRIBATI
Formerly the Gilbert Islands, separated from the Ellice Islands end of 1975, independent State in the British Commonwealth July 1979 and re-named KIRIBATI. Includes the Phoenix and Line Islands, and Ocean Island (now Banaba).
Issues of Gilbert and Ellice Islands 1911–1975.
Issues of Gilbert Islands 1976–1979. Issues of Kiribati 1979–

AMERICAN SAMOA
Eastern group of the islands of Samoa, under USA administration 1900 with limited self-government 1960.

GALAPAGOS ISLANDS (ISLAS GALAPAGOS)
Island group belonging to Ecuador 1832, and a Province of Ecuador Feb. 1973.
Issues 1957–1973.

POLYNÉSIE FRANÇAISE
Formerly the Établissements Français de l'Océanie (French Oceanic Settlements), an Overseas Territory of France (T.O.M.) Nov. 1958 and re-named Polynésie Française (French Polynesia).
Issues 1958–

WESTERN SAMOA
A former German Colony and under the administration of New Zealand 1920–1961, independent Republic of Western Samoa Jan. 1962 and member of the British Commonwealth Aug. 1970.
Republic issues 1962– (inscr. Samoa i Sisifo).

TERRITORY OF PITCAIRN, HENDERSON, DUCIE AND OENO ISLANDS
British Dependent Territory, formerly under the administration of Fiji 1952–1970.
Issues 1940–

ANTARCTICA

An international Antarctica Treaty came into effect in 1961 to promote international scientific co-operation in the region south of Lat. 60° S., the participants being: Argentina, Australia, Belgium, Chile, France, Great Britian, Japan, New Zealand, Norway, Republic of South Africa, the USSR, and the USA. Territorial claims are not affected by the Treaty, though new permanent claims are not allowed by it.

VICTORIA LAND
Capt.Scott's ill-fated expedition to the South Pole 1910–1913.
Special issue 1911.

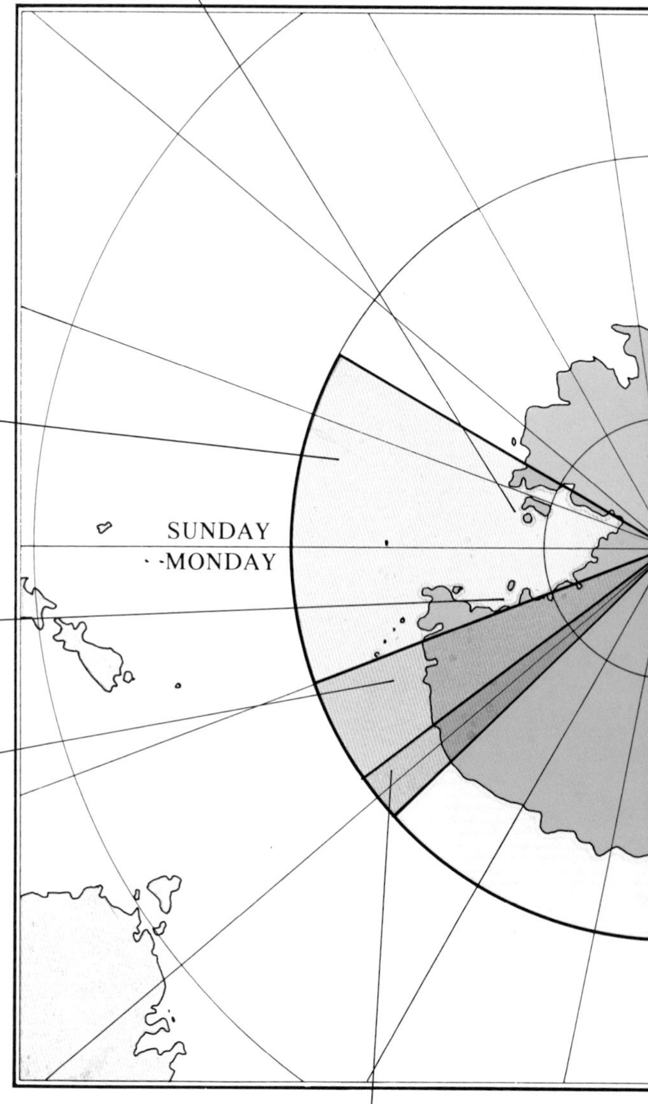

ROSS DEPENDENCY
Territory under the jurisdiction of New Zealand, established 1923, in the region south of Lat. 60°S. It includes EDWARD VII LAND and parts of VICTORIA LAND.
Issues 1957–

KING EDWARD VII LAND
Ernest Shackleton's expedition to the Ross barrier 1907–1909.
Special issue 1908.

AUSTRALIAN ANTARCTIC TERRITORY

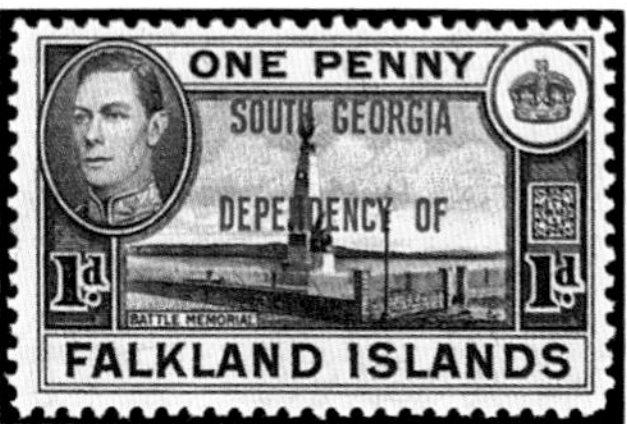

ADELIE LAND (TERRES AUSTRALES ET ANTARCTIQUES FRANÇAISES)-
Established in 1955 (defined 1938), it includes the Kerguelen and Crozet Islands and Terre Adélie, within the region south of Lat. 60°S. and between Long. 136°E. and 142°E.
Issues 1955–

Chinese station established 1984–1985 on King George Island, with a Post Office.

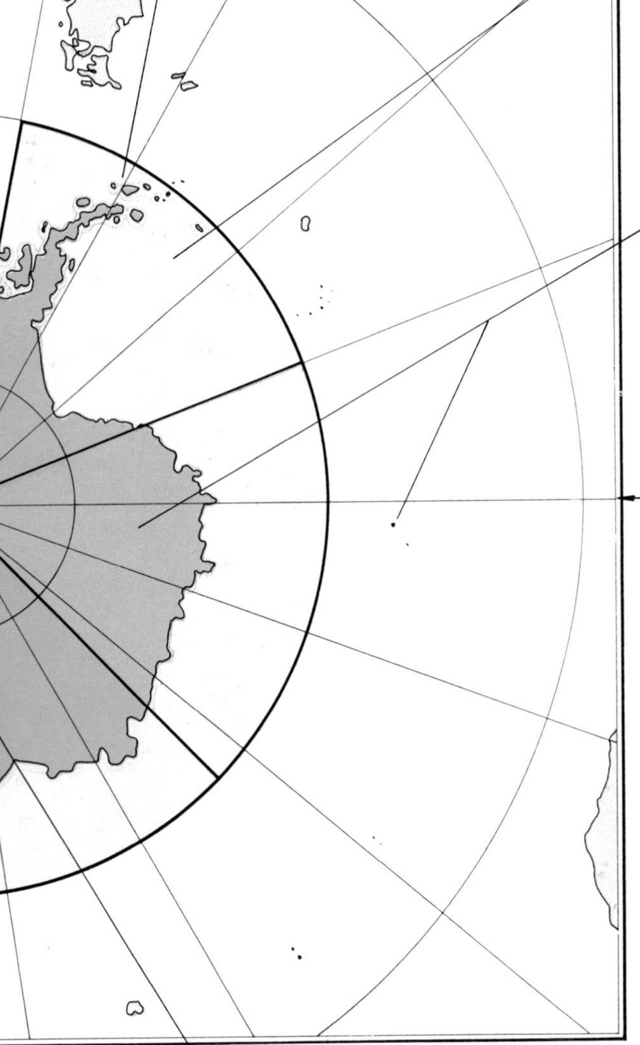

BRITISH ANTARCTIC TERRITORY
A British Dependent Territory established 1962 in the area south of Lat. 60° S. and between Long. 20° W. and 80° W. It includes the South Orkneys and South Shetland Islands, which were formerly part of the Falkland Islands Dependencies.
Issues 1963–

NORWEGIAN ANTARCTIC
Norwegian territories have been established between 1930 and 1939: Bouvet Island, Peter the First Land, Princess Ragnhild Land, and Queen Maud Land.
Special issue inscr. BOUVET ØYA 1934.

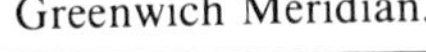

Greenwich Meridian.

AUSTRALIAN ANTARCTIC TERRITORY
Established in 1933, it covers the area south of Lat. 60° S. and between Long. 45° E. and 160° E. (excepting the French Territory of Adélie Land).
Issues 1955–

INDIAN AND ATLANTIC OCEAN ISLANDS

Many changes in the political status of Indian Ocean Islands took place since 1945. These relate to the former French possessions, notably the Comoros and Madagascar, both independent Republics. Several former British possessions are now independent States: the Maldive Islands, Mauritius and the Seychelles, while the new Dependent Territory of the British Indian Ocean Territory was formed in 1965. The former British possessions of Christmas Island (Indian Ocean) and the Cocos (Keeling) Islands are now part of Australia. All these changes are reflected in postage stamp issues.

BRITISH INDIAN OCEAN TERRITORY
British Dependent Territory established 1965, it includes some islands previously administered by Mauritius and the Seychelles. Since 1976, comprises only the Chagos Archipelago, including the island of Diego Garcia.
Issues 1968–

SEYCHELLES
Archipelago of 99 islands, British 1814 and administered by Mauritius till 1903, when they became a separate Colony. Independent Republic in the British Commonwealth 1976.
Issues 1890–

ZIL ELOIGNE SESEL (or other spellings)
Part of the Seychelles group of islands, with separate stamp issues. *Issues 1980–*

MALDIVE ISLANDS
Sultanate under British protection till 1952, Republic 1968, member of the British Commonwealth 1985 (special member 1982).
Issues 1906–1968.
Republic issues 1968–

COMORO ISLANDS
French possession 1841/43, under administration of Madagascar 1914, autonomous 1946 and Overseas Territory (T.O.M.) of France 1958. Republic independent of France 1974 (except the island of Mayotte).
Issues of Grande Comore 1897–1923.
Issues of Archipel des Comores 1950–1976.
Republic issues 1976–

CHRISTMAS ISLAND
(Indian Ocean)
Part of the former Colony of Singapore till 1957, separate British Colony till Oct.1958, when it came under the administration of Australia.
Issues 1958–

MAYOTTE
Island of the Comoros, under the administration of Madagascar 1914–1946 and part of the Comoros 1947. Seceded from these 1974 when they became a Republic, and Mayotte became an Overseas Département of France 1974.
Issues 1892–1914.

COCOS (KEELING) ISLANDS
British possession 1857, under the administration of Ceylon (now Sri Lanka) 1878 and later part of the former Colony of Singapore. Under the administration of Australia 1955 and integrated with Australia 1964.
Issues 1963 –

RÉUNION
French possession 1642, a Département of France (D.O.M.) 1946.
Issues 1852–1947 (French stamps used since then).

DIEGO-SUAREZ
French naval base on northern tip of Madagascar, under administration of Madagascar 1898.
Issues 1890–1896.

MADAGASCAR
French possession 1686 and Colony in 1896. Independent Republic in the French Community 1958 and fully independent 1960 (République Malgache, or Repoblika Malagasy).
Issues 1889–1958.
Republic issues 1958–

STE.-MARIE DE MADAGASCAR
Small island off northeast coast of Madagascar, part of Madagascar 1900.
Issues 1894–1896 (Stamps of Madagascar used from 1896).

NOSSI-BÉ
French island possession 1841 off the northwest coast of Madagascar, of which it became part in 1901.
Issues 1889–1901.

MAURITIUS
British possession since 1810, independent State in the British Commonwealth Mar. 1968.
Issues 1847–

BERMUDA
British Colony 1684, now a British Dependent Territory.
Issues 1865–

ST. PIERRE ÈT MIQUELON
French possession 1816, and an Overseas "Département" (D.O.M.) of France July 1976.
Issues 1885–1978.(Stamps of France used since 1978).

AZORES (AÇORES)
Islands administratively part of Portugal.
Issues 1868–1931 1980–

MADEIRA
Islands administratively part of Portugal.
Issues 1868–1929 1980–

SAO TOMÉ AND PRINCIPE
(St. Thomas & Principe)
Formerly Portuguese islands and Overseas Province of Portugal. Independent Republic of Sao Tomé e Principe in July 1975.
Issues 1870–1975. Republic issues 1975–

CAPE VERDE (CABO VERDE)
Formerly Portuguese Colony, Overseas Province of Portugal 1951, independent Republic 1975–
Issues 1877–

ASCENSION
Island administration by the British Admiralty 1815 to 1922, when it became a Dependency of St. Helena, and now a part of the British Dependent Territory of St. Helena and Dependencies.
Issues 1972–

ST. HELENA
British Colony 1834, now British Dependent Territory. Includes the Dependencies of Ascension Island and Tristan da Cunha, and known as St. Helena Dependencies. (Island on which Napoleon Bonaparte was exiled in 1815 till his death in May 1821.)
Issues 1856–

FALKLAND ISLANDS DEPENDENCIES
Formerly included the island Dependencies of Graham Land, South Georgia, South Orkneys and South Shetlands. The dependencies now consist only of South Georgia and South Sandwich and form a British Dependent Territory.
Separate issues of former Dependencies 1944–1946. General issues 1946–1963. (Replaced by issues of the British Antarctic Territory 1963– and separate issues of South Georgia (1963–).

TRISTAN DA CUNHA
Main island of a group (incl. Gough Island), British Colony 1816, Dependency of St. Helena 1938. Population evacuated Oct. 1961 due to volcanic eruptions, (when current stamp stocks were destroyed) and returned in 1963.
Issues 1952–1961. 1963–

BOUVET ISLAND (BOUVET ØYA)
Norwegian Dependency 1930.
Special Norwegian issue, opr. 1934.

BRITISH ANTARCTIC TERRITORY
British Dependent Territory formed in 1962 from the former Falkland Islands. Dependencies south of Lat. 60°S. and including the islands of South Orkney and South Shetland, and the British Antarctic Peninsula (incl. Graham Land).
Issues 1963–

FALKLAND ISLANDS
British possession in 1833, now a British Dependent Territory.
Issues 1878–

SOUTH GEORGIA
One of the two Falklands Islands Dependencies.
Separate issues 1944–1946 1963–

GRAHAM LAND
Part of the British Antarctic Territory, 1962.

SOUTH SHETLANDS
Formerly part of the Falkland Islands. Dependencies, now part of the British Antarctic Territory.
Separate issues 1944–1946.

SOUTH ORKNEYS
Formerly part of the the Falkland Islands. Dependancies, now part of the British Antarctic Territory.
Separate issues 1944–1946.

SOUTH SANDWICH ISLANDS
Together with South Georgia, forms the British Dependent Territory of the Falkland Islands Dependencies.

DICTIONARY OF WORLD STAMPS

Abbreviations: inscr. inscription on stamp (eg Helvetia, Espana, etc). This term includes inscriptions which are overprints or surcharges.
P.O. Post Office.

Explanatory note:

Stamp issue dates: The first date denotes when a stamp was first issued. A single date followed by a hyphen (eg 1840-) indicates that an issue is still continuing. The second date (when applicable) is that of the last issue or the obsolescence of a stamp. For better clarification, brief notes on political events are given where necessary.

Page numbers: Numbers in bold give the relevant atlas page. Numbers in lighter type indicate that an entry is located in the map shown, though not named in it.

51 **Abu Dhabi**
One of the Trucial States in Arabia and later a State in the United Arab Emirates (U.A.E.).
Issues *1964-1972*
See Trucial States for earlier issues, U.A.E. for later.

35,37 **Abyssinia** — See Ethiopia.

63 **Açores** — See Azores.

60 **Adelie Land** — See Terres Australes et Antarctiques Françaises (French Antarctica)

47,49, 51 **Aden**
British possession till 1967, when it became part of Yemen (South) (PDRY).
Issues *1937-1963*
For later issues, see Federation of South Arabia, of which Aden formed part 1963-1967.

49,51 **Aden Protectorate States**
Issues of Kathiri State of Seiyun *1942-1967*
Issues of Qu'aiti State of Shihr and Mukalla, or Qu'aiti State in Hadramaut *1942-1967*
For later issues, see Yemen (South) (PDRY), in which the States were incorporated 1967.

34 **A.E.F.** — See Afrique Equatoriale Française (French Equatorial Africa).

22 **Aegean Islands**
The Aegean (or Dodecanese) Islands were part of the Ottoman Empire, occupied by Italy 1912, ceded to Italy 1920, restored to Greece 1947.
Italian issues inscr. Isole Italiano dell'Egeo *1912-1944*
The following islands had their own separate issues 1912-1932 (except Rodi, which issued till 1935):
Calino (Calimno) *1912-1932*
Carchi (Karki) *1912-1932*
Caso *1912-1932*
Castelrosso *1922-1932*
Cos (Coo) *1912-1932*
Lero (Leros) *1912-1932*
Lipso (Lisso) *1912-1932*
Nisiro (Nisyros) *1912-1932*
Patmo (Patmos) *1912-1932*
Piscopi *1912-1932*
Rodi (Rhodes) *1912-1935*
Scarpanto *1912-1932*
Simi *1912-1932*
Stampalia *1912-1932*
British Military Issues *1945-1947*
Greek occupation issues *1947*

35,37 **Afars et Issas** — See Territoire Français des Afars et des Issas (now Djibouti, Africa).

38 **Afghanistan**
Issues (some inscr. in French: Postes Afghanes, or Afghan Post). *1870-*

34-37 **Africa, Correios**
Inscr. on some stamps of Portuguese territories in Africa *1898*

34,36 **Africa Occidental Española** — See Spanish West Africa.

37 **Africa Orientala Italiana** — See Italian East Africa.

34 **Afrique Equatoriale Française (A.E.F.)**
Federation of French territories of French Equatorial Africa: Gabon, Moyen Congo (Middle Congo) and Oubangui-Chari-Tchad. These became autonomous in 1958 and independent States in 1960: République Centrafricaine, République du Congo, République Gabonaise, and République du Tchad.
Issues *1936-1958*
Some issues Moyen Congo inscr. A.E.F. *1924-1930*
For later issues, see Central African Republic, Congo (French), Gabon, Tchad.

36,37 **Afrique Française Libre (Free French Africa)**
Issues of French territories in Africa indicating adherence to the Free French Government in exile during the 1939-1945 war. *1940-1945*

34 **Afrique Occidentale Française (A.O.F.)**
Federation of French territories in West Africa in the period 1895-1958.
Issues *1945-1959*
For earlier and later issues, see Côte d'Ivoire (Ivory Coast), Dahomey, Guinée (French Guinea), Haute Volta (Upper Volta, now Burkina), Mauritanie, Niger, Sénégal, and Soudan Français (French Sudan, now Mali).

36 **Agüera** — See La Agüera (in the former Spanish Sahara, Africa).

57,59 **Aitutaki**
Pacific island, part of the Cook Islands administration (Associated State of New Zealand).
Issues as part of the British Protectorate of the Cook Islands. (under N.Z. administration) *1903-1932*
Separate issues as part of the present administration *1972-*

51 **Ajman**
Formerly one of the Trucial States in southeast Arabia, formed part of the United Arab Emirates (U.A.E.) 1971.
Issues as part of the Trucial States *1964-1967*
See Manama for separate issues of dependent territory.
See U.A.E. for later issues.

48 **Alaouites/Lattaquié**
Territory of Syria under French Mandate 1919-1937, with town of Lattaquié (now the Syrian town of Al Ladhiqiyah).
Issues of Alaouites *1925-1930*
Issues of Lattaquié *1931-1935*

13,22 **Albania**
Issues *1913-*
As a result of changing political events in Albania, various inscriptions are found on postage stamps, with variants in spelling, among which are:
Korçë (Republic of Korytsa in eastern Albania) *1917-1918*
Albanie Centrale (Central Albania) *1915*
Shqipënie *1920*
Republika Shqiptare *1925-1928*
Mbretnia Shqiptare (Kingdom issues) *1928-1939*
Shqipni *1937-1938*
Italian occupation issues (inscr. Mbretnija Shqiptare) *1939-1942*
Greek occupation issues (of part of Albania) *1940-1941*
German occupation issues *1943-1944*
Independence restored, issues *1945-1946*
Republic issues *1946-*

22 **Albania**
Issues of Italian POs *1902-1916*
Variously inscr. Albania, Durazzo, Janina, Scutari di Albania, Valona.

34 **Alcazar a Quazzan, or Alcazar Wazan** — See Maroc (Morocco), local issues.

11 **Alderney**
One of the Channel Isles in the Bailiwick of Guernsey.
Separate stamp issues *1983-*

48 **Alexandrette**
Capital of region ('Sanjak') detached from Syria and returned to Turkey 1939, now the Turkish town of Iskenderun. It included the town of Hatay, now Antakya in Turkey.
French issues inscr. Sandjak d'Alexandrette 1938
Turkish issues inscr. Hatay 1939

24 **Alexandria (Virginia, USA)**
Postmaster's Provisional issues 1846

23 **Alexandrie (Alexandria, Egypt)**
French PO issues 1899-1930

34,36 **Algérie (Algeria)**
French possession 1830/1882, independent Republic outside the French Community 1962.
French administration issues 1924-1962
Republic issues (République Algérienne) 1962-

14 **Allemagne (Germany)**
Issues of Belgian occupation of Germany 1919-1921

19 **Allenstein (Olsztyn)**
Plebiscite July 1920, when the territory remained part of Germany (East Prussia) until 1945, when that part of East Prussia (Ostpreussen) was incorporated in Poland, town renamed Olsztyn.
Plebiscite issues 1920

16 **Alsace-Lorraine**
French territory annexed to Germany 1871, returned to French sovereignty 1918, under German occupation 1940-1945, returned to France 1945.
German issues of the Norddeutscher Postbezirk (North German Confederation Postal Administration) 1871
German occupation issues, inscr. Elsass (Alsace) and Lothringen (Lorraine) 1940-1941
Special issue inscr. Saverne 1944

42 **Alwar**
Indian State issues 1877-1902

25 **America** — See Confederate States of.

16,17 **A.M.G. F.T.T.**
Inscr. on issues of Allied Military Govt., Free Territory of Trieste — See Trieste, Zone A 1947-1954

16,17 **A.M.G. V.G.**
Inscr. on issues of Allied Military Govt., Venezia Giulia — See Venezia Giulia and Istria. 1945-1947

14 **Andorra**
Small Principality in the Pyrenees under the suzerainty of both France and the Spanish bishop of Urgel.
Spanish PO issues, inscr. Andorra 1928-
French PO issues, inscr. Andorre, or Vallées d'Andorre 1931-

34,36 **Angola**
Portuguese possession in Africa, independent Republic 1975.
Portuguese issues 1870-1975
Republic issues 1975-

63 **Angra**
Portuguese island in the Azores (Atlantic).
Issues inscr. Angra 1892-1905
Issues of the Azores (Açores) 1905-1931
Superseded by stamps of Portugal 1931

31 **Anguilla**
Caribbean island formerly part of the associated British island group of St. Christopher (St. Kitts), Nevis, Anguilla. Seceded from these 1967 and now a British Dependent Territory
Issues 1967-
For earlier issues, see St. Kitts-Nevis.

62 **Anjouan**
Indian Ocean island of the Comoro Archipelago, French Protectorate 1866, under administration of Madagascar 1911, and of the Comoro Islands 1947, now an autonomous territory of France since 1961.
Issues 1892-1912

43,45 **Annam et Tonkin**
Empire, French Protectorate 1883, under the administration of French Indochina 1887, now incorporated in Vietnam.
Issues — For later issues, see Indochine 1888

24 **Annapolis (Maryland, USA)**
Postmaster's Provisional issues 1846

31 **Antigua**
British Caribbean possession and Presidency of the Leeward Islands 1871, together with Barbuda and Redonda. Independent State of Antigua and Barbuda in the British Commonwealth, 1981.
Issues of Antigua 1862-1981
Issues of Antigua and Barbuda 1981-

30 **Antillas**
Name of former Spanish West Indies (comprising Cuba and Puerto Rico) — See Cuba.

32 **Antioquia**
State of Colombia (S. America)
Issues 1868-1904

34 **A.O.F.** — See Afrique Occidentale Française (French West Africa).

15 **Apolda, Stadtpost**
Germany (GDR), *local town issue* 1945

50-51 **Arabie Soudite, Royaume**
French inscr. on stamps of Saudi Arabia, see Saudi Arabia for details.

17 **Arbe**
Inscr. on some issues of Fiume Free City 1920
See Fiume (now Rijeka, Yugoslavia).

62 **Archipel des Comores** — See Comores (Comoro Archipelago, Indian Ocean).

32 **Arequipa**
Peru, *provisional local issues* 1881-1885

32-33 **Argentina**
Issues 1858-
Local issues of Buenos Aires, Cordoba and Corrientes 1858

38 **Armenia**
A National Republic in Russia 1918-1920, Soviet Republic 1920-1922 (with one intermission), later part of the Transcaucasian Federation, and now the Armenian SSR in the USSR.
National Republic issues 1919-1922
Soviet Republic issues 1921-1922
Armenia issues within the Transcaucasian Federation (Stamps of the USSR current from 1924). 1923

63 **Ascension**
British island possession in the Atlantic, now part of the British Dependent Territory of St. Helena Dependencies
Issues 1922-

22 **Astypalaia** — See Aegean (Dodecanese) Islands, Stampalia.

25 **Athens (Georgia, USA)**
Confederate States of America.
Postmaster's Provisional issues 1861

14 **Aunus (Olonets)**
Russian town temporarily held by Finland, now Olonets in the USSR.
Finnish occupation issues 1919

60-61 **Australes, Terres** — See Terres Australes et Antarctiques Françaises (French Antarctica).

52-53 **Australia**
Issues of the Federal Commonwealth of Australia 1913-
Issues of component former Colonies and Territories of Australia:
New South Wales 1850-1910
Queensland 1860-1911
South Australia 1855-1911
Tasmania (Van Diemens Land) 1853-1913
Victoria 1850-1912
Western Australia 1854-1912

52 **Australia**
Australian administration issues of Papua 1906-1939

55 *Australian issues of Territory of New Guinea* 1925-1939
See Papua New Guinea for later issues.

41 **Australia, British Commonwealth Occupation Force, Japan (BCOF Japan).**
Occupation issues 1946

61 **Australian Antarctic Territory**
Issues 1957-

12,14 **Austria (Österreich)**
Empire till Nov. 1918, Republic since then, first called Deutschösterreich (German Austria) 1918-1919, then Republik Österreich. Absorbed into Germany 1938-1945, sovereignty restored 1945.
Issues of Austrian Empire (inscr. K. K. Post Stempel, or Kais.-Königl. Österr. Post=Imperial and Royal Mail) 1850-1918
Issues of Deutschösterreich 1918-1921
Issues of Österreich 1922-1938

14 *Stamps of Germany (Deutsches Reich) current in Austria 1938-1945.*
Issues of Republik Österreich 1945-
Austria

14,15 *Local issues were made in the period 1918-1923, variously inscr. or hand-stamped:*
Burgenland, Kärnten, Knittelfeld, Osttirol, Radkerskburg, Salzburg, Spielfeld, Tirol.
In 1945, local issues were made for:
Frankenfels, Gmünd, Horn, Leibnitz, Losenstein, Mondsee, Raabs a.d. Thaya, Raxendorf, Scheibbs, Schwarzenbach a.d.Pielach, Waidhofen a.d.Ybbs, Weitra NÖ.

12 **Austria**
Special stamps of the Danube Steamship Company, inscr. Donau Dampfschiffahrt-Gesellschaft (DDSG) 1866-1870
Special local issues of the Danube-Black Sea Railway, inscr. DBSR 1867

19 **Austria**
Special plebiscite issues of Kärnten (Carinthia) — Austrian issues 1920
Yugoslav issues (Koruška) inscr. KGCA 1920

Austria — Austrian Military Field Post
16,17 *General issues of Austro-Hungarian Military mail (K.u.K. Feldpost)* *1915-1918*
Occupation of Italy issues *1918*
13 *Occupation of Montenegro (K.u.K. Militärverwaltung)* *1917*
13 *Occupation of Romania (Rumänien)* *1917-1918*
13 *Occupation of Serbia (Serbien)* *1916*
Austrian POs abroad
22-23 *Ottoman Empire (Levant)* *1867-1914*
13,23 *Crete* *1903-1914*
13,14 *Bosnia and Herzegovina* *1879-1918*
23 *(Bosnien-Herzegowina)*
13 *Liechtenstein* *1912-1918*
20 **Austrian Italy (Lombardei-Venetien)**
Kingdom of Lombardy-Venetia (Lombardia-Veneto) under the rule of the Emperor of Austria.
Issues, inscr. K.K. Poststempel *1850-1864*
32 **Ayacucho**
Peru, *local issues* *1881*
42 **Azahind**
Name for India on a war-time stamp issue printed in Germany for a possible Nationalist Indian government, but stamps not issued *(1943)*
38 **Azerbaidzhan**
National Republic 1918-1920, later part of the Transcausasian Federation, now the Azerbaidzhan SSR in the USSR.
National Republic issues (early ones with French inscr. République d'Azerbaidjan) *1919-1920*
Soviet Republic issues *1921-1923*
Superseded 1923 by issues of the Transcausasian Federation, and in 1924 by those of the USSR.
63 **Azores (Açores)**
Atlantic islands administratively part of Portugal.
Issues of Açores *1868-1931*
1980-
Stamps of Portugal current 1931-1980.

12 **Baden, Grossherzogtum (Grand Duchy)**
Issues *1851-1871*
Stamps of Germany (Deutsches Reich) current from 1871.
15 **Baden**
French occupation of Germany issues *1947-1949*
48,49 **Baghdad**
British occupation of Iraq issues *1917*
30 **Bahamas**
British islands possessions, independent Commonwealth State 1973.
Issues *1859-*
42 **Bahawalpur**
Former State of India, now in Pakistan.
Issues *1948-1949*
47,49, **Bahrain**
51 Sheikhdom in Treaty with Great Britain 1882, independent State 1971.
Issues *1933-1971*
Independent State issues *1971-*
30 **Baja California**
Mexican civil war issues *1915*
42 **Bamra**
Indian State issues *1888-1894*
14 **Bánát Bacska**
Issues of Romanian occupation of Hungary *1919*
39 **Bando**
German Prisoner of War camp in Japan.
Issues with German inscr. Lagerpost (Camp Mail) *1918*
42 **Bangkok**
Issues of British POs in Siam (Thailand) *1882-1885*
44 **Bangladesh**
Formerly in British India, from 1947 to 1971 was the East Pakistan part of the Dominion (later Republic) of Pakistan, independent Republic 1971.
Issues *1971-*
14 **Baranya**
Issues of Serbian occupation of Hungary *1919*
31 **Barbados**
British Caribbean island possession, independent Commonwealth State 1966.
Issues *1852-*
31 **Barbuda**
With the island of Redonda, was part of the Presidency of Antigua in the Leeward Islands Federation 1871-1956, and with Antigua became the independent Commonwealth State of Antigua and Barbuda, 1981.
Issues of Barbuda *1922-1981*
Issues of Antigua and Barbuda *1981-*
See also Antigua.

42 **Barwani**
State of India issues *1921-1948*
12 **Basel**
Local Swiss city and Canton issues *1845-1850*
Superseded by Swiss Federal Post stamps, 1850-
34,36 **Basutoland**
Territory in southern Africa under British administration till 1966, when it became an independent State (indigenous Monarchy) in the British Commonwealth and named Lesotho.
Issues *1933-1966*
See Lesotho for later issues.
25 **Baton Rouge (Louisiana, USA)**
Confederate States of America,
Postmaster's Provisional issues *1861*
13,46 **Batum**
Russian town on Black Sea under British occupation.
British occupation issues *1919-1920*
12 **Bayern (Bavaria)**
Kingdom till 1918, Republic 1919 and later Province of Germany.
Kingdom issues *1849-1919*
Republic issues, inscr. either Volksstaat (People's State) or Freistaat Bayern *1919-1920*
Bavaria had its own stamps till 1920, since when stamps of Germany (Deutsches Reich) have been current.
35 **B.C.A.** — See British Central Africa.
41 **B.C.O.F. Japan**
Issues of British Commonwealth Occupation Force, Japan *1946*
25 **Beaumont (Texas, USA)**
Confederate States of America,
Postmaster's Provisional issues *1861*
34,36 **Bechuanaland**
British Territory and Protectorate 1885/1888, part of Cape of Good Hope 1895 including its annexed territory of Stellaland. Independent Republic in the British Commonwealth 1966 and renamed Botswana.
Issues of British Bechuanaland *1885-1893*
Issues of Bechuanaland Protectorate *1888-1965*
See Botswana for later issues.
34,36 **Belgian Congo** — See Congo Belge.
13 **Belgien (Belgium)**
Issues of German occupation of Belgium *1914-1916*
12 **Belgium (Belgique, Belgie)**
Issues, inscr. Belgique (French) and Belgie (Flemish) *1849-*
Belgium
Issues of Overseas territories:
(See individual entries for details)
35,37 *Congo Belge (Belgian Congo, now Zaïre)* *1909-1960*
35,37 *Ruana-Urundi (now Rwanda, and Burundi)* *1916-1962*
16 **Belgium**
Issues of Belgian occupation of Germany, inscr. Allemagne *1919-1921*
Inscr. Eupen and Malmédy *1920-1921*
(For issues of German occupation of Belgium, see Germany, Occupation issues.)

30 **Belize**
Former Colony of British Honduras, re-named Belize 1973, independent Commonwealth State 1981.
Issues of British Honduras *1866-1973*
Issues of Belize *1973-*
35,37 **Benadir**
Inscr. on early stamps of Italian Somaliland. See Somalia.
35 **Bengasi**
Issues of Italian POs in the Ottoman Empire (Libya) *1901*
34,36 **Bénin**
Formerly part of the French Settlements of the Gulf of Benin, which became the Colony of Dahomey and Dependencies 1899, and later part of French West Africa (A.O.F.).
Issues *1892-1894*
(Issues of Dahomey used 1899-1942)
(Issues of A.O.F. used 1944-1959)
For later issues, see Dahomey, A.O.F., Benin, Republic.

36 **Benin, Republic**
Independent Republic 1960 and named Dahomey Republic, re-named Bénin 1975.
Issues of Dahomey Republic *1960-1975*
Issues inscr. Bénin *1976-*

12 **Bergedorf**
Town in north Germany under joint administration of Hamburg and Lübeck till 1867, when it came under Hamburg.
Town issues *1861-1867*
Stamps replaced 1868 by issues of the Norddeutscher Postbezirk (North German Confederation Postal Administration).

15 **Berlin**
Issues of West Sectors administration, inscr. Deutsche Bundespost, Berlin *1948-*
Issues of East Sector, inscr. Berlin-Brandenburg *1945*
See also Germany.

30 **Bermuda**
British islands in the Western Atlantic, but often considered a part of the British West Indies. Now a British Dependent Territory
Issues *1865-*

23,46 **Beyrouth** — See Levant, French POs.

44 **Bhopal**
Indian State issues:
inscr. H. H. Nawab Shah Jahan Begam *1876-1901*
inscr. H. H. Nawab Sultan Jahan Begam *1902-1908*
Bhopal State issues *1908*

42 **Bhor**
Indian State issues *1879-1901*

39,40 **Bhutan**
Issues *1962-*

36 **Biafra**
Eastern part of Nigeria, issued stamps during the 1967-1970 civil war, when it proclaimed itself a Republic, overrun in 1970.
Issues *1968-1970*

14 **Bialystok**
Town at that time in Russia, now in Poland.
German occupation issues *1916*
See Postgebiet Ober-Ost (German occupation of Eastern Areas).

42 **Bijawar**
Indian State issues *1935-1937*

42,44 **B.M.A. (British Military Administration of Malaya) — See Malaya, Federation.**

14,17 **Böhmen und Mähren** (Bohemia and Moravia)
German issues, inscr. Böhmen u.Mähren, and Čechy a Morava *1939-1945*

17 *Local German issue Mährisch-Ostrau* *1939*

17 *Local German issue for prison camp of Theresienstadt (Czech town of Terezin) (ingoing mail only)* *1943*

14 **Boka Kotorska**
Town and area of Boka Kotorska (Cattaro), Yugoslavia.
German occupation issues *1944*

32 **Bolivar**
Colombia, State issues *1863-1904*

32 **Bolivia**
Issues *1866-*

36 **Bophuthatswana**
"Homeland" Republic within the Republic of South Africa, formed 1977.
Issues *1977-*

43,45 **Borneo, British North** — See North Borneo.

13,14 **Bosnia-Herzegovina**
Formerly in the Ottoman Empire, occupied by Austria 1878 and annexed to Austria 1908, part of the Kingdom of Yugoslavia 1918.
Issues of Austrian POs, inscr. Bosnien-Herzegowina or Bosnien-Hercegovina *1879-1918*

13,14 *Early regional issues of Yugoslavia, inscr. Bosna i Hercegovina* *1918*

36 **Botswana**
Formerly Bechuanaland Protectorate, independent Republic in the British Commonwealth 1966.
Issues — See Bechuanaland for earlier issues *1966-*

61,62 **Bouvet Island (Bouvet Øya)**
Norwegian island in South Atlantic.
Special Norwegian issue *1934*

32 **Boyaca**
Colombia, State issues *1899-1904*

39 **B.R.A.** — See British Railway Administration, China.

33 **Brasil** — See Brazil.

24 **Brattleboro (Vermont, USA)**
Postmaster's Provisional issues *1846*

12 **Braunschweig (Brunswick, Germany)**
Duchy, in union with Germany (Deutsches Reich) 1871.
Issues *1852-1867*
Superseded 1868 by those of the Norddeutscher Bund (North German Confederation).

33 **Brazil (Brasil)**
Formerly Portuguese, United Kingdom with Portugal 1815-1822, independent Empire 1822-1889, Republic since then.
Empire issues *1843-1889*
Republic issues *1890-*

12 **Bremen**
German Hanseatic City.
Issues *1855-1867*
Superseded 1868 by stamps of the North German Confederation.

25 **Bridgeville (Alabama, USA)**
Confederate States of America,
Postmaster's Provisional issues *1861*

61 **British Antarctic Territory**
British Dependent Territory established 1962, includes the former Falkland Islands Dependencies of South Orkney and South Shetland Islands.
Issues *1963-*
See Falkland Islands Dependencies for earlier issues.

34,36 **British Bechuanaland**
British Territory and Protectorate 1885/88, annexed to Cape of Good Hope 1895, including Stellaland. Independent Republic in the British Commonwealth 1966 and re-named Botswana.
Issues of British Bechuanaland *1885-1893*
Issues of Bechuanaland Protectorate *1888-1965*
See Botswana for later issues.

35,37 **British Central Africa (B.C.A.)**
Became the Nyasaland Protectorate, independent in the British Commonwealth 1964 and Republic of Malawi 1966.
Issues of British Central Africa *1891-1908*
For later issues, see Nyasaland Protectorate, and Malawi.

28,29 **British Columbia**
Joined by Vancouver Island 1866 and both part of the Dominion of Canada 1871.
Issues of British Columbia *1865-1871*
Issues of British Columbia and Vancouver Island *1860-1865*

41 **British Commonwealth Occupation Force, Japan**
Issues, inscr. B.C.O.F. *1946*

35,37 **British East Africa**
Protectorate formed during the period 1885/95, later becoming Kenya, and Uganda.
Issues *1890-1903*
Stamps of East Africa and Uganda Protectorate used 1903-1922.
For later issues, see Kenya, Tanganyika and Uganda.

32 **British Guiana**
British Colony 1850-1966, when it became independent 1966 and re-named Guyana, Republic in the British Commonwealth 1970.
Issues *1850-1966*
See Guyana for later issues.

30 **British Honduras**
British Colony 1862, re-named Belize 1973, independent Commonwealth State 1981.
Issues — See Belize for subsequent issues *1866-1973*

62 **British Indian Ocean Territory**
British Dependent Territory, now consists of the islands of the Chagos Archipelago, including the island of Diego Garcia.
Issues *1968-*

22-23 **British Levant**
British POs in the Ottoman Empire were active till 1914.
Issues *1885-1914*
Issues were used during the British occupation after the 1914-1918 war.
Issues of British office at Salonica (now Thessaloniki, Greece), inscr. Levant *1916*

42,44 **British Military Administration Malaya (BMA)**
Issues *1945-1948*
Stamps gradually replaced by those of the States of the Federation of Malaya after 1948.
For details, see Malaya, Federation.

52,55 **British New Guinea (Papua)**
Issues *1901-1906*
For later issues, see Papua, and Papua New Guinea.

43,45 **British North Borneo** — See North Borneo.

British occupation of former Italian Colonies

22,35 *Middle East Forces (included Eritrea, Italian Somaliland, Cyrenaica, Tripolitania, and some of the Dodecanese islands).*
Issues, inscr. M.E.F. *1942-1947*

35,37 **Eritrea**
British Military and Administration issues *1941-1952*

35,37 **Somalia**
British occupation and Administration till Dec. 1950, when it reverted to Italian Administration.
Issues *1943-1950*

35,37 **Tripolitania (Libya)**
Issues *1948-1951*

13,23 **British POs in Crete**
Crete was administered jointly by France, Great Britain, Italy and Russia in the period 1898-1913, when it became part of Greece.
Issues *1898-1899*

51 **British Postal Agencies in Eastern Arabia**
British stamps were used in the territories which included Abu Dhabi, Doha, Dubai, Muscat, and Umm Said, dates varying with the territory.
Issues during period: *1948-1963*

39 **British Railway Administration (B.R.A.) (China)**
Special issue of stamps for mail on the Peking-Taku Railway *1901*

56,58 **British Solomon Islands**
British Protectorate in the Pacific 1893/99, independent Commonwealth State 1978.
Issues of British Solomon Islands. *1907-1975*
Issues of Solomon Islands. *1975-*

35,37 **British Somaliland Protectorate**
Protectorate formed 1884/88. In 1960, together with the Italian Trust Territory of Somalia, became the independent Republic of Somalia.
Issues — See Somalia for later issues *1903-1960*

35 **British South Africa Company**
Administered the British territory of Rhodesia, which was divided in 1924 into Northern and Southern Rhodesia.
Issues — See Rhodesia for later issues *1890-1925*

31 **British Virgin Islands**
Part of the Leeward Islands group 1871 and, together with the US Virgin Islands (formerly Danish), part of the Virgin Islands Archipelago. The main British islands are Tortola, Anegada, Virgin Gorda and Jost Van Dyke. Now a British Dependent Territory.
Issues *1866-*
General issues Leeward Islands, used also up to 1956.

43,45 **Brunei**
Independent Sultanate under British protection 1888, sovereign independent State in the British Commonwealth 1983.
Issues *1906-*
Japanese occupation issues *1942-1945*

12 **Brunswick** — See Braunschweig (Germany).

32 **Buenos Aires**
Argentina, local issues *1858-1862*

13,14 **Bulgaria**
23 Principality in the Ottoman Empire, united 1885 with Eastern Roumelia, independent Kingdom 1908, Republic 1946.
Issues *1879-*
Issues of Eastern Roumelia inscr. Rouméllie Orientale, or RO *1880-1884*
Issues of South Bulgaria, inscr. Yuzhna Bulgariya *1885*

14 **Bulgaria**
Issues of Bulgarian occupation of Romania (Dobrogea strip) *1916-1917*

15 **Bundesrepublik Deutschland (BRD)**
Inscr. on stamps of the Federal Republic of Germany *1949-*
See Germany for other details.

42 **Bundi**
Indian State issues *1894-1947*

34,36 **Burkina (Burkina Faso)**
Formerly called Haute Volta (Upper Volta), which see for details.

42,44 **Burma**
Formerly part of British India, autonomous under British rule 1937-1947, independent Republic outside the British Commonwealth 1947.
British Dominion issues *1937-1947*
Japanese occupation issues *1942-1945*
Issues of independent Union of Burma *1948-*

35,37 **Burundi**
Part of the Belgian Trust African territory of Ruanda-Urundi till 1962, when Urundi became an independent Kingdom, and Republic in 1967.
Kingdom (Royaume) issues *1962-1967*
Republic issues *1967-*
See Ruanda-Urundi for earlier issues.

47 **Bushire**
Town in Persia (now Iran).
British occupation issues *1915*

42 **Bussahir**
Indian State issues *1895-1901*

36 **Cabo Juby (or Jubi)** — See Cape Juby.

63 **Cabo Verde** — See Cape Verde.

56,58 **Calédonie** — See Nouvelle Calédonie (New Caledonia).

22 **Calino (Kalymnos)**
Island in the Aegean (Dodecanese) group.
Italian issues *1912-1932*
(some inscr. Calimno). See also Aegean Islands.

43,45 **Cambodia (Cambodge)**
French Protectorate 1863, later part of French Indochina, independent Kingdom 1953, Republic 1970/71 and country named Khmer Republic (République Khmère). Following hostilities, government overrun and country re-named Kampuchea (though not universally recognized).
Issues of Kingdom *1951-1971*
Issues of Khmer Republic *1971-1975*
Issues of Kampuchea *1980-*
See Indochine for earlier issues.

34,36 **Cameroon**
German Colony 1884-1919 (Kamerun), British and French occupation 1915-1920/21. Greater part of Territory under French Mandate 1921-1960 (Cameroun). The British Mandate region of Southern Cameroons was annexed to the new Republic of Cameroon, 1961.
German Colonial issues (Kamerun) *1897-1914*
British & French occupation issues *1915-1921*
French Mandate issues (Cameroun) *1921-1960*
British issues, inscr. Cameroons UKTT *1960*
Independent Republic issues *1960-*

30 **Campeche**
Mexico, local provisional issues *1875*

14,15 **Campione**
Small Italian enclave in Switzerland along Lake Lugano.
Local issues for mail to Switzerland only, inscr. Commune di Campione (under the aegis of the Italian Postal Administration, ie. Poste Italiane) *1944-1952*
Stamps of Italy and Switzerland used since 1952.

28,29 **Canada**
Dominion of Canada founded July 1867 by the union of Canada, New Brunswick and Nova Scotia, later joined by British Columbia, Prince Edward Island, and Newfoundland.
Issues of Canada *1851-1868*
Issues of Dominion of Canada *1868-*
Issues of component Territories:
Vancouver Island *1865*
British Columbia and Vancouver Island *1860-1865*
British Columbia *1865-1871*
New Brunswick *1851-1868*
Newfoundland *1857-1949*
Nova Scotia *1851-1868*
Prince Edward Island *1861-1873*

23 **Canal Maritime de Suez**
Suez Canal Company issues *1868*

27 **Canal Zone**
Territory of Panama Canal Zone leased to USA 1903-1979.
Issues *1904-1979*

39 **Canton**
Issues of French PO in China *1901-1922*

34 **Cape of Good Hope**
Territory in southern Africa, later a component part of the Union of South Africa, 1910.
Issues *1853-1910*
Special issues:
Vryburg, temporary Boer occupation issues (inscr. on Cape of Good Hope stamps) *1899*
Siege of Mafeking (March-May 1900) *1900*
British re-occupation issues (inscr. on stamps of Transvaal) — See South Africa for later issues *1900*

36 **Cape Juby (Cabo Juby or Jubi)**
Small Spanish Colony, annexed to Rio de Oro (later named Spanish Sahara).
Issues *1916-1948*

63 **Cape Verde (Cabo Verde)**
Portuguese islands in the Atlantic, Overseas Province of Portugal 1951, independent State 1975.
Issues *1877-*

22 **Carchi (or Karki)**
Island in the Aegean (Dodecanese) group.
Italian issues — See also Aegean Islands *1912-1932*
19 **Carinthia** — See Austria, Plebiscite of Kärnten.
56,58 **Caroline Islands**
German Colony 1899-1914, Japanese occupation 1914 and Mandate till 1945, Trust Territory of the USA 1945.
German Colonial issues (Karolinen) *1899-1915/19*
22 **Caso (Kasos)**
Island in the Aegean (Dodecanese) group.
Italian issues — See also Aegean Islands *1912-1932*
22 **Castellorizo**
Island in the Aegean (Dodecanese) group, formerly Turkish and occupied by France 1915-1920 when it was ceded to Italy, to Greece after 1945 and named Kastelorizon.
French issues *1920*
Italian issues (Castelrosso) *1922-1932*
32 **Cauca**
Colombia, State issues *1879-1903*
22 **Cavalle**
Port on the Aegean Sea, formerly Turkish and annexed to Greece 1914 (Kavalla).
Issues of French PO — (active 1874-1914) *1893-1914*
30 **Cayman Islands**
British islands in the Caribbean, now a British Dependent Territory.
Issues *1901-*
17 **Cechy a Morava (Bohemia and Moravia)**
Inscr. on German occupation issues of Czechoslovakia, also German inscr. Böhmen und Mähren *1939-1945*
34,36 **C.E.F. (Cameroons Expeditionary Force)**
British occupation issues *1915*
See Cameroon for other issues.
39 **C.E.F. (China Expeditionary Force, India)**
Issues *1900-1921*
14 **Cefalonia e Itaca**
Greek islands of Cephalonia and Ithaca.
Italian occupation issues *1941*
34,36 **Central African Republic**
Formerly French Colony of Oubangui-Chari, independent Republic 1960, became an Empire 1976 to 1979, when it reverted to a Republic.
Republic issues (République Centrafricaine) *1959-1976*
Empire issues (Empire Centrafricain) *1977-1979*
Republic issues *1979-*
14 **Ceskoslovensko** — See Czechoslovakia.

42,44 **Ceylon**
British Colony, independent Commonwealth State 1948, Republic in 1972 and re-named Sri Lanka.
British Colonial issues *1857-1948*
Dominion issues *1949-1972*
See Sri Lanka for later issues.
36 **Chad** — See Tchad.
32 **Chala**
Peru, provisional local issues *1884*
42 **Chamba**
Indian Convention State issues *1886-1950*
11 **Channel Islands**
German occupation 1940-1945, the Islands have their own Postal Administration since 1969.
Issues under German occupation (1940-1945):
Guernsey *1941-1944*
Jersey *1941-1946*
General issue for the Islands *1948*
Great Britain regional issues for Guernsey and Jersey (no inscr.) *1958-1969*
Issues of Guernsey Bailiwick *1969-*
Issues of Alderney (Bailiwick of Guernsey) *1983-*
Issues of Jersey *1969-*
42 **Charkhari**
Indian State issues *1894-1943*
25 **Charleston (S. Carolina, USA)**
Confederate States of America,
Postmaster's Provisional issues *1861*

32 **Chile**
Issues *1853-*
Local issue of Tierra del Fuego *1891*
39,41 **China**
Empire till 1912, Republic till 1949, when it became a People's Republic
Empire issues *1878-1912*
Republic issues *1912-1949*
Issues of People's Republic *1949-*
Some regional issues were made 1949-1950 by the Chinese Communist Administration for Central, East, North, Northwest, South, and Southwest China.

39,41 **China** — Other issues:
Local issues of Shanghai *1865-1898*
Sinkiang (Chinese Turkestan) *1915-1949*
Szechwan Province *1933-1934*
Yunnan Province *1926-1934*
41 **China** — Japanese occupation issues:
Kwantung *1942-1945*
Mengkiang (Inner Mongolia) *1941-1945*
North China *1941-1945*
Nanking *1941-1945*
Shanghai *1941-1945*
China — POs of other countries:
39 British POs *1917-1930*
British Railway Administration (B.R.A.)
Special stamp issue for mail on the Peking-Taku Railway *1901*
French POs *(inscr. Chine):* *1894-1922*
Offices were active at Canton, Hoi-Hao, Kouang-Tchéou, Mongtseu, Pakhoi, Tchong-King, Yannanfou (Yunnansen). They issued stamps at
43 *various times in the period 1894-1922, except Kouang-Tchéou (1906-1946). (Spellings are French forms).*
German POs: 1898-1917
Offices were active at Amoy, Canton, Chingkiang, Fuchau, Hankow, Ichang, Kiautschou, Nanking, Peking, Shanghai, Swatow, Tchifu, Tientsin.
Italian POs:
Offices active at Peking (Pechino) and Tientsin *1918*
Japanese POs *1900-1922*
Russian POs *(stamps inscr. Kitay)* *1899-1920*
USA PO at Shanghai *1919-1922*
China Expeditionary Force, India (C.E.F.) *1900-1921*
38 **Chinese POs in Tibet** *1911*
Offices at Gyantse, Lhasa, Phari Jong, Shigatse, Yatung.
62 **Christmas Island (Indian Ocean)** *1958-*
Under the administration of Australia since 1958.
23 **Cilicie** *1919-1921*
Province of Turkey twice occupied by France, in 1919 and 1920-1921.
36 **Ciskei** *1981-*
"Homeland" Republic formed 1981 within the Republic of South Africa.
30 **Coamo** — See Puerto Rico.
42 **Cochin**
Indian State issues *1892-1950*
See Travancore-Cochin for later issues.
43 **Cochinchine (Cochinchina)**
Territory part of French Indochina 1887/1888, later absorbed into Vietnam 1946/1949.
Issues *1886-1892*
(Stamps of Indochina current after 1892).
62 **Cocos (Keeling) Islands**
Formerly British, integrated with Australia in 1964.
Issues *1963-*
32 **Colombia**
Former Spanish territory till 1819, formed successively Greater Colombia, New Granada, the Granada Confederation, and the United States of Colombia 1861.
Issues:
Granada Confederation *1859-1860*
United States of New Granada (E.U. de Nueva Granada). *1861*
United States of Colombia (E.U. de Colombia) *1862-1886*
Republic of Colombia *1886-*

32 **Colombia**
States issues:
Antioquia 1868-1904
Bolivar 1863-1904
Boyaca 1899-1904
Cauca 1879-1903
Cundinamarca 1870-1904
Panama 1878-1903
(independent Republic 1903)
Santander 1884-1903
Tolima 1870-1903
The States became Departments in 1886.

28,29 **Columbia, British** — See British Columbia.

62 **Comoros (Comores)**
French Indian Ocean islands, include Anjouan, Grande Comore, Mayotte and Mohéli. An Overseas Territory of France 1958, independent Republic 1974 (except the island of Mayotte, which became a "Département" of France).
Issues inscr. Grande Comore 1897-1923
Archipel des Comores 1950-1976
Republic issues 1976-
(early issues inscr. État Comorien).

35,37 **Companhia de Moçambique** — See Mozambique Company.

25 **Confederate States of America**
Postmaster's Provisional stamps were issued 1861 for a short period in some 100 cities, among which are:

Athens (Georgia)	*Lynchburg (Virginia)*
Baton Rouge (Louisiana)	*Macon (Georgia)*
Beaumont (Texas)	*Madison (Florida)*
Bridgeville (Alabama)	*Marion (Virginia)*
Charleston (S. Carolina)	*Memphis (Tennessee)*
Danville (Virginia)	*Mobile (Alabama)*
Emory (Virginia)	*Nashville (Tennessee)*
Fredericksburg (Virginia)	*New Orleans (Louisiana)*
Goliad (Texas)	*New Smyrna (Florida)*
Gonzales (Texas)	*Petersburg (Virginia)*
Greenville (Alabama)	*Pittsylvania (Virginia)*
Greenwood (Virginia)	*Pleasant Shade (Virginia)*
Grove Hill (Alabama)	*Rheatown (Tennessee)*
Helena (Texas)	*Salem (Virginia)*
Independence (Texas)	*Spartanburg (S. Carolina)*
Jetersville (Virginia)	*Tellico Plains (Tennessee)*
Knoxville (Tennessee)	*Uniontown (Alabama)*
Lenoir (N. Carolina)	*Unionville (S. Carolina)*
Livingston (Alabama)	*Victoria (Texas)*

25 **Confederate States of America**
General issues 1861-1864

12 **Confoederatio Helvetica (Swiss Confederation)**
Inscr. on stamps of Switzerland, also inscr. Helvetia 1862-
See Switzerland.

34 **Congo**
Independent State issues 1886-1908
(État Indépendent du Congo). See Congo Belge for later issues.

34,36 **Congo Belge (Belgian Congo)**
Formerly independent, territory became the Belgian Congo (Congo Belge) 1908, with capital at Léopoldville (now Kinshasa).
Issues — See Congo, République for later issues 1909-1960

34,36 **Congo, République (Léopoldville, now Kinshasa)**
Formerly Belgian Congo, independent Republic 1960, followed by a period of uncertain administration and civil war. Republic re-named Zaïre in 1971.
Issues 1960-1971
Issues inscr. Katanga were made 1960-1962 for the proposed breakaway State of Katanga. It was reunited to Congo 1963. See Zaïre for later issues.

34,36 **Congo Français (French Congo)**
Formed in 1888 by the union of the territories of Congo and Gabon. These, together with Moyen Congo and Oubangui-Chari-Tchad, formed French Equatorial Africa (A.E.F.) in 1910.
Independent Republic 1960 (known sometimes as Congo, Brazzaville).
Issues of Congo Français 1891-1907
Issues of Moyen Congo (Middle Congo) 1907-1937
(Stamps of A.E.F. current 1937-1958).
See Congo (Brazzaville) for later issues.

36 **Congo, République (Brazzaville)**
Former French Congo, independent Republic 1960.
Issues 1959-

34 **Congo, Portuguese**
Small Portuguese territory north of the Congo River, now named Cabinda.
Issues 1894-1920

22 **Coo** — See Cos (Aegean islands)

57,59 **Cook Islands**
Islands in the Pacific administered by New Zealand 1901, an Associated State of New Zealand 1965.
Issues 1892-
(Some early issues inscr. Rarotonga, one of the islands in the group).

32 **Cordoba**
Argentina, local issues 1858

23 **Corfu**
Greek island in the Ionian Sea.
Italian occupation issues 1923
Issues inscr. Corfu and Paxos 1941

32 **Corrientes**
Argentina, local issues 1856-1858

22 **Cos (also Coo)**
Island in the Aegean (Dodecanese) group.
Italian issues — See also Aegean Islands 1912-1932

22 **Costantinopoli (Constantinople, now Istanbul)**
Issues of Italian POs in the Levant 1909-1910

30 **Costa Rica**
Issues 1863-
Local issues inscr. Guanacaste 1885-1889

35,37 **Côte Française des Somalis (French Somaliland)**
French Colony 1984, re-named Afars et Issas in 1967, independent Republic of Djibouti 1977.
Issues 1894-1967
Early issues inscr. Côte des Somalis, also Obock, then DJ or Djibouti. See Djibouti for later issues.

34,36 **Côte d'Ivoire (Ivory Coast)**
French Colony, territory first named Assinie, then Établissements de la Côte d'Or, named Côte d'Ivoire 1895. Later was part of the administration of French West Africa (A.O.F.) Independent Republic 1960.
Issues 1892-1944
Republic issues 1959-
(A.O.F. stamps current 1944-1958).

15 **Cottbus**
Germany (GDR), local town issues 1945-1946

13,23 **Crete (Kriti)**
Island under Turkish rule till 1898, joint administration by France, Great Britain, Italy and Russia 1898-1913, when it was annexed to Greece.
Greek issues, inscr. Ellas (Greece) 1900-1910
Austrian Po issues 1903-1914
British issues 1898-1899
French issues 1902-1903
Italian issues, inscr. La Canea 1900-1911
Russian issues, some inscr. Retymno 1899

14 **Croatia**
Inscr. Hrvatska S.H.S. on early issues of Yugoslavia 1918-1941
Regional issues of Yugoslavia, inscr. N. D. Hrvatska 1941-1945

30 **Cuba**
Formerly Spanish and known as Antillas (comprising Cuba and Puerto Rico), under USA rule 1899-1902, autonomous under USA control 1902-1934, independent 1934.
Spanish issues (Antillas) 1855-1871
Spanish issues (Cuba only) 1871-1898
(some inscr. Ultramar=Overseas).
USA administration issues 1899-1902
Republic of Cuba issues 1902-

30 **Cuernavaca**
Mexico, local issues 1867

32 **Cundinamarca**
Colombia, States issues 1870-1904

31 **Curaçao**
Caribbean island and part of the Netherlands Antilles, so-named in 1948.
Issues inscr. Curaçao 1873-1948
See Netherlands Antilles for later issues.

32 **Cuzco**
Peru, provisional local issues 1881-1885

13,23
50 **Cyprus**
Formerly Turkish, British island 1878, independent Republic in the British Commonwealth 1960, politically divided 1974/75 between Greek and Turkish elements.
British Colonial issues 1880-1960
Republic issues, inscr. Cyprus, Kibris (Turkish), Kipros (Greek) 1960-
Issues of the breakaway northern "Turkish State of Cyprus" 1974-

36 **Cyrenaica**
Incorporated in Italian Libya 1939 (Libia), became part of the State of Libya 1951.
Italian administration issues *1923-1939*
(inscr. Cirenaica).
British occupation issues *1942-1947*
(Middle East Forces).
Cyrenaica issues *1950*

14 **Czechoslovakia (Československo)**
Republic 1918/19, German occupation 1939-1945, restored sovereignty 1945.
Republic issues *1918-1939*
Issues of Czech Army in Russia *1919-1920*
(Intermission of issues 1939-1945.)
German occupation issues *1939-1945*
(inscr. Böhmen und Mähren, and Čechy a Morava).
"Independent" issues of Slovakia *1939-1945*
(inscr. Slovensko).
Issues of restored independent Republic *1945-*

34,36 **Dahomey**
French Colony of Dahomey and Dependencies formed 1899 and also part of the administration of French West Africa (A.O.F.) Independent Republic 1960, name changed 1975 to Benin, People's Republic.
Issues *1899-1942*
Issues of Dahomey Republic *1960-1975*
See Benin, Republic for later issues.
(Stamps of A.O.F. current 1944-1959).

31 **Danish West Indies (Dansk-Vestindien)**
Danish Caribbean islands purchased by the USA in 1917 and named US Virgin Islands.
Danish issues *1855-1917*
(Early issues inscr. Dansk Vestindiske Oer).
(Stamps of the USA current since then).

12 *Danmark* — See Denmark.

31 **Dansk-Vestindien** — See Danish West Indies.

25 **Danville (Virginia, USA)**
Confederate States of America,
Postmaster's Provisional issues *1861*

14,17 **Danzig**
Formerly part of Germany (East Prussia), independent Free City 1920-1939, annexed by Germany 1939-1945, part of Poland 1945 and city re-named Gdansk.
Issues of Free city (Freie Stadt) *1920-1939*
Issues of Polish PO, inscr. Gdansk *1925-1939*

42 **Datia** — See Duttia (State in India).

22 **Dédéagh**
Present Greek port of Alexandroupolis in Thracia.
Issues of French PO *1893-1914*

34 **Demnat Marrakech**
Morocco, local issues *1891-1912*

12 **Denmark (Danmark)**
Issues *1851-*
Denmark — Other stamp issues:
Danish West Indies (now US Virgin Islands) *1855-1917*
Iceland (independent Republic 1944) *1873-1948*
Greenland (Grønland) *1938-*

15 **Deutsche Bundespost**
Inscr. on stamps of the Federal Republic of Germany (FRG) (Bundesrepublik Deutschland=BRD) *1949-*

15 **Deutsche Demokratische Republik (DDR)**
Inscr. on stamps of the German Democratic Republic (GDR) *1949-*

14 **Deutsche Post Osten**
German occupation of Polish issues *1939*
See also Generalgouvernement.

12 **Deutsches Reich**
Inscr. on stamps of Germany 1871-1945. See Germany.
Deutschland — See Germany.

52,55 **Deutsch-Neuguinea (German New Guinea)**
German Colony 1884-1914, Australian Mandate 1920, and together with Papua formed the independent State of Papua New Guinea in 1975.
German Colonial issues *1897-1916*
British issues *1914-1918*
For later issues, see New Guinea and Papua New Guinea.

35 **Deutsch-Ostafrika (German East Africa)**
German Colony 1885/1890, British Mandate 1920 and re-named Tanganyika.
German Colonial issues *1893-1916*
British occupation issues *1915*
See Tanganyika and Tanzania for later issues.

14 **Deutschösterreich (German Austria)**
Inscr. on stamps of the new Republic of Austria used in period 1918-1921.

34 **Deutsch-Südwestafrika (or Südwest-Afrika)**
German Colony of Southwest Africa 1884, British occupation 1915, and under Mandate of the Union (now Republic) of South Africa since 1919.
German Colonial issues *1897-1915*
See South West Africa for later issues (also unofficially named Namibia).

42 **Dhar**
Indian States issues *1897-1901*

62 **Diego-Suarez**
French base in Madagascar, under the administration of Madagascar 1898.
Issues *1890-1896*

35,37 **Djibouti**
Port in French Somaliland (Côte Française des Somalis).
French issues, some inscr. DJ *1894-1902*
Replaced by stamps of Côte des Somalis, see for later issues, also Territoire Français des Afars et Issas (present Republic of Djibouti). See Obock for earlier issues.
Issues of "Vichy France" (non-occupied France) *1941*
"Free French" issues (Administration of France in Exile) *1943*

37 **Djibouti, Republic**
Formerly French Somaliland (Côte Française des Somalis), re-named 1967 Territoire des Afars et des Issas, independent Republic of Djibouti 1977.
Issues *1977-*

15 **Döbeln**
Germany (GDR), local town issues 1945

22 **Dodecanese** — See Aegean Islands.

31 **Dominica**
British Colony and part of the Leeward Islands administration, later of that of the Windward Islands. Independent Commonwealth State 1978.
Issues *1874-1978*
Independent Commonwealth of Dominica issues *1978-*

30 **Dominican Republic (Republica Dominicana)**
Eastern part of the island of Haiti (Hispaniola), successively under French, Haitian and Spanish rule, independent Republic 1865.
Issues *1865-*

14 **Država S.H.S. (State of the Serbs, Croats and Slovenes)**
Inscr. on some early stamp issues of Yugoslavia.

51 **Dubai**
Territory forming part of the Trucial States till end of 1963, and later part of the United Arab Emirates (U.A.E.) in 1971.
Issues — See U.A.E. for later issues *1963-1973*

22 **Durazzo**
Albanian town of Durrës.
Issues of Italian POs in the Ottoman Empire *1909-1915*

33 **Dutch Guiana** — See Surinam.

52,54 **Dutch New Guinea** — See Netherlands New Guinea.

42 **Duttia (also Datia)**
Indian States issues *1893-1920*

37 **E.A.F. (East African Forces)**
British occupation of Somalia
Issues *1943-1948*
Superseded by British Military Administration issues 1948, later by those of the Italian Administration.
For later issues, see Somalia, and Somali Republic.

35 **East Africa, German** — See Deutsch-Ostafrika, and Tanganyika (now Tanzania).

35,37 **East Africa and Uganda Protectorate** — See British East Africa.

15 **Eastern Karelia (Itä-Karjala)**
Region of Russia under temporary Finnish Administration, now part of the USSR.
Finnish issues *1940-1947*

13,23 **Eastern Roumelia** — See Roumélie Orientale.

48 **East of Jordan (also E.E.F.)**
Inscr. on early stamp issues of British Military Administration of Palestine *1918*
See also E.E.F., Jordan, and Palestine.

32 **Ecuador**
Republic 1830, includes the Pacific islands of Galapagos
Issues *1865-*
Separate issues of Galapagos Isds. *1957-1959*

48 **E.E.F. (Egyptian Expeditionary Force)**
Inscr. on early stamp issues of British Military Administration of Palestine *1918*
See also Jordan, and Palestine.

14 **Eesti** — See Estonia.

22 **Aegeo** — See Aegean Islands.

23,35 **Egypt**
37 Formerly a Viceregency in the Ottoman Empire, British occupation 1882 and Protectorate 1914-1922, independent Kingdom 1922-1953, Republic 1953. Member of the United Arab Republic (UAR), together with Syria, 1958-1961. Federated with Libya and Syria 1971, country re-named Arab Republic of Egypt.
Khedive issues *1866-1914*
(Khedive = "Prince").
British Protectorate issues *1914-1925*
Kingdom issues *1922-1953*
(some with French inscr. Royaume d'Égypte).
Republic issues *1953-1958*
Egypt issues of the UAR *1958-1971*
Egypt, Arab Republic issues (A.R.Egypt) *1971-*
Egypt — Other stamp issues:
23 *Suez Canal Company (Canal Maritime de Suez)* *1868*
23 *Issues of French POs at Alexandria and Port Said (Alexandrie, and Port-Saïd)* *1899-1930*
Issues of British Forces in Egypt *1936-1951*
50 *Egyptian issues of Egyptian occupation of Palestine (Israel) (inscr. Palestine 1948-1958, and UAR 1958-1967)* *1948-1967*

14 **Eire (Irish Republic)**
Inscr. on stamps of the Republic of Ireland *1922-*

30 **El Salvador**
Former Spanish Colony, independent 1821, Republic 1839
Issues *1867-*

12,13 **Ellas** — See Greece and Crete.

34 **Elobey, Annobon, and Corisco**
Spanish territories in the Gulf of Guinea, united as one postal region 1909 with Spanish Guinea and Fernando Poo (now Equatorial Guinea).
Spanish Colonial issues *1903-1909*

16 **Elsass (Alsace)**
Inscr. on German occupation issues of Alsace (France) *1940-1941*

16 **Elsass-Lothringen** — German form for Alsace-Lorraine, which see for details.

25 **Emory (Virginia, USA)**
Confederate States of America.
Postmaster's Provisional issues *1861*

12 **Empire Français (French Empire)** — See France.

22 **Empire Ottoman (Ottoman Empire)** — See Turkey.

13 **Epirus (Ipeiros)** — See Greece.

22 **Episkopi** — Greek form for Piscòpi, also Telos.
See Aegean Islands.

36 **Equatorial Guinea**
Previously Spanish Guinea, independent Republic 1968 consisting of the territory of Rio Muni (now Mbini) and the Atlantic island of Fernando Poo (now Macias Nguema).
Issues *1968-*
For earlier issues, see Fernando Poo and Rio Muni.

35,37 **Eritrea**
Italian Colony 1890, part of Italian East Africa 1938-1942, British occupation and administration 1941-1952, autonomous as part of Federation of Ethiopia and Eritrea 1952-1962, when it was absorbed in the Empire of Ethiopia.
Italian Colonial issues *1893-1938*
(Stamps of Italian East Africa current 1938-1941).
British Military and Administration issues *1941-1952*

38 **E.S.F.S.R.**— See Transcaucasian Federation.

12 **Espana** — See Spain.

14 **Estland** — See Estonia.

14 **Estonia (Eesti)**
Independent State 1918, under Russian occupation Aug. 1940, then under German occupation 1941-1944. Annexed by USSR 1945, and now the Estonskaya SSR.
Republic issues (inscr. Eesti) *1918-1940*
German occupation issues (inscr. Estland) *1941-1942*

42 **Établissements Français dans l'Inde (French Settlements in India)** — See Inde Française.

57 **Établissements Français de l'Océanie (French Settlements in the Pacific, now French Polynesia)** — See Océanie, and Polynésie Française.

61 **État Comorien** — See Comoros.

35,37 **Ethiopia**
Formerly known as Abyssinia, independent Empire, under Italian occupation 1936-1941, independence restored 1942. Military administration since 1974 (deposition of the Emperor).
Empire issues *1894-1936*
Italian occupation issues (inscr. Etiopia) *1936-1938*
(Stamps of Italian East Africa current 1938-1941).
Issues of restored independence *1942-*

32 **E.U. de Colombia (United States of Colombia)** — See Colombia.

32 **E.U. de Nueva Granada (United States of New Granada)** — See Colombia.

16 **Eupen**
Territory formerly German, annexed to Belgium 1920.
Belgian issues of Belgian occupation of Germany, inscr. Eupen, and Malmédy *1920-1921*

15 **Falkensee**
Germany (GDR), *local town issue, inscr. Gemeinde Falkensee* *1945*

61,63 **Falkland Islands**
British possession 1833, now British Dependent Territory
Issues *1878-*

61,63 **Falkland Islands Dependencies**
The Dependencies now include only South Georgia and South Sandwich Islands.
Separate issues of the Dependencies of Graham Land, South Georgia, South Orkneys, and South Shetlands *1944-1946*
General issues for all Dependencies *1946-1963*
Separate issues of South Georgia *1963-*
Replaced 1963 by stamps of the British Antarctic Territory, except the current separate issues of South Georgia (one of the two Falkland Islands Dependencies).

42 **Faridkot**
Indian State issues *1879-1887*
Indian Convention State issues *1887-1931*

14 **Faröe Islands**
Danish islands in the North Atlantic.
British issues during the 1939-1945 war, inscr. Foroyar *1940*
Separate issues of Foroyar *1975-*

42 **Federated Malay States** — See Malaya.

44 **Federation of Malaya** — See Malaya, and Malaysia.

51 **Federation of South Arabia**
Formed 1963 from the British Colony of Aden and other Aden Protectorate States. Part of the South Yemen Republic (PDRY) in 1967.
Issues *1963-1966*

34 **Fernando Poo**
Spanish island in the Gulf of Guinea which, together with the mainland territory of Rio Muni and other areas, became the independent Republic of Equatorial Guinea (Guinea Equatorial) in 1968, island now named Macias Nguema
Issues *1868-1929, 1960-1968*
See Equatorial Guinea for later issues.

34 **Fez Mequinez, and Fez a Sefrou**
Morocco, local issues *1891-1912*

37 **Fezzan**
Formerly Turkish, territory acquired by Italy 1912, later by France in 1943. Part of the independent Kingdom of Libya, 1951.
Issues — (some inscr. Fezzan Ghadamès) *1943-1951*

56,58 **Fiji**
British Colony 1874, independent State in the British Commonwealth Oct. 1970.
Issues *1870-*

43,45 **Filipinas** — See Philippines.

13 **Finland (Suomi)**
Grand Duchy under Russian administration, independent Republic 1917.
Issues under Russian rule *1856-1917*
Republic issues *1917-*
Finland — Special issues:
Finnish occupation of the town of Aunus (now Olonets, USSR) *1919*
Issues of Finnish administration of Eastern Karelia (Itä-Karjala) (now part of the USSR) *1940-1947*

15 **Finsterwalde**
Germany (GDR), *local town issues, inscr. Sängerstadt Finsterwalde* *1945-1946*

17,21 **Fiume**
Formerly Austrian, Free City 1919/1920, annexed to Italy 1924, city ceded to Yugoslavia 1947 and re-named Rijeka.
Allied occupation issues *1918-1919*
Free City issues *1919-1924*
(some inscr. Arbe, or Veglia).
Italian issues *1924*
Italian occupation issues — (inscr. Fiume and Kupa) *1941*
Yugoslav occupation issues *1945*
(occupation of Venetia Giulia and Istria).

39,41 **Formosa (Taiwan)**
Former name for island State of China (Taiwan).
Issues of the Chinese Nationalist Government, some with inscr. Republic of China. *1945-*
Japanese occupation issues *1945*

14 **Foroyar** — See Faroe Islands.

12 **France**
Second Republic 1848, Second Empire 1852, Third Republic 1870, (French State=État Français 1940-1944, Government of Vichy in non-occupied France), Fourth Republic 1947, Fifth Republic 1959.
Republic issues (République Française, or R.F.) *1849-1852*
Empire issues (Empire Français) *1853-1871*
Republic issues *1870-1940*
War-time Vichy Government issues, inscr. État Français, or Postes Françaises *1940-1944*
Stamps of "France Libre" (Free France Government in Exile under General de Gaulle) printed in London 1942, but not issued.
48 *Special issues of the "Comité Français de la Libération Nationale" (French Committee of National Liberation) were made in 1943 and used in Corsica and in most of the French Colonies, with various inscr., among which was 'Forces Françaises Libres, Levant"* *1942-1944*
"Liberation" issues in France, with various inscr. on existing stamps *1944*
(Fourth Republic) Provisional Government issues *1944-1946*
Regular issues *1947-*

France — Colonies and Territories under French administration: (See individual entries for details)
General Colonial issues *1859-1910*

34 *Afrique Équatoriale Française=A.E.F. (French Equatorial Africa)*
34 *Afrique Occidentale Française=A.O.F. (French West Africa)*
48 *Alaouites, Territoire (Syria)*
48 *Alexandrette, Sandjak (Antakya, Turkey)*
34,36 *Algérie (Algeria)*
62 *Anjouan (Comoros)*
43,35 *Annam et Tonkin (in French Indochina)*
34,36 *Bénin*
43,45 *Cambodge (Cambodia)*
34,36 *Cameroun (Cameroon)*
43 *Cochinchine (Cochinchina, in French Indochina)*
62 *Comores (Comoros)*
34,36 *Congo Français (French Congo)*
35,37 *Côte Française des Somalis (French Somaliland)*
34,36 *Côte d'Ivoire (Ivory Coast)*
34,36 *Dahomey (now Bénin, Republic)*
62 *Diego Suarez (Madagascar)*
34,36 *Gabon*
48 *Grand-Liban (Lebanon)*
31 *Guadeloupe*
34,36 *Guinée Française (French Guinea)*
33 *Guyane Française (French Guiana)*
34,36 *Haute-Volta (Upper Volta, now Burkina)*
34,36 *Haut-Sénégal et Niger (Senegal and Niger)*
42 *Inde Française (French India)*
43,45 *Indochine (French Indochina)*
43,45 *Laos*

62 *Madagascar*
34,36 *Maroc (Morocco)*
31 *Martinique*
34,36 *Mauritanie (Mauritania)*
62 *Mayotte*
17 *Memel*
34,36 *Niger*
62 *Nossi-Bé*
56,58 *Nouvelle Calédonie (New Caledonia)*
57,59 *Océanie, Établissements Français (French Polynesia)*
34,36 *Oubangui-Chari (now Central African Republic)*
62 *Réunion*

63 *St. Pierre et Miquelon*
34,36 *Sénégal*
34,36 *Soudan Français (French Soudan*

48 *Syrie (Syria)*
34,36 *Tchad (Chad)*
60 *Terres Australes et Antarctiques Françaises (French Antarctic Territory, Adélie Land)*
34,36 *Togo*
34,36 *Tunisie (Tunisia)*
56,58 *Wallis et Futuna (New Caledonia)*
France — POs in other countries:
39 China — *General issues, inscr. Chine* 1894-1922
Offices at: Canton, Hoi-Hao, Kouang-Tchéou, Mong-Tzeu, Pakhoi,
43 *Tchong-King, Yunnanfou. All closed 1922, except Kouang-Tchéou which closed in 1946 (territory returned to China 1943).*
Ottoman Empire and Levant —
22 *POs in Greece at Cavalle (Kavalla),*
Dédéagh (Alexandroupolis) 1893-1914
Port-Lagos (Porto Lago) 1893-1898
2 *POs in the Levant, with various inscr. including Beyrouth* 1885-1923
22 *Vathy (Aegean island of Samos)* 1885-1923
23 Crête *(when under joint administration of France, Great Britain, Italy and Russia, 1898 to 1913)* 1902-1903
23 Egypt —*POs at Alexandria and Port Said* 1899-1930
46 Ile Rouad *(French occupation of island off the coast of Syria)* 1916-1920
Zanzibar 1894-1904

15 **Frankenberg, Sachsen**
Germany (GDR), *local town issue* 1946
25 **Fredericksburg (Virginia, USA)**
Confederate States of America,
Postmaster's Provisional issues 1861
15 **Fredersdorf**
Germany (GDR), *local town issues, inscr. FM* 1945-1946
French Colonies and Territories —See France.
51 **Fujeira (Fujairah)**
One of the former Trucial States till 1971, when it formed part of the new State of the United Arab Emirates (UAE).
Issues — See UAE for later issues 1964-1972
63 **Funchal**
Portuguese island in the Atlantic. 1892-1905
Stamps of the Azores current 1905-1931 and of Portugal from 1931.

34,36 **Gabon**
Part of French Congo 1888 and of French Equatorial Africa (A.E.F.) 1910-1958, independent Republic 1960
Issues 1886-1936
(A.E.F. stamps current 1937-1959).
Republic issues (République Gabonaise) 1959-
59 **Galapagos (Islas Galapagos)**
Pacific islands belonging to Ecuador, Province of Ecuador 1973.
Issues 1957-1973
34,36 **Gambia**
British Colony and Protectorate, independent Republic of The Gambia in the British Commonwealth 1970.
Issues 1869-
50 **Gaza**
Gaza Strip occupied by Israel 1967, and previously occupied by Egypt.
Egyptian issues, inscr. Palestine 1948
17 **Gdansk (Poland)** —See Danzig.

14 **Generalegouvernement**
Inscr. on German occupation issues of Poland 1940-1944
Preceded by stamps inscr. Deutsche Post Osten.
12 **Genève**
Local Swiss city and Canton issues 1843-1850
Superseded by Swiss Federal Post stamps, 1850-
38 **Georgia**
National Republic established 1918-1921 in the wake of the Russian Revolution of 1917, later part of the Transcaucasian Federation.
Issues — (some inscr. in French: Géorgie) 1919-1923
German Colonies and Territories — See Germany.
12 **Germany** — Pre-unification period
Several States and local authorities had their own postal administration before the unification of Germany in 1871. From 1868 to 1871, several States combined to form the North German Confederation Postal Administration (Norddeutscher Postbezirk).
Stamp-issuing authorities:
(see individual entries for details)
Baden, Grossherzogtum (Grand Duchy) 1851-1871
Bayern (Kingdom of Bavaria) 1849-1920
Bergedorf — town issues 1861-1867
Braunschweig, Herzogtum (Duchy of Brunswick) 1852-1867
Bremen, Hansestadt (Hanseatic City) 1855-1867
Hamburg, Hansestadt (Hanseatic City) 1859-1867
Hannover, Königreich (Kingdom of Hanover) 1850-1866
16 *Helgoland (Heligoland)*
British and German issues 1859-1890
(See Heligoland for details)
Holstein, Herzogthum (Duchy) 1864-1867
Lübeck, Hansestadt (Hanseatic City) 1859-1868
Mecklenburg-Schwerin, Grossherzogtum (Grand Duchy) 1856-1867
Mecklenburg-Strelitz, Grossherzogtum (Grand Duchy) 1864-1867
Oldenburg, Grossherzogtum (Grand Duchy) 1852-1867
Preussen, Königreich (Kingdom of Prussia) 1850-1867
Sachsen, Königreich (Kingdom of Saxony) 1850-1867
Schleswig, Herzogthum (Duchy) 1865-1867
(see for details)
Schleswig-Holstein, Herzogthum (Duchy) 1850-1867
(see for details)
Thurn und Taxis (Principality) 1852-1867
(see for details)
Württemberg, Königreich (Kingdom) 1851-1918
(see for details)
Norddeutscher Postbezirk:
(see for details)
Issues of the North German Confederation Postal Administration 1868-1871
Superseded 1872 by stamps of the unified Kingdom of Germany.
12 **Germany (Deutsches Reich)**
Second Reich founded 1871. Republic 1918/1919 to 1933, when the Third Reich was established till 1945 (Nazi Government). Republic restored 1945.
Kingdom issues (Reichspost) 1871-1919
Republic and Third Reich issues 1919-1945
(some issues 1943-1945 inscr. Grossdeutsches Reich).
15 **Germany, Federal Republic (FRG)**
(Bundesrepublik Deutschland = BRD)
Issues, inscr. Deutsche Bundespost 1949-
Berlin, Western Sectors 1948-
(Bundespost stamps inscr. Berlin).
15 **Germany, Democratic Republic (GDR)**
(Deutsche Demokratische Republik = DDR)
Issues 1949-
Berlin, Eastern Sector 1945
(inscr. Berlin-Brandenburg)
15 **Germany** — Allied occupation:
General issues (Deutsche Post) 1945-1949
Issues of Anglo-American Bizone 1945-1949
(not thus inscr.)
15 French issues:
inscr. Zone Française 1945-1946
(included the Provinces of Baden, Pfalz, Rheinland, Saargebiet, Württemberg).
Issues followed by those of the several Provinces (now Länder):
Baden 1947-1949
Rheinland-Pfalz 1947-1949
Württemberg 1947-1949
Saar — (Economic attachment to France) 1947-1956
15 Soviet Occupation Zone issues:
Berlin-Brandenburg (Stadt Berlin) 1945
Mecklenburg-Vorpommern 1945-1946
Ostsachsen (East Saxony) 1945-1946
Provinz Sachsen (Saxony) 1945-1946
Thüringen 1945-1946
West-Sachsen (West Saxony) 1945-1946
General Soviet Zone issues: 1948-1949
For later issues, see Germany (GDR).
Germany — Local issues:
These were either a hand-stamped label, an inscr. on an existing stamp, or a distinct postage stamp printed as such. The latter are preceded by an * and are cross-referenced in the Dictionary.
14 *Period* 1918-1923

Bad Suderode	Leverkusen
Berg. Gladbach	Preussich-Gladbach
Halle a.d. Saale	Schliersee
Leipzig	

15 *Period* *1945-1948*

Altdöbern
* Apolda, Stadtpost
Arnsberg
Aschaffenburg
Bad Nauheim
Bad Saarow (Markt)
Barsinghausen
Chemnitz
* Cottbus
Demnin (Vorpommern)
* Döbeln
Dresden
Eckartsberga (Thur.)
* Falkensee, Gemeinde
* Finsterwalde
Flensburg
Frankenau
* Frankenberg (Sa.)
* Fredersdorf (b. Berlin)
Freudenstadt
* Glauchau, Kreis
* Görlitz, Stadt
Gottleuba
* Grossräschen
Hamburg
* Herrnhut
Holzhausen (Sa.)
Kiel
Köln/Rhein
Lauterbach (Hessen)
Löbau (Sachsen)
Löhne (Westfalen)
Lohne (Oldenburg)
* Lübbenau, Stadt
Lütjenburg
* Meissen
Memelland (1939)
Mindelheim (Bayern)
Mühlberg
Naumburg/Saale
Netzschkau-Reichenbach
* Niesky, Stadt (Oberlausitz)
Perleberg
* Plauen i.V.
* Rosswein (Sa.)
* Ründeroth
Saulgau
* Schwarzenberg
Spremberg
* Storkow, Stadt
* Strausberg, Stadt
Titisee
Unna
Westerstede
Wittenberg, Lutherstadt
Wurzen

Germany — POW camps:
41 *German POW camp at Bando, Japan* *1918*
inscr. Bando Lagerpost.
13 *British POW camp at Ruhleben, Germany* *1915*
inscr. Ruhleben Postage.
18,19 **Germany** — Plebiscite areas
(see individual entries for details).
Allenstein (East Prussia, now Olsztyn, Poland) *1920*
Marienwerder (East Prussia, now Kwidzyn, Poland) *1920*
Oberschlesien (Upper Silesia, Haute-Silésie, Gorny Slask) *1920-1922*
Saar (with variants: Saargebiet, Saarland, Saare) *1934*
1955
Schleswig (Slesvig) *1920*
Germany — Former Colonies and Territories under German administration:
(see individual entries for details).
52 *Deutsch-Neuguinea* *(German New Guinea)*
35 *Deutsch-Ostafrika* *(German East Africa)*
34 *Deutsch-Südwestafrika* *(German South-West Africa)*
34 *Kamerun* *(Cameroons)*
56 *Karolinen* *(Caroline Islands)*
39 *Kiautschou* *(Tsingtau, China)*
56 *Marianen* *(Mariana Islands)*
56 *Marschall-Inseln* *(Marshall Islands)*
56,57 *Samoa*
34 *Togo*
35 *Witu-Schutzgebiet* *(Suaheliland Protectorate)*
Germany — POs in other countries:
39 China — *Issues, inscr. China* *1897-1917*
Offices at Amoy, Canton, Chingkiang, Fuchau, Hankow, Ichang, Nanking, Peking, Shanghai, Swatow, Tchifu, Tientsin (Field POs were also active at Pechili, northern China, during the Boxer Rebellion of 1900).
22-23 Levant — *German issues with value inscr.* *1884-1914*
Offices at Beirut, Constantinople (Istanbul), Jaffa (Tel Aviv-Yafo), Jerusalem, Smyrna (Izmir). (Stamps cancelled with name of the town of issue).
34 Morocco — *Issues, inscr. Marocco, or Marokko* *1899-1914*
Offices active in French territory 1899-1914, and till 1919 in Spanish territory. Offices at Alcassar, Arsila, Asimmur, Casablanca, Fez, Fez-Mellah, Larache, Marrakesh, Mazagan, Meknes, Mogador, Rabat, Safi, Tetouan.
Germany — German occupation of other countries:
Period 1914-1918:
13 *Belgien (Belgium)* *1914-1916*
13 *Postgebiet Ober-Ost (Eastern Postal areas)* *1916-1918*
13 *Russisch-Polen (Russian Poland)* *1915*
13 *Gen.-Gouv. Warschau (General Admin. Warsaw)* *1916*
13 *Rumänien (M.V.i.R.) (Romania)* *1917-1918*
Period 1939-1945:
14 *Albanien (Albania) — (some inscr. Shqipnija)* *1943-1944*
14 *Belgien (Belgium) — Field Post issues of the Flemish and Walloon Legions* *1941-1942*
14,17 *Böhmen und Mähren (Bohemia and Moravia)* *1939-1945*
14 *Dänemark (Denmark) — Field post of the Danish Legion* *1944*
16 *Elsass (Alsace)* *1940-1941*
14 *Estland (Estonia)* *1941-1942*
14 *France — Early issues hand-stamped "Besetztes Gebiet Nordfrankreich" (Occupied area of Northern France)* *1940*
14 *Special issues "Festung Lorient" ("Lorient" Fortification) and* *1944*
14 *"Front Atlantique" (Atlantic Front)* *1945*
Issues of the French Voluntary Legion ("Légion Volontaires Français") *1941-1942*
14 *Generalgouvernement (Poland)* *1940-1944*
(early issues inscr. Deutsche Post Osten).
14 *Boka Kotorska (Territory of Cattaro, Yugoslav Adriatic coast)* *1944*
14 *Kurland (in Latvia)* *1945*
14 *Laibach (Province of Ljubljana, Yugoslavia)* *1944-1945*
14 *Lettland (Latvia)* *1941*
14 *Litauen (Lithuania, Lietuva)* *1941*
16 Lothringen (Lorraine) 1940-1941
14 *Luxemburg* *1940-1942*
14 *Mazedonien (Macedonia)* *1944*
14 *Montenegro* *1943-1944*
14 *Ostland (general German occupation of eastern areas, including Estonia, Latvia, Lithuania and White Russia)* *1941-1943/44*
14 *Pleskau (town of Pskov, USSR)* *1941-1942*
14 *Serbien (Serbia)* *1941-1942*
14 *Ukraine* *1941-1943*
14 *Zante (Greek Ionian Islands)* *1943*
17 *Zara (town of Zadar, Yugoslavia)* *1943-1944*
14,17 *Several Military issues were also made in various theatres of war with special inscr., among which are "Feldpost", "Luftfeldpost" (Military Air Mail), "Inselpost" (Island post). Special issues Mar. 1945 for submarine mail to beleaguered troops on the Hela Peninsula (Bay of Gdansk, Poland) inscr. "durch U-Boat" (by U-boat).*
23 **Gerusalemme**
Inscr. on issues of Italian PO at Jerusalem *1909*
37 **Ghadamès**
Inscr. on issues of Fezzan (Libya) *1949*
See Fezzan for earlier issues.
36 **Ghana**
Former British Colony of the Gold Coast, independent 1957 and Commonwealth State of the Republic of Ghana, 1960.
Issues — See Gold Coast for earlier issues *1957-*
13 **Gibraltar**
British territory 1713, now British Dependent Territory.
Issues *1886-*
57,59 **Gilbert and Ellice Islands**
British Protectorate in the Pacific 1892, Colony in 1916. Administrative connection between the island groups severed 1975, the Ellice Islands becoming independent as Tuvalu in 1978, and the Gilbert Islands becoming the Republic of Kiribati in 1979, both States in the British Commonwealth.
Gilbert and Ellice Islands issues *1911-1976*
For later issues, see Kiribati and Tuvalu respectively.
14 **Glauchau**
Germany (GDR), *local town issues* *1945*
34,36 **Gold Coast**
British Colony 1874/1896, independent and Republic of Ghana in 1960.
Issues — See Ghana for later issues *1875-1957*
34,36 **Golfo de Guinea** — See Spanish Guinea.
25 **Goliad (Texas, USA)**
Confederate States of America,
Postmaster's Provisional issues *1861*
25 **Gonzales (Texas, USA)**
Confederate States of America,
Postmaster's Provisional issues *1861*
14 **Görlitz**
Germany (GDR), *local town issues* *1945*
19 **Gorny Slask (Upper Silesia)**
Polish inscr. on Plebiscite stamp issues of Upper Silesia (Oberschlesien) *1920-1922*
63 **Graham Land**
Formerly one of the Falkland Islands Dependencies, now part of the British Antarctic Territory.
Issues *1944-1946*
32 **Granada Confederation**
Formerly New Granada and later the United States of Colombia
Issues *1859-1860*
See Colombia for later issues.
62 **Grande Comore** — See Comoros.
48 **Grand-Liban (Lebanon)**
French Mandate territory of Lebanon (Grand-Liban) 1922-1926, when it became a Republic under French Mandate.
Issues, inscr. Grand-Liban *1924-1927*
11 **Great Britain**
Issues *1840-*
Regional issues (without inscr.) for: *1958-*
Guernsey (till 1969)
Jersey (till 1969)
Isle of Man (till 1973)
Northern Ireland
Scotland
Wales and Monmouthshire.
See also Channel Islands.

12,14 **Greece (Ellas)**
23 Monarchy 1832, revolution followed by a Republic in 1924, Monarchy restored 1935, Italian occupation 1940, German occupation 1942, liberation 1944 and Monarchy restored 1946, later abolished and Republic in 1973.
Monarchy issues, inscr. Ellas 1861-1924
Issues of revolutionary elements in northern Epirus, inscr. Ell. Auton.
Ipeiros (Autonomous Greek Epirus) 1914-1915
Revolutionary administration issues 1922
Republic issues 1924-1935
Restoration Monarch and Republic, issues 1935-
(issues continued through period of 1939-1945 war).
German occupation issues 1941-1944

14,22,23 **Greece**
Greek occupation of adjoining territories during the Balkan Wars of 1912 and 1913.
Greek provisional issues at various dates during period 1913-1916 for the localities, territories or islands of:
Cavalla (Kavalla)
Chios (Khios)
Dédéagatz (Alexandroupolis)
Icaria (Ikaria)
Lemnos (Limnos)
Mytilene (Lesbos)
Samos
Thrace (temporary autonomous government of Western Thrace, 1913).

14 **Greece**
Issues of Greek occupation of part of Albania 1940-1941
Occupation of the Dodecanese (Aegean) Islands 1947

27 **Greenland (Grønland)**
Danish territory, became a part of the Kingdom of Denmark 1963
Issues 1938-

25 **Greenville (Alabama, USA)**
Confederate States of America,
Postmaster's Provisional issues 1861

25 **Greenwood (Virginia, USA)**
Confederate States of America,
Postmaster's Provisional issues 1861

31 **Grenada**
British possession in the Windward Islands which includes islands of the Grenadines group. Independent Commonwealth State 1974.
Issues 1861-
Separate issues of the Grenada 1973
Grenadines (Grenadines of Granada)

31 **Grenadines of Grenada**
That part of the island group belonging to Grenada.
Issues 1973-

31 **Grenadines of St. Vincent**
Island group belonging to St. Vincent.
Issues of St. Vincent and the Grenadines 1973-
See also St. Vincent.

34 **Griqualand West**
Former British territory in southern Africa, annexed to the Cape of Good Hope and now part of the Republic of South Africa.
Issues, inscr. G. or G.W. on Cape stamps 1874-1880

27 **Grønland** — See Greenland.

14 **Grossdeutsches Reich (Greater Germany)**
Inscr. on some stamps of Germany (Third Reich) in period 1943-1945.

14 **Grossräschen**
Germany (GDR), *local town issues* 1945-1946

25 **Grove Hill (Alabama, USA)**
Confederate States of America,
Postmaster's Provisional issues 1861

30 **Guadalajara**
Mexico, *local issues* 1867-1868

31 **Guadeloupe**
French Colony 1814, and a "Département" of France 1946.
Issues 1884-1947
(Stamps of France current since 1947).

56,58 **Guam**
Island in the Mariana group in the Pacific, formerly Spanish, USA Territory 1898.
Issues of USA Administration 1899
Local post service issues, inscr. Guam Guard 1930

30 Guanacaste
Costa Rica, *local issues* 1885-1889

30 **Guatemala**
Republic 1844
Issues 1871-

11 **Guernsey**
Channel Islands Bailiwick, with own Postal Administration 1969.
Regional issues of Great Britain (no inscr.) 1958-1969
Separate issues of Guernsey Bailiwick 1969-
German war-time occupation issues 1941-1944
See also Channel Islands.

32,33 **Guiana, British** — See British Guiana.

33 **Guiana, French** — See Guyane Française.

33 **Guiana, Dutch** — See Suriname.

34,36 **Guiné Portuguesa** — See Portuguese Guinea, and Guinea-Bissau.

34,36 **Guinea, Republic** — See Guinée, République, and Guinée Française for earlier issues.

36 **Guinea-Bissau**
Formerly Portuguese Guinea, independent State 1974.
Issues 1974-
See Portuguese Guinea for earlier issues.

36 **Guinea Ecuatorial** — See Equatorial Guinea.

36 **Guinea Española** — See Spanish Guinea.

34,36 **Guinée**
French territory, of Guinée Française, under the administration of French West Africa (A.O.F.) in 1895, independent Republic 1958.
Issues 1892-1944
(AOF stamps used 1944-1958)
Independent Republic issues 1959-

32,33 **Guyana**
Former Colony of British Guiana, independent 1966 and re-named Guyana, Republic in the British Commonwealth 1970.
Issues — See British Guiana for earlier issues 1966-

33 **Guyane Française**
French Colony, Overseas "Département" of France 1946.
Issues 1886-1947
(Stamps of France current from 1947).
See Inini for separate issues.

42 **Gwalior**
Issues of Convention State of India 1885-1951

51 **Hadramaut, Qu'aiti State in** — See Aden.

30 **Haiti**
Issues, inscr. République d'Haïti 1881-

12 **Hamburg, Hansestadt (Hanseatic City)**
Issues 1859-1867

16 *Hamburg issues of PO on island of Heligoland* 1859-1867
Superseded 1868 by stamps of Norddeutscher Postbezirk.

12 **Hannover**
Kingdom till 1866, when it became Province of Prussia.
Kingdom issues 1850-1866
Replaced 1866 by stamps of Prussia.

48 **Hatay**
Town in the former Sandjak d'Alexandrette, then in Syria and now the town of Antakya in Turkey.
Turkish administration issues, inscr. Hatay Devleti 1939
See also Alexandrette.

19 **Haute-Silésie (Upper Silesia)**
French inscr. on Plebiscite issues of Oberschlesien (Upper Silesia) 1920-1922

34 **Haut-Sénégal et Niger**
French African territory formed 1904 from the Sénégambie and Niger, part of which became Haute-Volta (Upper Volta) in 1919, the eastern part became the Territoire du Niger. The remainder became French Sudan.
Issues 1906-1921
French Sudan stamps used after 1921.

34 **Haute-Volta (Upper Volta)**
French Colony formed 1919 from Haut-Sénégal and Niger. Part of French West Africa (AOF) 1932-1947 and under the administration of Ivory Coast (Côte d'Ivoire) 1932-1947. Independent Republic 1960, name changed to Burkina, 1984.
Issues *1920-1933*
Republic issues *1959-*

26,57 **Hawaii**
59 Independent Kingdom till 1893, possession of the USA 1898, Territory of the USA 1900 and promulgated as the 50th State of the USA in 1959.
Issues *1851-1899*
Stamps of the USA current since 1899.

56,58 **Hébrides, Nouvelles** — See New Hebrides.

46,49 **Hedjaz-Nejd**
Kingdom of Hejaz-Nejd, formed from the Kingdom of Hejaz and the Sultanate of Nejd, re-named Saudi Arabia 1932.
Issues of Hejaz *1916-1925*
Issues of Nejd *1925*
Issues of Hejaz-Nejd *1926-1934*
Issues of Kingdom of Saudi Arabia *1934-*

25 **Helena (Texas, USA)**
Confederate States of America,
Postmaster's Provisional issues *1861*

16 **Heligoland**
British Colony 1814-1890, when it was exchanged with Germany for the island of Zanzibar (now part of Tanzania).
British issues *1867-1890*
Hamburg Postal Agency issues, inscr. or stamped "Helgoland" *1859-1867*

12 **Helvetia**
Inscr. on stamps of Switzerland, also sometimes inscr. Confoederatio Helvetica. *1862-*
See Switzerland.

14 **Herrnhut**
Germany (GDR), *local town issue* *1945*

42 **H.H.Nawab Shah**
Inscr. on stamps of Indian State of Bhopal, which see for details.

39 **Hoï-Hao**
Issues of French PO in China *1901-1922*

42 **Holkar** — See Indore (Indian State).

12 **Holstein, Herzogthum**
German Duchy annexed to Prussia in 1866, together with the Duchy of Schleswig. The southern part of Holstein became a part of Prussia in 1865 under the name of Herzogthum Lauenburg.
Issues *1864-1867*
Superseded 1868 by stamps of the Norddeutscher Postbezirk.

30 **Honduras, British** — See British Honduras, and Belize.

30 **Honduras**
Central American Republic 1839.
Issues *1866-*

39,41 **Hong Kong**
With its Territories, British Colony since 1841 leased from China till 1997. With its Territories of Kowloon Peninsula and numerous islands, it is now a British Dependent Territory.
Issues *1862-*
Japanese occupation issues *1945*
(occupied 1941-1945).

63 **Horta**
Portuguese island in the Azores
Issues *1892-1905*
(Superseded by stamps of the Azores 1905-1931, and those of Portugal since then).

14 **Hrvatska S.H.S. (Croatia)**
Inscr. on early issues of Croatia *1918*
Regional issues of Yugoslavia, inscr. N. D. Hrvatska *1941-1945*

12 **Hungary (Magyarorszag)**
Kingdom within the Austro-Hungarian Empire till end of 1918, period of political upheaval 1919-1920, became a Regency 1920-1944, and a Republic 1945/1946.
Kingdom issues *1871-1918*
(some inscr. Magyar Posta, or Magyarorszag).
Republic issues (Bolshevist regime) *1919-1921*
Szegedin issues (anti-Bolshevist administration) *1919-1921*
Regency issues *1921-1945*
Liberation issues *1945-1946*
Republic issues *1946-*

Hungary — Allied occupation:
French issues, inscr. Occupation Française *1919*
14 *Romanian issues, inscr. Bánát Bacska* *1919*
(Romanian occupation of Debreczin, Temesvar, Transylvania).
Serbian issues, inscr. Baranya, and Temesvar *1919*

42 **Hyderabad**
Indian States issues *1869-1949*

13,14 **Iceland**
Under Danish rule 1814-1918, autonomous State in union with the Kingdom of Denmark 1918-1944, independent Republic 1944.
Issues of Denmark, inscr. Island *1873-1948*
Republic issues *1944-*

42 **Idar**
Indian States issues *1939-1944*

42 **I.E.F. (Indian Expeditionary Forces)**
Issues *1914*

36 **Ifni**
Small Spanish enclave on coast of Morocco, ceded by Spain to Morocco 1969.
Issues *1941-1969*

48 **Île Rouad** — See Rouad (Eastern Mediterranean).

35 **Imperial British East Africa Company**
Inscr. on issues of stamps of British East Africa *1890-1895*
See British East Africa for later issues.

42 **Inde Française (French India)**
French possessions in India, also named Établissements Français dans l'Inde (French Settlements in India), consisted of the territories of Chandernagore, Karikal, Mahé, Pondichéry, and Yanaon. Territories transferred to India 1954.
Issues *1892-1954*

25 **Independence (Texas, USA)**
Confederate States of America,
Postmaster's Provisional issues *1861*

42,44 **India**
British Empire of India until 1947, when it was divided into the two separate Dominions of India and of Pakistan. India became a Republic within the British Commonwealth Jan. 1950.
Issues of East India Company, inscr. Scinde District Dawk *1852-1854*
Issues inscr. India *1854-1946*
Dominion of India issues *1947-1949*
Republic of India issues *1950-*
See also Pakistan, and Bangladesh.

42 **India — Convention States**
This was a non-political Postal Convention, whereby the States used stamps of India with the name of the State inscr. on them. The other States of India issued their own stamps.
Convention States issues:
Chamba *1886-1951*
Faridkot *1887-1931*
Issues previous to Convention *1879-1887*
Gwalior *1885-1951*
Jind *1885-1950*
Nabha *1885-1951*
Patiala (early issues inscr. Puttialla) *1884-1951*

42 **India** — *Issues of Indian States:*
Alwar *1877-1902*
Bahawalpur (now in Pakistan) *1948-1949*
Bamra *1888-1894*
Barwani *1921-1948*
Bhopal *1876-1908*
Bhor *1879-1901*
Bijawar *1935-1937*
Bundi (part of Rajasthan, 1948) *1894-1947*
Bussahir *1895-1901*
Charkhari *1894-1943*
Cochin *1892-1950*
See Travancore-Cochin for later issues.
Dhar *1897-1901*
Duttia (also spelt Datia) *1893-1920*
Faridkot *1879-1887*
Issues as Convention State *1887-1931*
Holkar — See Indore
Hyderabad *1869-1949*
Idar *1939-1944*
Indore (Holkar) *1886-1947*
Jaipur — See Rajasthan for later issues *1904-1948*
Jammu and Kashmir *1866-1894*
Jasdan — Part of Union of Saurashtra, 1948 *1942*
Jhalawar *1887-1890*
Jind *1874-1885*
Kishangarh — Part of Rajasthan, 1948 *1899-1947*
Las Bela (now in Pakistan) *1897-1907*
Morvi *1931-1948*
Part of Union of Saurashtra, 1948.
Nandgaon *1892-1895*
Nawanagar *1877-1895*
Part of Union of Saurashtra, 1948.
Orchha *1913-1942*
Poonch *1876-1894*
Rajasthan *1949*
Rajpipla *1880-1886*

Sirmoor (Sirmur) *1879-1902*
Soruth (Saurashtra) *1864-1950*
Travancore *1888-1949*
See Travancore-Cochin for later issues.
Travancore-Cochin *1949-1950*
Wadhwan *1888-1892*
Part of Union of Saurashtra, 1948.

India — Special issues:
China Expeditionary Force (C.E.F.) *1900-1921*
Indian Expeditionary Forces (I.E.F.) *1914*
Indian Custodian Forces in Korea *1953*
International Commission in Indo-China *1954-1957*
See also Azahind.

42,44 **India Portuguésa** — See Portuguese India.

43,45 **Indochina (Indochine)**
French Indochina formed 1882-1888, uniting the French Colonies and Protectorates of Cochinchina (Cochinchine), Cambodia (Cambodge), Annam et Tonkin, joined later by Laos (1893) and the territory of Kouang-Tchéou (in China).
Japanese occupation 1940-1945.
Component States autonomous 1946-1949:
Kingdoms of Cambodia and Laos. Vietnam (comprising Tonkin, Annam and Cochinchina), became the State of Viet-Nam within the French Community, and following years of conflict became divided in 1954 into the two separate States of North and South Vietnam. (See Vietnam for other details).
French Indochina (Indochine) issues *1889-1946*
Issues inscr. Viet-Nam *1946*
See also Cambodia, Laos, Vietnam.

43,45 **Indonesia, Republic**
Dutch Colony of the Netherlands Indies 1816-1941 (Japanese occupation 1941-1945). Republic proclaimed 1945, independent State 1949 (except western part of New Guinea, which became part of Indonesia 1963 and named Irian Jaya). Netherlands-Indonesian Union dissolved 1954.
Republic issues (Java and Sumatra) *1945-1950*
Parallel issues of Netherlands Indies *1864-1948*
United States of Indonesia (1945-1950) issues *1949-1950*
Republic of Indonesia issues *1950-*

45 **Indonesia**
Special issues:
Riau-Lingga Archipelago, inscr. Riau *1954*
Issues of West Irian *1963-1970*
(Irian Barat, formerly Netherlands New Guinea).

42 **Indore (Holkar)**
Indian State issues *1886-1947*

14 **Ingermanland (Pohjois Inkeri)**
Small region in Russia northwest of Leningrad and bordering Finland, for some months in 1920 temporarily independent of the Bolshevist regime, but part of the USSR Oct. 1920.
Issues *1920*

35 **Inhambane**
Town in Portuguese East Africa (Mozambique).
Issues *1895-1920*
Superseded by stamps of Mozambique.

33 **Inini**
Territory in French Guiana (now Guyane) with autonomous administration 1932-1946.
Issues, inscr. Territoire de l'Inini *1932-1946*

23 **Ionian Islands**
Republic under British protection 1815-1863, ceded to Greece 1864.
Issues, inscr. Ionikon Kratos *1859-1864*
Italian occupation issues, *1941-1943*
inscr. Isole Jonie.
(continued under later German occupation in 1943).

47,49,51 **Iran**
Kingdom up to 1979, when it became an Islamic Republic. Country formerly named Persia, name changed to Iran 1935.
Issues of Persia *1868-1935*
(some with French inscr. Postes Persannes).
Issues of Iran — (some inscr. Postes Iraniennes) *1935-*

48,50 **Iraq**
Formerly in the Ottoman Empire, British Mandate 1920-1932, Kingdom 1921-1932 and independent Kingdom 1932-1958, Republic since then.
British occupation and Mandate issues *1918-1923*
Kingdom issues (under Mandate) *1923-1932*
Independent Kingdom issues *1934-1958*
Republic issues *1959-*

14 **Ireland, Republic**
Issues, inscr. Eire *1922-*

52,54 **Irian Jaya** — See Netherlands New Guinea.

13,14 **Island** — See Iceland.

11 **Isle of Man**
Has its own Postal Administration since 1973.
Regional issues of Great Britain (no inscr.) *1958-1973*
Separate issues of Isle of Man *1973-*

48,50 **Israel**
State of Israel founded in May 1948.
Issues *1948-*

16,17 **Istria (or Istra)**
Formerly Austrian, then Italian (1919/1920), ceded to Yugoslavia 1947.
Yugoslav occupation, provisional issues *1945*
(some inscr. Istra, Trst, etc.)
Yugoslav Military Government issues *1945-1947*
(some inscr. Istria, and V.U.J.A.) See also Venetia Giulia.

15 **Itä-Karjala** — See Eastern Karelia.

20,21 **Italy**
Several States and Duchies had their own postal administration before Italy was united as one Kingdom in 1861 (excepting the Roman, or Papal States and the remainder of the Austrian Kingdom of Lombardo-Venetia.)
Italy became a Republic in 1946.
Stamp-issuing authorities:
(see individual entries for details)
Naples (Napoli), Kingdom *1858-1861*
Naples, Province (Province Napoletane) *1861-1862*
Modena, Duchy *1852-1859*
Modena, Provisional Government *1859-1860*
(superseded by issues of Sardinia 1860).
Parma, Duchy *1852-1859*
Parma, Provisional Government *1859-1860*
(superseded by issues of Sardinia 1860).
Romagna, provisional issues *1859-1860*
(See Roman States for earlier issues.
Superseded by issues of Sardinia 1860).
Roman (Papal) States *1852-1870*
(superseded by Kingdom of Italy stamps 1870).
Sardinia, Kingdom *1851-1862*
Sicily, Kingdom *1859-1862*
(together with the Kingdom of Naples, formed the Kingdom of the Two Sicilies).
Tuscany (Toscana), Grand Duchy *1851-1859*
Tuscany, Provisional Government *1860-1861*
(superseded by issues of Sardinia, 1861).

20,21 **Italy — Kingdom**
Issues, inscr. Poste Italiane *1862-1946*
14 *Issues during 1939-1945 war:*
Allied Military Government *1943-1944*
14 *Fascist Provisional Government in parts not occupied by the Allies, inscr. Republica Sociale Italiana* *1943-1944*
15 *Republic issues* *1945-*
15 *Issues of Campione, Italian enclave in Switzerland (see for details)*

Italy — Italian occupation: *1944-1952*
Districts acquired from Austria 1919/1920:
16,17 *Trentino* *1918*
21 *(some inscr. Venezia Tridentina, also Trentino).*
16,17,21 *Trieste (some inscr. Venezia Giulia)* *1918-1919*
Occupation of Greek islands:
Corfu *1923*
Corfu and Paxos *1941*
Cephalonia and Ithaca (Cefalonia e Itaca) *1941*
Ionian Islands (Isole Jonie) *1941-1943*
Other issues:
Saseno island (Sazan, Albania) *1923*

Italy — Former Colonies and Territories:
General issues (Poste Coloniale Italiane) *1932-1934*
22 *Aegean (Dodecanese) Islands* *1912-1944*
(Isole Italiane dell'Egeo) (See Aegean Islands for details)
37 *Cyrenaica (Cirenaica)* *1923-1939*
35,37 *Eritrea* *1893-1938*
35,37 *Ethiopia (Etiopia)* *1936-1938*
35,37 *Italian East Africa (Africa Orientale Italiana)* *1938-1941*
(Included Ethiopia, Eritrea and Italian Somaliland)
35,37 *Italian Somaliland (Somalia)* *1903-1936*
Italian Administration issues: *1950-1960*
37 *Jubaland (Oltre Giuba)* *1925-1926*
35,37 *Libya (Libia)* *1912-1941*
35,37 *Tripolitania* *1923-1935*
Italy — POs in other countries:
Ottoman Empire — General issues of the Levant *1874-1908*
22,23 *Issues of POs at what is now Istanbul, Jerusalem, Thessaloniki and Izmir, inscr. respectively Costantinopoli, Gerusalemme, Salonicco, Smirne* *1908-1914/1923*
(See individual entries).
22 **Albania**
Variously inscr. Albania, Durazzo, Janina (now in Greece), Scutari di Albania, Valona *1902-1916*
35 *Bengasi (Libya)* *1901*
13,23 *Crete — inscr. La Canea* *1900-1911*
39 *China - inscr. Pechino, Tientsin* *1918*
35 *Tripoli di Barberia (Libya)* *1910*
34,36 **Ivory Coast** — See Côte d'Ivoire.

42 **Jaipur**
Part of State of Rajasthan, 1948.
Issues *1904-1948*
30 **Jamaica**
British Colony 1655, independent Commonwealth State 1962.
Issues *1860-*
42 **Jammu and Kashmir**
Indian State issues *1866-1894*
22 **Janina**
Issues of Italian POs in Albania *1915*
(Now the Greek town of Ioannina).
39,41 **Japan**
Issues *1871-*
Japan — POs in other countries:
39 *China* *1900-1922*
39 *Korea* *1900-1901*
Japan — Japanese occupation:
43 *Brunei* *1942-1944*
42 *Burma* *1942-1944*
39 *China (see China for details)* *1941-1945*
39 *Formosa (Taiwan)* *1945*
39 *Hong Kong* *1945*
42 *Kelantan (Malaya)* *1942-1943*
42 *Malaya* *1942-1945*
43 *Netherlands Indies (Java and Sumatra)* *1943-1944*
43 *North Borneo* *1942-1945*
43 *Philippines* *1942-1945*
43 *Sarawak* *1942*
Japan — Allied occupation:
British Commonwealth Occupation Force (B.C.O.F.) *1946*
42 **Jasdan**
Part of Union of Saurashtra, 1948.
Issues *1942*
11 **Jersey**
Channel Islands, with own Postal Administration 1969.
German occupation issues *1941-1944*
Regional issues of Great Britain (no inscr.) *1958-1969*
Separate issues of Jersey *1969-*
48 **Jerusalem**
Foreign POs:
Italian issues, inscr. Gerusalemme *1909*
German POs active 1900-1914.
Issues of French Consulate *1948*
25 **Jetersville (Virginia, USA)**
Confederate States of America.
Postmaster's Provisional issues *1861*
42 **Jhalawar**
Indian State issues *1887-1900*
42 **Jind**
Indian State issues *1874-1885*
Issues as Indian Convention State *1885-1950*
42 **Johore**
A State of Malaya, in Treaty with Great Britain 1885 and British Protectorate 1914, incorporated in Malaysia 1963.
Issues *1876-*

23 **Jonie, Isole** — See Ionian Islands.
48,50 **Jordan**
Formerly Transjordan, British Mandate 1920-1946, independent Hashemite Kingdom of Jordan 1946.
British Mandate issues *1920-1947*
(early issues inscr. E.E.F., East of Jordan, or Transjordan).
Issues of the Hashemite Kingdom of Jordan *1949-*
50 **Jordan**
Issues of Jordanian occupation of Palestine (Israel) *1948-1949*
37 **Jubaland (Oltre Giuba)**
Previously a part of Kenya, ceded to Italy as part of Italian Somaliland, 1925.
Italian Colonial issues *1925-1926*
(Issues of Italian East Africa used later).
36 **Juby** — See Cape Juby.
14 **Judenpost (Jewish Mail)** — See Litzmannstadt.
14 **Jugoslavia** — See Yugoslavia

12 **Kaiserliche — Königliche Österreichische Post (Imperial and Royal Austrian Mail), sometimes abbreviated K.u.K.Königl. Österr.Post.**
Inscr. on Austrian stamps. See Austria.
22 **Kalymnos** — See Calino.
34 **Kamerun** — See Cameroon.
15 **Karelia, Eastern** — See Eastern Karelia.
22 **Karki (or Carchi)**
Island in the Aegean (Dodecanese) group.
Italian issues *1912-1932*
19 **Kärnten (Carinthia, Austria)**
Plebiscite held 1920, the southern part of Carinthia remaining part of Austria.
Austrian issues, some inscr. Kärnten Abstimmung *1920*
Yugoslav issues (Koruška), inscr. KGCA *1920*
56 **Karolinen** —See Caroline Islands.
22 **Karpathos** — See Scarpanto (Aegean Islands).
22 **Kasos** — See Caso (Aegean Islands).
22 **Kastelorizon** — See Castelrosso (Aegean Islands).
36 **Katanga**
Temporary breakaway State of Katanga in the Congo Republic (Kinshasa) during period of civil war, reunited to Congo (now Zaïre) 1963.
Issues *1960-1962*
49 **Kathiri State of Seiyun** — See Aden Protectorate.
42 **Kedah**
A State of Malaya, part of Malaysia 1963.
Issues *1912-*
41 **Keeling Islands** — See Cocos Islands.
42 **Kelantan**
A State of Malaya, part of Malaysia 1963.
Issues *1911-*
Japanese occupation issues *1942-1943*
35,37 **Kenya**
Former British Colony and part of the British East Africa Protectorate which later included Uganda and Tanganyika, independent 1963 and Republic in the British Commonwealth 1964.
Issues *1963-*
For earlier issues, see Kenya, Uganda and Tanganyika.
35,37 **Kenya, Uganda and Tanganyika**
Territories with a common postal service 1935-1977, though each had its own separate issues from the dates of their respective independence.
Issues of Kenya and Uganda *1922*
Issues of Kenya, Tanganyika *1922-1964*
Issues of Kenya, Uganda, Tanzania *1965-1977*
(inscr. in varying order)
For earlier issues, see British East Africa, and each State for later ones.
19 **K.G.C.A.**
Inscr. on Yugoslav (Slovene) issues of the Plebiscite of Kärnten (Carinthia, Austria) in Oct. 1920 *1920*
39 **Kiautschou**
Territory of China leased to Germany 1897. Occupied by Japan 1914, port reverting to Chinese administration 1922 (now the town of Tsingtau).
German issues *1900-1914*
50 **Kibris**
Turkish inscr. on stamps of Cyprus. See Cyprus.
60 **King Edward VII Land**
Antarctica expedition of Ernest Shackleton to the Ross Barrier 1907-1909.
New Zealand issue *1908*
35 **Kionga**
Region of German East Africa (Deutsch-Ostafrika) occupied by Portuguese Forces.
Portuguese issues *1916*

50 **Kipros**
Greek inscr. on stamps of Cyprus. See Cyprus.

58,59 **Kiribati**
Formerly the Gilbert Islands (of the Gilbert and Ellice Islands group, West Pacific), independent Republic in the British Commonwealth 1979.
Issues *1979-*
See Gilbert and Ellice Islands for earlier issues.

41 **Kirin and Heilungchang** — See Manchuria.

42 **Kishangarh**
Indian State issues *1899-1947*
Part of Rajasthan, 1948.

17 **Klaipeda** — See Memel (Lithuania, now USSR).

25 **Knoxville**
Confederate States of America.
Postmaster's Provisional issues *1861*

13,22 **Korçë**
Republic of Korytsa, Eastern Albania.
Issues — See also Albania *1917-1918*

39,41 **Korea**
Autonomous under Chinese rule till 1895, Japanese Protectorate 1905 and annexed to Japan 1910. Formed into two separate Republics after 1945, North and South Korea.
Empire issues *1884-1905*
(Japanese Postal Administration 1905).

41 **Korea (North)**
Republic formed after Russian occupation of Korea north of Lat.38 deg.N. in 1945.
Russian administration issues *1946-1948*
People's Republic issues *1948-*

41 **Korea (South)**
The Republic of Korea was formed after occupation by the USA of the area south of Lat.38 deg.N. in 1945.
USA Military administration issues *1946-1948*
Republic of Korea issues *1948-*
North Korean occupation issues *1950*

22 **Kos** — See Cos (Aegean Islands).

43 **Kouang-Tchéou**
Chinese territory leased to France 1898, returned to China 1943.
French issues *1906-1944*
(early issues inscr. Kouang Tchéou-Wan).

13,14 **Kraljestvo S.H.S.**
(also Kraljevina Srba, Hrvata i Slovenaca=Kingdom of the Serbs, Croats and Slovenes).
Inscr. on stamps of Yugoslavia, which see for details.

13,23 **Kriti** — See Crete.

16,17 **K.u.K Feldpost**
(also K.u.K. Militärpost=Imperial and Royal Military Mail).
Inscr. on Austrian Military mail. See Austria.

14 **Kurland**
Issues of German occupation of Latvia *1945*

49,51 **Kuwait**
Sheikhdom in Treaty with Great Britain 1899, independent State under British protection 1914, sovereign independent State 1961.
Sheikhdom issues *1923-1961*
Independent State issues *1961-*

41 **Kwantung**
Regional issues of Japanese occupation of China *1942-1945*

36 **La Agüera**
Former Spanish territory, part of Rio de Oro (re-named Spanish Sahara), now Morocco.
Issues *1920-1923*

42,43 **Labuan**
44,45 British territory off the coast of North Borneo, part of Colony of North Borneo 1946, and of Malaysia 1963.
Issues *1879-1905*

13 **La Canea**
Inscr. on Italian stamps of Crete *1900-1911*

34 **Lagos**
British territory amalgamated with the Southern Nigeria Protectorate.
Issues *1874-1905*

14 **Laibach (Ljubljana, Yugoslavia)**
Inscr. on German occupation issues of Slovenia, also inscr. Ljubljanska Pokrajina.

43,45 **Laos**
Kingdom and French Protectorate 1893, part of French Indochina, independent Kingdom 1953, Republic 1975.
Issues — See Indochine for earlier issues *1951-*

42 **Las Bela**
Indian State issues — Now in Pakistan *1897-1907*

48 **Latakia (Lattaquié)**
Town in the French Mandate territory of Alaouites. Part of Syria 1937 and now the Syrian town of Al Ladhiqiyah.
Issues — See also Alaouites *1931-1935*

14 **Latvija (Latvia)**
Independent Republic 1918, under Russian administration 1940 and German occupation 1941-1944, annexed by the USSR and now the Latviyskaya SSR.
Republic issues *1918-1940*
Soviet 'Republic' issues (Russian occupation), inscr. Latvijas P.S.R. *1940-1941*
German occupation issues (Lettland, though not so inscr.) *1941*
Issues inscr. Ostland *1941-1944*
(Stamps of the USSR current since 1944).

League of Nations — See United Nations.

31 **Leeward Islands**
British Caribbean islands federated into one Colony 1871, dissolved 1956.
Issues *1890-1956*
See also separate issues of Anguilla, Antigua, British Virgin Islands, Dominica, Montserrat, St. Christopher (St. Kitts)-Nevis.

25 **Lenoir (N. Carolina, USA)**
Confederate States of America.
Postmaster's Provisional issues *1861*

22 **Lero (Leros)**
Island in the Aegean (Dodecanese) group.
Italian Colonial issues *1912-1932*

36 **Lesotho**
Formerly the territory of Basutoland, independent indigenous Monarchy in the British Commonwealth 1966.
Issues *1966-*
See Basutoland for earlier issues.

14 **Lettland** — German form for Latvia — See Latvija.

22,23 **Levant**
Geographical region comprising the immediate borders of the Eastern Mediterranean, though the term is often used to include the area in the Ottoman (Turkish) Empire between Greece and Egypt.
For details of foreign POs in the Levant, see Austria, British Levant, France, Germany, Italy, Romania, Russia.

48 **Liban (Lebanon)**
Formerly French Mandate territory of Grand-Liban (1922-1943), Republic under French Mandate 1926-1943, independent Republic 1944.
Issues of Grand-Liban *1924-1927*
Republic issues *1927-*

34,36 **Liberia**
Independent Republic 1847.
Issues *1860-*

35,37 **Libya**
Part of the Ottoman Empire till 1912, Italian occupation 1911, becoming Italian Libya 1912, under British and French administration 1945-1951, including the territories of Cyrenaica, Fezzan and Tripolitania, independent Kingdom 1951-1969, when it became a Republic.
Italian Colonial issues inscr. Libia *1912-1941*
Kingdom issues *1951-1970*
Republic issues *1970-*

13 **Liechtenstein, Fürstentum**
Principality issues *1912-*
Issues of Austrian PO in Liechtenstein *1912-1918*

14 **Lietuva (Lithuania)**
Independent State 1918, under Russian occupation 1940, then German occupation 1941-1944. Annexed by the USSR 1945 and now the Litovskaya SSR.
Republic issues *1918-1940*
Polish occupation issues, inscr. Litwa *1920-1922*
(ara of central Lithuania).
Russian occupation issues, inscr. Lietuva *1919*
(part of south Lithuania).
German occupation issues *1941*
(there were several local issues, including environs of the city of Vilnius).
Issues inscr. Ostland *1941-1944*
(Stamps of the USSR current since 1944).

32 **Lima**
Peru, local issues *1871-1873*

22 **Lipso (or Lisso)**
Island in the Aegean (Dodecanese) group.
Italian Colonial issues *1912-1932*

14 **Lithuania** — See Lietuva.

14 **Litwa** — See Lietuva.

14 **Litzmannstadt, Judenpost (Jewish Mail, Lodz)**
Stamp issued by the Jewish Ghetto at Lodz, Poland, and used for a few days only *1944*

25 **Livingston (Alabama, USA)**
Confederate States of America.
Postmaster's Provisional issues *1861*

14 **Ljubljanska Pokrajina (Ljubljana, Yugoslavia)**
Inscr. on German occupation issues of Slovenia, also inscr. Provinz Laibach *1944-1945*

31 **L.Mc.L. (Lady McLeod Steamship)**
Inscr. on early issues of Trinidad.

24 **Lockport, (New York, USA)**
Postmaster's Provisional issues *1846*

20 **Lombardia-Veneto (Lombardy-Venetia)** — See Austrian Italy.

22 **Long Island (Aegean Sea)**
British issue *1916*

16 **Lothringen** — See Lorraine.

35 **Lourenzo Marques (Lourenço Marques)**
Town in Portuguese East Africa.
Issues *1894-1895*
(superseded by stamps of Mozambique).

14 **Lübbenau**
Germany (GDR), *local town issues* *1946*

12 **Lübeck**
Hanseatic town, Germany.
Issues *1859-1868*
Superseded by stamps of the Norddeutscher Postbezirk, 1868. *1859-1868*

12 **Luxembourg, Grand Duché**
Grand Duchy issues *1852-*
German occupation issues — (occupied 1940-1944) *1940-1942*

25 **Lynchburg (Virginia, USA)**
Confederate States of America.
Postmaster's Provisional issues *1861*

39,41 **Macao (Macau)**
Portuguese territory in China.
Issues *1884-*

14 **Macedonia**
Part of Bulgaria in 1944, German occupation Sep-Nov 1944, the region declared itself independent. Part of Yugoslavia end 1944.
Special issues, some inscr. Makedoniya *1944*

25 **Macon (Georgia, USA)**
Confederate States of America.
Postmaster's Provisional issues *1861*

62 **Madagascar**
French Colony 1896, independent Republic 1960.
Issues *1889-1958*
Republic issues *1958-*
(République Malgache, or Repoblika Malagasy).
British Consular Mail issues *1884-1895*
British inland mail *1895*
Special issues for town of Majunga *1895*
(See for details).
See Diego Suarez for separate issues before 1896.

63 **Madeira**
Atlantic islands administratively part of Portugal.
Issues *1868-1929*
1980-
(stamps of Portugal current in the intervening period).

25 **Madison (Florida, USA)**
Confederate States of America.
Postmaster's Provisional issues *1861*

34 **Mafeking**
Special issue during siege of Mafeking, Bechuanaland *1900*

12 **Magyar Posta** — See Hungary.

50 **Mahra State**
Sultanate in southern Arabia under British protection, incorporated in Yemen (South) 1967.
Issues *1967*

17 **Mährisch-Ostrau**
Local German issue of town of Moravska Ostrava, Czechoslovakia (occupied 1939) *1939*

62 **Majunga**
Port in northern Madagascar.
Special local issue made during a shortage of postage stamps in 1895 *1895*

14 **Makedonyia** — See Macedonia.

42,44 **Malacca**
Settlement in the Federation of Malaya, part of Malaysia, 1963.
Issues, later issues inscr. Melaka *1948-*

62 **Malagasy Republic** — See Madagascar.

37 **Malawi**
Former Nyasaland Protectorate, independent 1964 and re-named Malawi. Republic in the British Commonwealth 1966.
Issues *1964-*
For earlier issues, see Rhodesia and Nyasaland.

42,44 **Malaya — Straits Settlements**
British Colony comprising Christmas Island (Indian Ocean), the Cocos (Keeling) Islands, Labuan (off the coast of North Borneo), and the Malayan Settlements of Malacca, Penang, and Singapore.
Issues *1867-1941*

42,44 **Malaya — Federated Malay States**
Included the States of Negri Sembilan, Pahang, Perak, and Selangor.
Issues *1900-1934*
See these States for earlier issues, and for those after 1935.
See also separate issues of the following States: Johore, Kedah, Kelantan, Perlis, Trengganu.

42,44 **Malaya — Federation of Malaya**
Included the Malay States and the Settlements of Malacca and Penang, the States of Johore, Kedah, Kelantan, Negri Sembilan, Pahang, Perak, Perlis, Selangor, Singapore, Trengganu. Federation independent in 1957, and part of Malaysia 1963.
Issues *1957-1963*
See the separate States for earlier issues, and Malaysia for later ones.

44 **Malaya — Japanese occupation**
Issues for Malaya *1942-1945*
Issues for Kelantan *1942-1943*

44 **Malaya — British Military Administration**
Issues inscr. B.M.A. Malaya *1945-1948*
These gradually replaced after 1948 by separate issues of the States.

44 **Malaysia**
Federation formed 1963 from the former States of the Federation of Malaya, the State of Singapore, the Colonies of North Borneo (now Sabah) and Sarawak. It is an independent Commonwealth State. Singapore seceded from Malaysia in 1965 and became an independent sovereign State in the Commonwealth.
Issues *1963-*

62 **Maldive Islands**
Sultanate under British Protection till 1952, Republic 1968, member of the British Commonwealth 1985.
Issues *1906-1968*
Republic issues *1968-*

62 **Malgache, République** — See Madagascar.

36 **Mali**
Mali Federation formed 1959 as a Republic by the union of French Sudan and Senegal, and ended in 1960 when both became separate Republics and former French Sudan became the Republic of Mali.
Federation issues — (Fédération du Mali) *1959-1960*
Republic issues — (République du Mali) *1960-*

16 **Malmédy**
Territory annexed to Belgium, with Eupen, 1920.
Belgian occupation issues *1920-1921*
inscr. Eupen et Malmédy.

12 **Malta**
British Crown Colony 1814, independent Republic in the British Commonwealth Dec. 1974.
Issues *1860-*

11 **Man, Isle of** — See Isle of Man.

51 **Manama**
Dependent territory of Ajman (United Arab Emirates).
Issues *1966-1972*

39,41 **Manchuria (Manchukuo)**
Under Chinese rule till 1932, Japanese Protectorate 1932, Empire 1934–1945 (Manchukuo), Russian occupation 1945-1946, now part of China as the Province of Heilungkiang.
Issues under Chinese rule *1927-1929*
inscr. Kirin, and Heilungchang.
Issues of 'independent' Republic *1932-1934*
Empire issues (Manchukuo) *1934-1945*
Chinese administration issues *1946-1948*

56,58 **Mariana Islands**
Former Spanish islands in the Pacific, German Colony 1899-1914, Japanese occupation 1914 and under Japanese Mandate till 1945, Trust Territory of the USA since 1947.
Spanish Colonial issues *1899*
inscr. Marianas Española.
German Colonial issues, *1899-1916/1919*
inscr. Marianen.

19 **Marienwerder**
Plebiscite 1920 in territory in Germany (East Prussia), area remaining part of Germany. Incorporated in Poland 1945 and town re-named Kwidzyn.
Plebiscite issues *1920*

25 **Marion (Virginia, USA)**
Confederate States of America.
Postmaster's Provisional issues *1861*

34,36 **Maroc (Morocco)**
Independent Kingdom, French Protectorate 1912, the northern part becoming a Spanish Protectorate 1914. Independent Kingdom 1956.
Local issues in period 1891-1912, with various inscr.:

Alcazar a Ouazzan	*Saffi Marakech*
Alcazar Wazan	*Tanger Arzila*
Demnat Marrakech	*Tanger Elksar*
Fez Mequinez	*Tanger — Fez*
Fez a Sefrou	*Tangier — Laraiche*
Mazagan-Azemour-Marakech	*Tetouan — Chechouan (Sheshuan)*
Mazagan Marakech	*Tetouan a El-Ksar*
Mogador Agadir	
Mogador Marrakesch	

French Protectorate issues *1914-1955*
Spanish Protectorate issues *1914-1955*
Kingdom issues *1956-*

34,36 **Maroc (Morocco)** — POs of other countries:
British POs *1898-1956*
French POs *1891-1917*
German POs, inscr. Marocco, or Marokko *1899-1914*
Spanish POs *1903-1914*

56,58 **Marshall Islands**
German Colony 1885, Allied occupation 1914, Japanese Mandate 1920-1945, USA Mandate 1947.
German Colonial issues, inscr. Marschall-Inseln. *1897-1916*
British-New Zealand occupation issues, inscr. G.R.I. on German stamps. *1914-1915*
See Nauru Island for separate issues (part of the Marshall Islands group).

31 **Martinique**
Former French Caribbean Colony, a 'Département' of France 1946.
Issues *1886-1947*
(Stamps of France current since 1947).

34,36 **Mauritanie (Mauritania)**
French territory, under administration of French West Africa (A.O.F.) 1904, French Colony 1920, independent Republic 1960.
Issues *1906-1944*
(AOF stamps used after 1944).
Republic issues *1960-*
(République Islamique de Mauritanie).

62 **Mauritius**
British Colony 1810, independent Commonwealth State 1968.
Issues *1847-*

62 **Mayotte**
Island of the French Comoro Archipelago, Indian Ocean, a 'Département' of France 1974.
Issues *1892-1914*
(Stamps of Madagascar current after 1914).

34 **Mazagan-Azemour-Marakech** — See Maroc.

34 **Mazagan-Marakech-Morocco** — See Maroc.

14,22 **Mbretnia Shqiptare (Kingdom of Albania)** — See Albania.

12 **Mecklenburg-Schwerin, Grossherzogtum**
Grand Duchy, Germany.
Issues *1856-1867*
See Germany, Pre-unification period.

12 **Mecklenburg-Strelitz**
Grand Duchy, Germany.
Issues *1864-1867*
See Germany, Pre-unification period.

37, 22-23 **M.E.F. (Middle East Forces)**
Areas occupied by British Forces in former Italian Colonies: Cyrenaica, some of the Dodecanese (Aegean) Islands, Eritrea, Italian Somaliland, Tripolitania.
Issues at various times during the period *1942-1947*

14 **Meissen**
Germany (GDR), *local town issues* *1945-1946*

30 **Mejico** — See Mexico.

44 **Melaka** — See Malacca.

17 **Memel**
Formerly part of Germany (East Prussia), under international control 1919-1923 with French administration. Incorporated in Lithuania 1923 and re-named Klaipeda. Part of Germany again 1939, annexed by the USSR 1945 in the new Litovskaya SSR (former State of Lithuania).
French Mandate issues, inscr. Memel, or Memelgebiet. *1920-1922*
Lithuanian issues, inscr. Klaipeda *1923-1925*
Local German issues, inscr. Memelland *1939*

25 **Memphis (Tennessee, USA)**
Confederate States of America,
Postmaster's Provisional issues *1861*

41 **Mengkiang**
Japanese occupation of China (Inner Mongolia).
Japanese regional issues *1941-1945*

30 **Mexico**
Former Spanish possession, Empire 1822-1823, Republic 1824-1864, Empire 1864-1867, and Republic 1867.
Republic issues, inscr. Mejico *1856-1864*
Empire issues *1864-1867*
Republic issues *1867-*

Mexico —
Local and provisional issues:
Campeche *1875*
Cuernavaca *1867*
Guadalajara *1867-1868*
Civil war issues were made during 1913-1915, with various inscr., among which were:
Baja California, Mexico *1915*
Oaxaca *1915*
Sonora *1913-1914*

37 **Middle East Forces** — See M.E.F.

63 **Miquelon** — See St. Pierre et Miquelon.

25 **Mobile (Alabama, USA)**
Confederate States of America,
Postmaster's Provisional issues *1861*

35,37 **Moçambique** — See Mozambique.

20 **Modena**
Duchy of Italy.
Duchy issues *1852-1859*
Province issues — (Provisional Government) *1859-1860*
Superseded 1860 by issues of the Kingdom of Sardinia, and in 1862 by those of the Kingdom of Italy.

34 **Mogador Agadir** — See Maroc.

34 **Mogador Marrakesch** — See Maroc.

62 **Mohéli**
French island in the Comoro Archipelago, attached to Madagascar 1914-1946.
Issues — See also Comoros *1906-1914*

13 **Monaco**
Independent Principality 1860
Issues *1885-*

39,41 **Mongolia**
Under Chinese rule till 1911 (Outer Mongolia), after several changes of rule, autonomous 1921, and Mongolian People's Republic 1924.
Issues *1924-*

39 **Mongtseu**
Town in China.
Issues of French PO, early issues inscr. Mongtze. *1903-1922*

13,14, 23 **Montenegro**
Principality under Turkish rule till 1878, when it became independent, a Kingdom in 1910, united to Serbia 1918 as part of the new Kingdom of the Serbs, Croats and Slovenes, later named Yugoslavia.
Issues, inscr. Tsrnagora, or Tsr. Gora (= Black Mountains). *1874-1914*
Austrian occupation issues, inscr. K.u.K. Militär-Verwaltung. *1917*
(Kingdom of Yugoslavia issues 1918-)
Italian occupation issues *1941-1943*
German occupation issues *1943-1944*

31 **Montserrat**
British Caribbean island in the Leeward Islands group, now a British Dependent Territory.
Issues *1876-*
General issues of the Leeward Islands also used till 1956.

32 **Moquegua**
Peru, *local provisional issues* *1881-1885*

34,36 **Morocco** — See Maroc.

Morocco Agencies — See Maroc, POs of other countries.

42 **Morvi**
Indian State issues *1931-1948*
Part of the Union of Saurashtra, 1948.

46,48 **Mosul**
Now the town of Al Mawsil, Iraq.
British issues *1919*

34 **Moyen Congo**
French African territory, part of French Equatorial Africa (A.E.F.) 1910.
Issues of Moyen Congo *1907-1937*
(AEF stamps used 1937-1958).
See Congo Français for earlier issues, and Congo (Brazzaville) for later ones.

35,37 **Mozambique (Moçambique)**
Portuguese Colony, Overseas Province of Portugal 1951, independent State 1975.
Portuguese Colonial issues *1876-1975*
Republic issues *1975-*
Issues of the Mozambique Company *1892-1941*
(Companhia de Moçambique, whose charter ended 1942).

49,51 **Muscat**
Independent Sultanate in southern Arabia, later part of the Sultanate of Muscat and Oman 1966-1971, and the Sultanate of Oman in 1971.
Issues of Muscat *1944-1948*
(Issues of the British Postal Agencies in Arabia used up to 1966).

51 **Muscat and Oman**
Formerly the Sultanate of Muscat, becoming the Sultanate of Oman in 1971.
Issues of Muscat and Oman *1966-1971*

14 **M.V.i.R.**
German occupation of Romania (Militärverwaltung in Rumänien=Military Administration in Romania).
German occupation issues *1917-1918*

42 **Nabha**
Indian Convention State issues 1885-1950

Naciones Unidas — Spanish form for United Nations.

36 **Namibia** — See South West Africa.

42 **Nandgaon**
Indian State issues *1892-1895*

21 **Naples (Napoli)**
Kingdom, together with Sicily formed the Kingdom of the Two Sicilies.
Kingdom issues, inscr. Posta Napoletana *1858-1861*
Province issues *1861-1862*
(Superseded 1862 by Kingdom of Italy stamps).

25 **Nashville (Tennessee, USA)**
Confederate States of America,
Postmaster's Provisional issues *1861*

34 **Natal**
British Colony, part of the Union of South Africa 1910
Issues *1857-1909*
Nations Unies — French form for United Nations.

56,58 **Nauru**
Part of the Marshall Islands group, German Colony 1885-1914, under Allied Trusteeship 1916-1947 and administered by Australia. Independent Commonwealth Republic 1968.
British issues *1916-1968*
Republic issues *1968-*

42 **Nawanagar**
Part of the Union of Saurashtra, 1948.
Indian State issues *1877-1895*

14 **N.D.Hrvatska (Nezavisna Država Hrvatska)** — (Independent State of Croatia) — See Croatia.

12 **Nederland** — See Netherlands.

31 **Nederlandse Antillen** — See Netherlands Antilles.

42 **Negri Sembilan**
A State of the Federation of Malaya, and part of Malaysia 1963.
Issues *1891-*

46,49 **Nejd**
Sultanate in central Arabia, union with the former Kingdom of Hejaz in 1926 forming the Kingdom of Hejaz and Nejd, re-named Saudi Arabia 1932.
Issues of Nejd — See Hejaz for later issues *1925*

38,40 **Nepal**
Kingdom in the Himalayas.
Issues *1881-*

12 **Netherlands (Nederland)**
Issues *1852-*
Netherlands — Overseas Territories:

31 **Netherlands Antilles**
Colony of the Netherlands, the largest islands being Curaçao, Aruba and Bonaire. Autonomous in union with the Kingdom of the Netherlands 1954.
Issues, inscr. Curaçao *1873-1948*
Issues inscr. Nederlandse Antillen *1949-*

43 **Netherlands Indies**
Colony of the Netherlands 1816-1941, Japanese occupation 1941-1945, Republic proclaimed 1945.
Dutch issues, inscr. Nederlandsch-Indië, or Ned.Indie *1864-1950*
Issues inscr. Indonesia *1948-1949*
Japanese occupation issues (Java and Sumatra) *1943-1944*
See Indonesia for later issues.

52,54 **Netherlands New Guinea**
Western part of island of New Guinea, and administered as part of the Netherlands Indies till 1963, now part of the Republic of Indonesia and re-named at first West Irian, now Irian Jaya.
(Stamps of Netherlands Indies current 1864-1850).
Issues, inscr. Nederlands Nieuw Guinea *1950-1962*
Issues of the U.N. Administration of West New Guinea (U.N.T.E.A.) *1962-1963*
Indonesian issues of West Irian (Irian Barat) *1963-1970*

52 **Neu-Guinea**
Inscr. on some stamps of German New Guinea. See Deutsch-Neuguinea.

31 **Nevis**
British Caribbean island in the Leeward Islands. Independent Commonwealth State of St Kitts-Nevis, 1983. Separate Postal Administrations for Nevis and St. Kitts instituted 1980, although both islands are one State.
Issues of Nevis *1861-1903*
Issues of St. Kitts-Nevis *1903-1980*
Separate issues of Nevis *1980-*
See also Anguilla, St. Christopher, and St. Kitts-Nevis.

28 **New Brunswick**
Province of Canada, by its union with Canada and Nova Scotia in 1867, formed the Dominion of Canada
Issues *1851-1868*

56,58 **New Caledonia** — See Nouvelle Caledonie.

28,29 **Newfoundland**
Formed part of the Dominion of Canada in Apr. 1949.
Issues *1857-1949*

52,55 **New Guinea, British (Papua)**
British possession, administered by Australia 1906, Australian Mandate 1920-1973.
British issues *1901-1906*
Australian Administration issues (suspended 1906-1939, 1942-1945, and stamps of Australia current 1945-1952).
See Papua New Guinea for later issues from 1952.

52 **New Guinea, German (Deutsch-Neuguinea)**
German Colony 1884-1914, Australian Mandate 1920 together with British New Guinea, and named Territory of New Guinea (now Papua New Guinea).
German Colonial issues *1898-1916*
British occupation issues *1914-1918*
(some were Registered Letter labels used as stamps, inscr. G.R.I. and name of place of issue).
(Superseded by stamps of the Australian Administration).

24 **New Haven (Connecticut, USA)**
Postmaster's Provisional issues *1845*

56,58 **New Hebrides (also Nouvelles Hébrides)**
Anglo-French Protectorate of the island group 1887-1906, when it became an Anglo-French Condominium till 1980. Independent Commonwealth State 1980, and re-named Vanuatu.
Issues, inscr. in English and in French. *1908-1980*
See Vanuatu for later issues.

25 **New Orleans (Louisiana, USA)**
Confederate States of America.
Postmaster's Provisional issues *1861*

34 **New Republic, South Africa (Nieuwe Republiek)**
A Boer Republic first part of Zululand, incorporated in the South African Republic (Boer) in 1888, and part of Natal 1903.
Issues inscr. Nieuwe Republiek *1886-1887*

25 **New Smyrna (Florida, USA)**
Confederate States of America.
Postmaster's Provisional issues *1861*

53 **New South Wales**
A State in the Commonwealth of Australia, 1901.
Issues *1850-1913*
(Superseded by stamps of Australia, 1913).

53,55 **New Zealand**
Dominion of New Zealand formed Sep. 1907.
Issues *1855-*
New Zealand — Territories under New Zealand Administration:

56,58 **Aitutaki**
Part of the Protectorate of Cook Islands.
Issues *1903-1932*
1972-
(Stamps of Cook Islands used 1932-1972).

57,59 **Cook Islands**
Associated State of New Zealand 1965.
Issues — See Cook Islands *1892-*

56,58 **Niue**
Part of the Cook Islands group, Associated State of New Zealand 1974.
Issues *1902-*

56,58 **Penrhyn Island**
Also named Tongareva, part of the Cook Islands group.
Issues *1902-1932*
1973-
(Stamps of Cook Islands used 1932-1972).

60 **Ross Dependency**
Antarctic Territory under the jurisdiction of New Zealand since 1923.
Issues *1957-*

59 **Tokelau Islands**
Also named Union Islands, formerly part of the Gilbert and Ellice Islands, and part of New Zealand 1949.
Issues *1948-*

30 **Nicaragua**
Republic 1839.
Issues *1862-*

14 **Niesky, Stadt**
Germany (GDR), *local town issue* *1945*

34 **Nieuwe Republiek** — See New Republic, South Africa.

52,54 **Nieuw Guinea** — See Netherlands New Guinea.

36 **Niger, Territoire du**
French Colony formed 1919 and under the administration of French West Africa (A.O.F.). Independent Republic in the French Community, 1960.
Issues, inscr. Territoire du Niger *1921-1944*
(AOF stamps used 1944-1959).
Republic issues *1959-*
For earlier issues, see Haut-Sénégal et Niger.

34 **Niger Coast Protectorate**
District named Oil Rivers Protectorate 1885-1893, when it was re-named Niger Coast Protectorate, later becoming part of Southern Nigeria.
Issues, inscr. Oil Rivers *1892-1898*

34,36 **Nigeria**
British Colony including Lagos, Northern and Southern Nigeria, formed in the period 1861-1902. The Niger Coast Protectorate became part of Southern Nigeria. Independent Commonwealth State 1960, and Federal Republic in 1963.
Issues of Nigeria *1914-1960*
Republic issues *1960-*
See Northern and Southern Nigeria for earlier issues.

22 **Nisiro (Nisyros)**
Island in the Aegean (Dodecanese) group.
Italian Colonial issues *1912-1932*

56,58 **Niue**
Island in the Pacific and part of the Cook Islands, an Associated State of New Zealand 1974.
Issues *1902-*

12 **Norddeutscher Postbezirk**
(North German Confederation Postal Administration) The Confederation consisted of the following German States which had their own postal administration: Braunschweig, Bremen, Hamburg, Lübeck, Mecklenburg-Schwerin, Mecklenburg-Strelitz, Oldenburg, Sachsen, and Preussen.
Issues *1868-1871*
Superseded 1872 by stamps of the unified Kingdom of Germany.
See Germany for details on the Pre-unification period.

55 **Norfolk Island**
Pacific island under the administration of Australia 1914-1960, now a Dependent Territory of Australia.
Issues *1947-*

12 **Norge** — See Norway.

43,45 **North Borneo**
Territory administered by the British North Borneo Company till 1946, when it became a Crown Colony. Part of the Federation of Malaysia, 1963.
Issues *1883-1963*
Japanese occupation issues *1942-1945*
(used throughout British Borneo, ie, Brunei, Labuan, North Borneo, and Sarawak).

41 **North China**
Japanese occupation of China.
Regional issues *1941-1945*

12 **North German Confederation** — See Norddeutscher Postbezirk.

41 **North Korea** — See Korea (North).

11 **Northern Ireland**
Great Britain, *regional issues (no inscr.)* *1958-*

34 **Northern Nigeria.**
United with Southern Nigeria and Lagos in 1914 as the Colony of Nigeria
Issues *1900-1914*
See Niger Coast Protectorate for earlier issues, and Nigeria for later ones.

35,37 **Northern Rhodesia**
Independent Commonwealth State 1964, and re-named Zambia.
Issues *1925-1963*
See also British South Africa Company, Rhodesia, Rhodesia and Nyasaland, Zambia.

12,13 **Norway (Norge)**
Kingdom united to Sweden 1814-1905, independent Kingdom 1905.
Kingdom united to Sweden issues *1855-1905*
Issues of independent Kingdom *1905-*
(German occupation 1940-1945).

42 **Nossi-Bé**
French island off coast of Madagascar.
Issues, some inscr. NSB *1889-1901*
(Stamps of Madagascar current after 1901).

56,58 **Nouvelle-Calédonie (New Caledonia)**
French Pacific islands, with Dependencies which includes the islands of Wallis and Futuna. An Overseas Territory (T.O.M.) of France, 1958.
Issues *1860-*

56,58 **Nouvelles-Hébrides** — See New Hebrides.

28 **Nova Scotia**
Province of Canada, united with Canada and New Brunswick in 1867 to form the Dominion of Canada.
Issues *1851-1868*

35 **Nyasaland**
First, part of British Central Africa, it became the Nyasaland Protectorate 1907, part of the Central African Federation 1954-1963, independent Commonwealth State 1964 and re-named Malawi.
Issues of British Central Africa (B.C.A.) *1891-1908*
Issues of Nyasaland Protectorate *1908-1934*
Issues of Nyasaland *1934-1953*
(See Rhodesia and Nyasaland for later issues, and Malawi).

35 **Nyassa**
Territory of Portuguese East Africa, part of Mozambique 1929.
Issues, some inscr. Companhia do Nyassa *1897-1929*

30 **Oaxaca**
Mexico, *civil war issues* *1915*

Ob'edinennye Natsii — Russian for United Nations — See United Nations.

13 **Ober-Ost (or, Ob.-Ost) Postgebiet**
German occupation issues of Eastern Postal Areas *1916-1918*

19 **Oberschlesien (Upper Silesia)**
German inscr. on Plebiscite issues of Upper Silesia *1920-1922*

35 **Obock**
Seat of administration in French Somaliland in 1862, moved to Djibouti in 1888.
Issues *1892-1903*
For later issues, see Côte Française des Somalis.

57,59 **Océanie, Établissements Français**
French Pacific Settlements, being a group of archipelagos and islands, constituted as a French Protectorate in 1842, and Colony in 1880.
Issues *1892-1956*
For later issues, see Polynésie Française and Tahiti for separate issues.

34 **Oil Rivers Protectorate**
Inscr. on early stamps of Niger Coast Protectorate, inscr. Oil Rivers *1892-1898*

12 **Oldenburg, Grossherzogtum**
Grand Duchy, Germany.
Issues *1852-1867*
See Germany, Pre-unification period.

14 **Olonets** — See Aunus.

19 **Olsztyn** — See Allenstein.

37 **Oltre Giuba** — See Jubaland.

51 **Oman**
Independent Sultanate in Arabia, formerly the Sultanate of Muscat and Oman, re-named Oman Jan. 1971.
Issues of Muscat and Oman *1966-1970*
Issues of Sultanate of Oman *1971-*

48 **O.M.F. Cilicie (Occupation Militaire Française)**
French Military occupation of Cilicia, Turkey
Issues *1919-1921*

34 **Orange Free State**
Formerly a British possession, independent from 1854 to 1899, again British and later a Province in the Union of South Africa.
Issues, inscr. Oranje Vrij Staat *1868-1900*
British occupation issues *1900*
Issues of Orange River Colony *1900-1910*

42 **Orchha**
Indian State issues *1913-1942*

35 **Ostafrika, Deutsch** — See Deutsch Ostafrika (German East Africa).

12,14 **Österreich** — See Austria.

14 **Ostland**
General German occupation issues of Estonia, Latvia, Lithuania, and White Russia *1941-1944/1945*
See also Estonia, Latvia and Lithuania.

22,23 **Ottoman Empire** — See Turkey.

34,36 **Oubangui-Chari**
French possession, formerly part of the territory of Oubangui-Chari-Tchad 1905-1920, when Tchad seceded. Autonomous within French Equatorial Africa (A.E.F.) 1920.
Issues *1915-1933*
See Central African Republic for later issues.

42,44 **Pahang**
A State of the Federation of Malaya, part of Malaysia 1963.
Issues *1889-1899*
1935-
For earlier issues, see Malaya, Federated Malay States.

32 **Paita**
Peru, *local provisional issues* *1884*

39 **Pakhoi**
China, *French PO issues* *1903-1922*

44 **Pakistan**
Part of the British Empire of India till 1947, when the two separate Dominions of India and Pakistan were formed, Pakistan being divided into East and West Pakistan. Republic in 1956 (East Pakistan becoming the Republic of Bangladesh in 1971).
Issues *1947-*

23,48 **Palestine**
Formerly part of the Ottoman Empire, under British Mandate 1923-1948, independent State of Israel founded May 1948.
British Military issues, inscr. E.E.F. (Egyptian Expeditionary Force), *1918-1944*
and civil administration issues, inscr. Palestine.
Jordanian occupation of Palestine (Israel), issues *1948-1949*
Issues of Egyptian occupation of the Gaza Strip *1948-1967*
(inscr. Palestine 1948-1958, and UAR 1958-1967).
See Israel for later issues.

27,30 **Panama**
Formerly a State of Colombia till 1903, when it became an independent Republic. The Canal Zone was leased to the USA 1903-1979.
Issues of Panama as a State of Colombia *1878-1903*
Independent Republic issues *1903-*
See Canal Zone for separate issues.

20 **Papal States** — See Roman States (Italy).

52,55 **Papua** — See New Guinea, British.

52,55 **Papua New Guinea**
Formerly an Australian Mandate and combining the former territories of British New Guinea (Papua) and German New Guinea. Independent Commonwealth State 1975.
Issues *1952-*
For earlier issues, see New Guinea, British.

33 **Paraguay**
Issues *1870-*

20 **Parma**
Duchy of Italy.
Duchy issues *1852-1859*
Issues of Provisional Government *1859-1860*
Superseded 1860 by stamps of the Kingdom of Sardinia, and in 1862 by those of the Kingdom of Italy.

32 **Pasco**
Peru, *local provisional issues* *1884*

42 **Patiala**
Indian Convention States issues *1884-1951*
(early issues inscr. Puttialla).

22 **Patmo (Patmos)**
Island in the Aegean (Dodecanese) group.
Italian Colonial issues *1912-1932*

39 **Pechino (Peking)**
Issues of Italian PO in Peking, China *1918*

42,44 **Penang**
A State of the Federation of Malaya, and part of Malaysia 1963.
Issues *1948-*

56,58 **Penrhyn Island**
British island in the Pacific (also named Tongareva) and part of the Cook Islands group, under New Zealand administration 1901.
Issues *1902-1932*
1973-
(Stamps of Cook Islands current 1932-1973).

42,44 **Perak**
A State of the Federation of Malaya, and part of Malaysia 1963.
Issues *1878-1900*
1935-
For earlier issues, see Malaya, Federated Malay States, and Federation of Malaya.

42,44 **Perlis**
A State of the Federation of Malaya, and part of Malaysia 1963.
Issues *1948-*

47,49,51 **Persia** — See Iran.

32 **Peru**
Formerly Spanish, independent Republic 1828.
Issues *1858-*
Local provisional issues were made at various time in the period 1881-1885:
Arequipa, Ayacucho, Chala, Cuzco, Moquega, Paita, Pasco, Pisco, Piura, Puno, Yca.

25 **Petersburg (Virginia, USA)**
Confederate States of America.
Postmaster's Provisional issues *1861*

43,45 **Philippines**
Spanish Colony till 1898, USA Territory 1898, independent Republic 1946.
Spanish Colonial issues, *1854-1898*
inscr. Filipinas.
USA Administration issues *1899-1935*
USA Commonwealth issues *1935-1946*
Japanese occupation issues *1942-1945*
Republic issues, *1946-*
inscr. Republika Pilipinas.

32 **Pisco**
Peru, *local provisional issues* *1884*

22 **Piscopi (Episkopi)**
Island in the Aegean (Dodecanese) group.
Italian Colonial issues *1912-1932*

57,59 **Pitcairn Islands**
British Settlement 1887, now British Dependent Territory of Pitcairn, Henderson, Ducie and Oeno Islands.
Issues *1940-*

25 **Pittsylvania (Virginia, USA)**
Confederate States of America.
Postmaster's Provisional issues *1861*

32 **Piura**
Peru, *local provisional issues* *1884*

14 **Plauen**
Germany (GDR), *local town issues* *1945*

25 **Pleasant Shade (Virginia, USA)**
Confederate States of America.
Postmaster's Provisional issues *1861*

14 **Pleskau**
German occupation of the town of Pskov, USSR.
Local issues *1941-1942*

14 **Pohjois Inkeri (USSR)** — See Ingermanland.

12,13
14 **Poland**
Following a turbulent history, the country was divided between Austria, Prussia and Russia during most of the 19th century. Independent Republic Nov. 1918, divided between Germany and the USSR 1939-1941, occupied by Germany 1941-1944, liberated and restored as an independent Republic 1944.
Issues of Imperial Russia *1860-1915*
German occupation *1915-1918*
inscr. Russisch-Polen (Russian Poland), or Gen.-Gouv. Warschau (General Government, Warsaw).
Independent Republic issues *1918-1939*
German occupation issues, *1939-1945*
inscr. Generalgouvernement.
London issues of Government in Exile *1941-1944*
Independent Republic issues, inscr. Polska *1944-*

22 **Poland**
Issues of Polish Consulate office at Constantinople (Istanbul), inscr. Levant *1919*

14 **Poland**
Issues of Polish occupation of Lithuania (Lietuva), inscr. Litwa
1920-1922

57,59 **Polynésie Française (French Polynesia)**
Formerly the Établissements Français de L'Océanie (French Pacific Settlements), an Overseas Territory of France (T.O.M.) 1958 and re-named Polynésie Française.
Issues *1958-*
See Océanie, Établissements Français for earlier issues, and Tahiti for separate issues.

63 **Ponta Delgada**
Portuguese island in the Azores (Açores)
Issues *1892-1905*
(Stamps of the Azores current 1905-1931, and Portugal ones since then).

24 **"Pony Express"**
Horse-ridden mail system inaugurated by the USA Government in 1860, running from St. Joseph (Missouri) to the Pacific coast near San Francisco. Superseded some 2 years later by the telegraph.

42 **Poonch**
Indian State issues *1876-1894*

22 **Port-Lagos**
Issues of French PO at Port-Lagos (Porto Lago) in Greece *1893-1898*

23 **Port-Said**
Issues of French PO at Port Said *1899-1930*

12 **Portugal**
Kingdom till 1910, Republic since then.
Kingdom issues *1853-1910*
Republic issues *1910-*
(early issues inscr. Republica Portuguesa).

Portugal — Overseas Colonies and Territories:
The Colonies attained the status of Overseas Territories of Portugal, 1951 (see individual entries for details).
General issues for African possessions *1898*
34,36 *Angola* *1879-1975*
63 *Angra (Azores)* *1892-1905*
63 *Azores, inscr. Açores* *1868-1931*
1980-
63 *Cape Verde, inscr. Cabo Verde* *1877-*
34 *Congo (Cabinda)* *1894-1920*
63 *Funchal (Azores)* *1892-1905*
63 *Horta (Azores)* *1892-1905*
35 *Inhabane (East Africa)* *1895-1920*
35 *Kionga (occupation of German East Africa)* *1916*
35 *Lourenzo Marques (East Africa)* *1894-1895*
39,41 *Macao, inscr. Macau (China)* *1884-*
63 *Madeira* *1868-1929*
1980-
35,37 *Mozambique, inscr. Moçambique* *1876-1975*
Independent Republic issues *1975-*
35 *Mozambique Company, inscr. Companhia de Moçambique* *1892-1941*
35 *Nyassa (East Africa)* *1897-1929*
63 *Ponta Delgada (Azores)* *1892-1905*
34,36 *Portuguese Guinea (Guiné Portuguesa)* *1881-1973*
42,44 *Portuguese India (India Portuguésa)* *1871-1961*
35 *Quelimane (East Africa)* *1914-1922*
63 *St. Thomas and Principe Islands* *1870-1975*
(S. Thomé e Principe)
Independent Republic issues *1975-*
35 *Tete (East Africa)* *1913-1914*
43,45 *Timor (East Indies)* *1886-1973*
35 *Zambezia (East Africa)* *1894-1917*

34,36 **Portuguese Guinea (Guiné Portuguesa)**
Portuguese Colony on west coast of Africa, independent State 1974 and re-named Guinea-Bissau
Issues *1881-1973*
See Guinea-Bissau for later issues.

42,44 **Portuguese India (India Portuguésa)**
Portuguese possession on the west coast of India, consisting of Diu, Damao, and Goa. Territories incorporated in India, 1961.
Issues, inscr. India Portuguésa, and later Estado da India, Rep. Portugal *1871-1961*

11 **Postage Revenue**
Inscr. on many issues of Great Britain.

47,49 **Postes Persannes (Persian Mail)**
French inscr. on some issues of Persia (Iran). See Iran.

13 **Postbebiet Ober-Ost**
German inscr. on occupation issues of Eastern Areas *1916-1918*
Included a special issue for the town of Bialystok (at that time Russia, now Poland).

12 **Preussen (Prussia)**
German Kingdom, joined the North German Confederation Postal Administration (Norddeutscher Postgebiet), later was the pre-eminent Kingdom at the unification of Germany (Second Reich) in 1871.
Issues of Preussen *1850-1867*
Superseded 1868 by stamps of the Norddeutscher Postbezirk. See Germany.

28,29 **Prince Edward Island**
Province of the Dominion of Canada, July 1873.
Issues *1861-1873*
Stamps of Canada current after 1873.
13 **Principauté de Monaco** — See Monaco.
24 **Providence (Rhode Island, USA)**
Postmaster's Provisional issues *1846*
12 **Prussia** — See Preussen.
30 **Puerto Rico**
Spanish possession till 1898, USA sovereignty since then.
Spanish Colonial issues (Cuba and Puerto Rico) *1855-1873*
Spanish occupation issues *1873-1898*
Coamo issues (town in southern part of Puerto Rico) *1898*
USA issues *1899-1900*
32 **Puno**
Peru, *provisional local issues* *1881-1885*
42 **Puttialla** — See Patiala, Indian Convention State.

47,49 **Qatar**
51 Independent Emirate of Arabia, in Treaty with Great Britain 1916-1971, now an independent State.
Issues *1957-1971*
Independent State issues *1971-*
49,51 **Qu'aiti State of Shihr and Mukalla, or Qu'aiti State in Hadramaut (Arabia)** — See Aden Protectorate States.
52 **Queensland**
A separate Colony in Australia 1859, and a State in the Commonwealth of Australia 1901.
Issues *1860-1911*
(Superseded by stamps of Australia, 1913).
35 **Quelimane**
Part of Portuguese East Africa, previously named Zambezia,. later part of Mozambique.
Issues *1914-1922*
(Stamps of Mozambique current since).

42 **Rajasthan**
State in India formed in 1948 from several States in Rajputana, including Bundi, Jaipur and Kishangarh.
Issues *1949*
42 **Rajpipla**
Indian State issues *1880-1886*
57 **Rarotonga** — See Cook Islands.
51 **Ras al Khaimah**
Sheikhdom in southeastern Arabia, part of the Trucial States, and of the United Arab Emirates (UAE) in 1971.
Issues *1964-1972*
12 **Reichspost**
Inscr. on stamps of Germany. See Germany.
62 **Repoblika Malagasy** — See Madagascar.
14 **Republik Österreich** — See Austria.
36 **République Algérienne** — See Algeria.
36 **République Centrafricaine** — See Central African Republic.
12 **République Française** — See France.
48 **République Libanaise** — See Lebanon.
62 **République Malgache** — See Madagascar.
36 **République du Tchad** — See Tchad (Chad).
34,36 **République Tunisienne** — See Tunisia.
13,23 **Retymno**
Inscr. (among others) on Russian stamps of Crete. *1899*
See Crete.
62 **Réunion**
French island in the Indian Ocean, since 1946 a "Département" of France.
The island had various names: Mascareigne, Île Bourbon in 1740, Île de la Réunion in 1791, then Île Bonaparte, re-named Bourbon 1815, reverted to Île de la Réunion in 1849.
Issues *1852-1947*
(Stamps of France current since 1947).
12 **R.F.**
Abbreviation for République Française, inscr. on numerous French stamps.
25 **Rheatown (Tennessee, USA)**
Confederate States of America.
Postmaster's Provisional issues *1861*
15 **Rheinland-Pfalz (Rhine Palatinate)** — See Germany, Allied occupation.
35,37 **Rhodesia**
British territory in the period 1888/1899, at first administered by the British South Africa Company. Divided in 1924 into Northern and Southern Rhodesia. In 1954-1964 both Rhodesias formed part of the Central African Federation of Northern and Southern Rhodesia, with the Nyasaland Protectorate. Northern Rhodesia became the independent Commonwealth State of Zambia. Southern Rhodesia independent 1965-1979 and re-named Rhodesia. Under a new Administration in 1980, it was re-named Zimbabwe.
Issues of British South Africa Company — Rhodesia *1890-1925*
See also Northern Rhodesia, Rhodesia and Nyasaland, Zambia, Rhodesia (UDI), Zimbabwe, and Malawi.
35,37 **Rhodesia and Nyasaland**
Central African Federation 1954-1964 of both Northern and Southern Rhodesia, and the Protectorate of Nyasaland.
Issues, inscr. Rhodesia and Nyasaland *1954-1964*
37 **Rhodesia (UDI)**
Formerly named Southern Rhodesia.
Issues *1965-1979*
See Zimbabwe for later issues.
22 **Rhodos** — See Rodi (Aegean Islands).
45 **Riau**
Indonesian Archipelago of Riau-Lingga.
Issues, inscr. Riau *1954-*
34,36 **Rio de Oro**
Spanish Colony 1884, re-named Spanish Sahara 1924 (now part of Morocco)
Issues — See Spanish Sahara for later issues *1905-1924*
34,36 **Rio Muni**
Spanish Colony on the Gulf of Guinea, Province of Spain 1959, and part of the Republic of Equatorial Guinea in 1968, together with the Atlantic island of Fernando Poo.
Issues *1960-1968*
(Stamps of Spanish Guinea used up to 1960). See Equatorial Guinea for later issues.
22 **Rodi (Rhodos)**
Island in the Aegean (Dodecanese) group.
Italian Colonial issues *1912-1935*
20,21 **Romagna**
One of the Roman (Papal) States till 1860.
Provisional issues *1859-1860*
Superseded 1860 by stamps of the Kingdom of Sardinia, and by those of the Kingdom of Italy in 1862.
20 **Roman (Papal) States**
Consisted of the Church States of Latium, Marches, Romagna, and Umbria. States gradually absorbed in the Kingdom of Italy, the last one (Latium) in 1870.
Papal issues *1852-1870*
(Stamps distinguished by the Papal Insignia of Triple Mitre and Crossed Keys, inscr. with stamp value only).
(Stamps of Italy current 1870-1929).
See Vatican City for issues after 1929.
12,13 **Romania**
23 Became a Principality in the Ottoman Empire 1858/1861 by the union of Moldavia and Wallachia, independent Kingdom 1881, enlarged 1918/1920 by the annexation of Bessarabia from Russia and Transylvania (Siebenbürgen) from Austria. Republic in 1947.
Issues of Moldavia (not so inscr.) *1858-1862*
Issues of Moldo-Wallachia (not so inscr.) *1862-1865*
Kingdom of Romania issues *1865-1947*
(early issues inscr. Posta Romana).
Republic issues, inscr. Republica Populara Romana, or Romina. *1948-*
Romania — POs in other countries:
22 *Ottoman Empire, general issues* *1896*
PO at Constantinople, inscr. Constantinopol *1919*
Romania — Occupation issues:
14 Romanian occupation of Hungary:
Bánát Bacska (inscr.), Debreczin, Temesvar, Transylvania.
60 **Ross Dependency**
Antarctic Territory under New Zealand administration since 1923.
Issues *1957-*
14 **Rosswein (Sachsen)**
Germany (GDR), *local town issues* *1946*
48 **Rouad, Île**
French occupation of island off the coast of Syria.
Issues *1916-1920*
13,23 **Roumélie Orientale (Eastern Roumelia)**
Province in the Ottoman Empire, part of the Principality of Bulgaria 1885.
Issues *1880-1884*
(Superseded by stamps of Bulgaria). See Bulgaria.
43,45 **Royaume du Laos** — See Laos.
15 **R.P.E. Shqiperise (People's Republic of Albania).** See Albania.
36 **R.S.A. (Republic of South Africa)** — See South Africa, Republic.
38 **R.S.F.S.R.** — See Russia.
35,37 **Ruanda-Urundi**
Part of German East Africa till 1916, when it came under Belgian administration. The territory of Ruanda declared its independence 1962, name changed to Rwanda in 1982. Burundi an independent Kingdom in 1962, and Republic in 1967.
Issues of Ruanda-Urundi *1916-1962*
Republic issues, *1962-*
inscr. République Rwandaise. See also Burundi.
13 **Ruhleben, Postage**
British POW camp at Ruhleben, Germany.
Semi-official issues *1915*
Rumania — See Romania.
13 **Rumänien (Romania)**
German occupation of Romania.
Issues, some inscr. M.V.i.R. *1917-1918*

14 **Ründeroth**
Germany (FRG), *local town issues* *1945*

12 **Russia**
Empire until the Revolution of 1917. Bolshevist State of the Union of Soviet Socialist Republics (USSR), consolidated by about 1923.
12 *Empire issues* *1855-1917*
38 *Issues of Provisional Government* *1917-1918*
38 *Issues of RSFSR* *1917-1923*
(abbreviation for Russian Soviet Federal Socialist Republic, the largest of the federated Republics).
15 *Issues of the USSR* *1923-*
(inscr. "CCCP"=SSSR).

38 **Russia** — Post-Revolution period:
Northwest Russia *1919*
R.S.F.S.R. *1917-1923*
Siberia (several issues by various authorities in temporary power) *1919-1922*
South Russia (issues by authorities in temporary power) *1918-1920*
38 *Transcaucasian Federation (E.S.F.S.R.)* *1923*
38 *Ukraine (see Ukraine for details)* *1918-1923*
14 *Issues of Russian occupation of southern Lithuania, inscr. Lietuva* *1919*
Issues of Russian refugees *1920-1921*
Russia — POs in other countries:
14 *Wenden* *1863-1901*
District in former Province of Livonia, later Latvia and now in the USSR.
13,23 Crete, *some issues inscr. Retymno* *1899*
See Crete.
39 POs in China, *issues inscr. Kitay* *1899-1920*
22,23 POs in the Ottoman Empire *general issues* *1863-1914*

13 **Russisch-Polen (Russian Poland)**
German occupation of Poland.
Issues *1915*
Superseded by issues inscr. Gen-Gouv. Warschau).

37 **Rwanda**
Part of former Belgian Trust Territory of Ruanda-Urundi (now Burundi). Declared itself independent as the Republic of Rwanda, 1962.
Issues *1962-*
For earlier issues, see Ruanda-Urundi, also Burundi.

41 **Ryukyus**
USA administration of the Japanese Ryukyu Islands, China Sea. Reverted to Japan 1972 *1948-1972*

18 **Saar**
The territory of the Saar has been successively under the administration of France or Germany and has been the scene of two Plebiscites. It is now the German Federal "Land" of Saarland.
Issues under French administration *1920-1935*
French and German issues inscr. Saar or Saargebiet (German), or Sarre (French).
Plebiscite issues *1934*
French occupation issues *1945-1947*
Issues during period of economic attachment to France *1947-1956*
Plebiscite issues *1955*
Issues of Germany (FRG), inscr. Saarland *1957-1959*
(Superseded by regular German "Bundespost" issues from 1959).

12 **Sachsen (Saxony)**
German Kingdom issues *1850-1867*
See Germany, Pre-unification period.

34,36 **Saffi Marakech** — See Maroc, *local issues.*

34,36 **Sahara Espanol** — See Spanish Sahara.

31 **St. Christopher (St. Kitts)**
British Caribbean island in the Leeward Islands.
Issues *1870-1890*
See St. Kitts, Nevis, Anguilla for later issues and political details.

31 **St. Christopher, Nevis, Anguilla** — See St. Kitts-Nevis for details.

63 **St. Helena**
Atlantic island and British Colony 1834, now a British Dependent Territory. Includes the Dependencies of Ascension Island and the island of Tristan da Cunha.
Issues *1856-*

28,29 **St. John's Newfoundland** — See Newfoundland, and Canada.

31 **St. Kitts-Nevis**
British Colony 1623. St. Kitts (or St. Christopher) became a Presidency of the Leeward Islands, together with Nevis and Anguilla in 1871. Anguilla ended its association in 1967 and is now a British Dependent Territory since 1982. St Kitts-Nevis became an independent Commonwealth State in 1983. In 1980, each agreed to have a separate Postal Administration, though remaining one State.
Issues of St. Kitts-Nevis *1903-1951*
Issues of St. Christopher, Nevis, Anguilla *1952-1967*
Issues variously inscr. St. Kitts, Nevis, Anguilla or St. Christopher, Nevis, Anguilla *1967-1980*
Separate issues of St. Kitts *1980-*
Separate issues of Nevis *1980-*
See also Anguilla, Nevis, and St. Christopher.

24 **St. Louis (Missouri, USA)**
Postmaster's Provisional issues *1845-1847*

31 **St. Lucia**
British Colony in the Caribbean, 1814, independent Commonwealth State 1979.
Issues *1860-*

63 **Saint-Pierre et Miquelon**
French island in the Atlantic off the coast of Newfoundland, and an Overseas "Département" (D.O.M.) of France, 1976.
Issues, early ones inscr. S.P.M. *1885-1978*
(Stamps of France current since 1978).

63 **St. Thomas and Prince** — See Sao Tomé and Principe.

31 **St. Vincent**
British possession in the Windward Islands, Caribbean, includes the nearby part of the Grenadine islands belonging to St. Vincent. Independent Commonwealth State of St. Vincent and the Grenadines, 1979.
Issues inscr. St. Vincent *1861-*
Issues inscr. Grenadines of St. Vincent *1973-*

62 **Sainte-Marie de Madagascar**
Small French island off the coast of Madagascar and part of Madagascar, 1900.
Issues *1894-1896*
(Stamps of Madagascar current since 1896).

25 **Salem (Virginia, USA)**
Confederate States of America.
Postmaster's Provisional issues *1861*

22 **Salonicco**
Italian PO at Salonica, now Thessaloniki, Greece.
Issues *1909-1910*

30 **Salvador** — See El Salvador.

57,59 **Samoa**
An independent Kingdom, the islands were divided in 1900 between Germany (western part) and the USA (eastern part). Western Samoa occupied by New Zeland Forces 1914, and New Zealand Mandate 1920-1961, becoming the independent Commonwealth State of Western Samoa, 1970.
Kingdom issues *1877-1899*
German Colonial issues *1900-1915*
New Zealand occupation and Mandate issues, early ones inscr. G.R.I., later Samoa, and Western Samoa. *1914-1961*
Independent West Samoa issues inscr. Samoa i Sisifo. *1962-*

12 **San Marino**
Independent Republic
Issues *1877-*
(Stamps of Sardinia and of Italy used 1862-1877).

48 **Sandjak d'Alexandrette** — See Alexandrette.

32 **Santander**
Colombia, *State issues* *1884-1903*

63 **Sao Tomé and Principe**
Overseas Province of Portugal in the Atlantic, the islands became an independent Republic in 1975.
Issues (Sao Tomé e Principe) *1870-*

43,45 **Sarawak**
Independent State under British protection and Crown Colony 1946-1963, part of Malaysia 1963
Issues *1869-*
Japanese occupation issues *1945*

20 **Sardinia (Sardegna)**
Independent Kingdom, later united to the Kingdom of Italy.
Kingdom issues *1851-1862*
(Stamps of Sardinia temporarily used between 1859 and 1862 in other regions of Italy which were united with the Kingdom of Sardinia at one time or another during that period: Modena, Parma, Romagna, Toscana).

18 **Sarre** — *French inscr. on stamps of the Saar. See Saar.*

14 **Saseno**
Island in the Adriatic occupied by Italy, ceded to Albania 1947 (Sazan Island).
Italian issues *1923*

46,49 **Saudi Arabia**
Formerly the Kingdom of Hedjaz-Nejd, re-named Saudi Arabia 1932.
Issues, some with French inscr. Royaume Arabie Soudite. *1934-*

42 **Saurashtra** — See Soruth (Indian State).

14 **Saverne**
Inscr. on special issue of German occupation of Alsace, France *1944*

12 **Saxony** — See Sachsen.

22 **Scarpanto (Karpathos)**
Island in the Aegean (Dodecanese) Islands.
Italian Colonial issues *1912-1932*

12 **Schleswig, Herzogthum**
Duchy, Germany. Together with the Duchy of Holstein, annexed to Prussia in 1866.
Issues *1865-1867*

19 **Schleswig (Slesvig)**
Plebiscite in North Schleswig held 1920.
Plebiscite issues *1920*

12 **Schleswig-Holstein**
Duchy, Germany. Annexed to Prussia in 1866, together with the Duchy of Holstein. The frequent political changes in the region occasioned by Danish, then Prussian and Austrian occupations are reflected in the variety of postage stamps issued in that period.
Issues *1850-1867*

14 **Schwarzenberg**
Germany (GDR), *local town issues* *1945*

12 **Schweiz** — German form for Switzerland — See Switzerland.

42 **Scinde District Dawk**
Inscr. on issues of the East India Company *1852-1854*

11 **Scotland**
Great Britain, *regional issues — (no inscr.)* *1958-*

22 **Scutari di Albania**
Issues of Italian PO in Albania *1915*

49 **Seiyun, Kathiri State of** — See Aden Protectorate States.

42 **Selangor**
A State in the Federation of Malaya, part of Malaysia, 1963.
Issues — See Malaya, Federated States *1881-1900*

34,36 **Sénégal** *1935-*
French Colony 1817, part of French West Africa (A.O.F.) 1895. With French Sudan, formed the Mali Federation 1959, which ended 1960 when both became separate Republics.
Issues *1887-1944*
(Stamps of AOF used 1944-1959)
Republic issues *1960-*
inscr. République du Sénégal.

34 **Sénégal, Haut** — See Haut-Sénégal, and Niger

34 **Sénégambie et Niger.**
Hinterland territory of Senegal, so-named in period 1902-1904. Formed part of Haut-Sénégal et Niger in 1904.
Issues *1903*

13,14, 23 **Serbia (Srbiya)**
Independent Kingdom 1882 after a stormy history. In 1918 formed part of the union of Serbia, Slovenia, Croatia, Bosnia-Herzegovina and Montenegro, later known as Yugoslavia.
Issues — See Yugoslavia for later issues *1866-1918*

Serbia — Occupations:
13 Serbian occupation of Hungary:
Baranya (inscr.), Temesvar (not inscr.) *1919*
13 *Issues of Austrian occupation of Serbia, inscr. Serbien* *1916*
14 *Issues of German occupation, some inscr. Serbien, or Srbiya (in Cyrillic)* *1941-1943*

62 **Seychelles**
British islands in the Indian Ocean. Colony 1903, independent Republic in the British Commonwealth 1976.
Issues *1890-*
(Stamps of Mauritius used till 1890, with special cancellation)
Separate issues of islands group of Zil Eloigne Sesel (part of the Seychelles) *1980-*

39 **Shanghai**
China, *local issues* *1865-1898*
Issues of USA POs in China *1919-1922*

41 **Shanghai and Nanking**
Japanese occupation issues *1941-1945*

51 **Sharjah**
Sheikhdom in southeastern Arabia, formerly part of the Trucial States, and member of the United Arab Emirates (U.A.E.) 1971.
Issues, some inscr. Sharjah and Dependencies *1963-1971*

49,51 **Shihr and Mukkala, Qu'aiti State of** — See Aden Protectorate States.

13,22 **Shqiperise, Rep. Pop. (People's Republic of Albania)** — See Albania.

13,14 **S.H.S. Država (State, or Kingdom of the Serbs, Croats, Slovenes)**
Inscr. on early issues of the Kingdom *1918*
(later named Yugoslavia), sometimes in Latin alphabet or in Cyrillic, with variants for the different national languages.

42,44 **Siam** — See Thailand.

39 **Siberia** — See Russia.

21 **Sicily (Sicilia)**
Together with the Kingdom of Naples, formed the Kingdom of the Two Sicilies.
Issues *1859-1862*
Superseded 1862 by stamps of the Kingdom of Italy.
See also Naples.

34,36 **Sierra Leone**
British Colony 1787, independent Republic in the British Commonwealth 1971.
Issues *1859-*

19 **Silesia (Schlesien)** — See Haute-Silésie, and Oberschlesien (Upper Silesia).

22 **Simi**
Island in the Aegean (Dodecanese) group.
Italian Colonial issues *1912-1932*

42,44 **Singapore**
British Crown Colony till 1957, autonomous State of Singapore 1958, a State of the Federation of Malaya 1963, seceded 1965 as a separate Commonwealth State.
Issues *1948-*

39,41 **Sinkiang**
Chinese Turkestan.
China, *regional issues* *1915-1949*

42 **Sirmoor (Sirmur)**
Indian State issues *1879-1902*

19 **Slesvig** (Danish form for Schleswig) — See Schleswig, Plebiscite.

17 **Slovakia (Slovensko)**
"Independent" State established by Germany in Slovakia 1939-1945.
Issues, inscr. Slovensko *1939-1945*

14 **Slovenia (Slovenija)**
Italian occupation of Yugoslavia, when Slovenia was annexed to Italy 1941-1943. Occupied by Germany 1943.
Italian occupation issues *1941*
(Stamps of Italy used 1941-1943).
German occupation issues, with various inscr.: Provinz Laibach, Ljubljanska Pokraina *1944-1945*

17 **Slovensko** — See Czechoslovakia.

22 **Smyrna**
Issues of Italian PO in Smyrna (now Izmir, Turkey) *1909-1910*
Issues of German PO *1900-1914*

56,58 **Solomon Islands**
Formerly the British Solomon Islands, independent Commonwealth State 1978.
Issues *1975-*
See British Solomon Islands for earlier issues.

14,15 **Société des Nations (League of Nations)** — See United Nations for issues by Swiss Postal authorities.

35,37 **Somalia**
Territory of Italian Somaliland 1889, included the region of Jubaland (Oltre Giuba) ceded by Kenya to Italy 1925. British Military occupation 1943-1948, Italian Trust Territory 1950-1960, when Somalia became an independent Republic.
Italian Somaliland issues *1903-1936*
early issues inscr. Benadir.
(Stamps of Italian East Africa current 1938-1941).
British occupation issues, inscr. E.A.F. *1943-1948*
British administration issues *1945-1950*
Italian Administration issues *1950-1960*

37 **Somalia, Republic**
Independent Republic 1960, consisting of the former Italian Trust Territory of Somalia (Italian Somaliland) and the British Somaliland Protectorate.
Issues *1960-*

35,37 **Somaliland Protectorate (British Somaliland)** — See British Somaliland.

35,37 **Somaliland, French** — See Côte Française des Somalis, and Djibouti.

30 **Sonora**
Mexico, *Civil War issues* *1913-1914*

42 **Soruth (Saurashtra)**
The Union of Saurashtra included the Indian States of Jasdan, Morvi, Nawanagar, Soruth and Wadhwan.
Indian State issues *1864-1950*

34,36 **Soudan Français (French Sudan)**
French territory first known as Haut-Fleuve, then Soudan Français in 1894, Sénégambie et Niger in 1902, Haut-Sénégal-Niger in 1904, reverting to Soudan Français in 1920. Part of the administration of French West Africa (A.O.F.).
Formed part of the Mali Federation in 1959 by uniting with Senegal. This ended in 1960, Soudan becoming the Republic of Mali, Senegal remaining a separate Republic.
Issues of Soudan Français — See also Mali *1894-1944*

51 **South Arabian Federation** — See Federation of South Arabia.

34 **South Africa (Suidafrika)**
The Union of South Africa was formed in 1910 as a British Dominion by the union of Cape Province (Cape of Good Hope), Natal, Orange Free State, and Transvaal. Republic outside the British Commonwealth 1961.
Issues 1910-1961
Republic issues, some inscr. R.S.A. 1962-

35 **South Africa Company, British** — See Rhodesia.

34 **South African Republic (Z.Afr.Republiek)** — See Transvaal.

52 **South Australia**
British Province 1836, part of the Commonwealth of Australia 1901.
Issues 1855-1911

13,23 **South Bulgaria (Yuzhna Bulgariya)**
Known as Roumélie Orientale (Eastern Roumelia) till 1885, when it became part of the Principality of Bulgaria.
Issues — See Bulgaria for later issues 1885

63 **South Georgia**
One of the Falkland Islands Dependencies.
Issues 1944-1946
1963-

41 **South Korea** — See Korea (South).

61,63 **South Orkneys**
One of the Falkland Islands Dependencies till 1962, when it became part of the British Antarctic Territory.
Issues 1944-1946

61,63 **South Shetlands**
One of the Falkland Islands Dependencies till 1962, when it became part of the British Antarctic Territory.
Issues 1944-1946

34,36 **South West Africa**
Former German Colony 1884-1915, Mandate Territory of the Union (now Republic) of South Africa 1919. Territory also unofficially known as Namibia.
German Colonial issues, (Deutsch-Südwestafrika). 1897-1915
Issues 1923-

50 **South Yemen** — See Yemen (South) (PDRY).

34 **Southern Nigeria**
Part of the Colony of Nigeria by the merging of Northern and Southern Nigeria and Lagos.
Issues 1901-1914
See also Niger Coast Protectorate, and Nigeria.

35,37 **Southern Rhodesia** — See Rhodesia, Rhodesia and Nyasaland, Rhodesia (UDI), and Zimbabwe.

12,38,40 **Soviet Union** — See Russia.

12 **Spain (España)**
Kingdom till 1873, Republic 1873-1875, Kingdom 1875-1931, Republic 1931-1939, Civil War 1936-1939, National State 1938, Monarchy 1975.
Kingdom issues 1850-1867
Issues of Revolutionary Government 1868-1870
Kingdom issues 1872-1873
Republic issues 1873-1875
Issues of Carlist (Royalist) authorities (northern Spain) 1873-1874
Kingdom issues 1875-1931
Republic issues 1931-1939
National State issues 1936-
(continued through to the present Monarchy period).
Spain — Overseas Colonies and Territories:
(see individual entries for details)
36 *Cape Juby (Cabo Juby, or Jubi)* 1916-1948
30 *Cuba and Puerto Rico, general issues* 1855-1871
30 *Cuba* 1871-1898
34 *Elobey, Annabon and Corisco* 1903-1909
34 *Fernando Poo* 1868-1929
36 *Ifni* 1941-1969
36 *La Aguëra* 1920-1923
56 *Mariana Islands (Marianas Española)* 1899
43 *Philippines (Filipinas)* 1854-1898
30 *Puerto Rico* 1873-1898
34,36 *Rio de Oro (later Spanish Sahara* 1905-1924
34,36 *Rio Muni* 1960-1968
34 *Spanish Guinea (Guinea Español)* 1902-1959
34,36 *Spanish Morocco (Marruecos)* 1914-1955
34,36 *Spanish Sahara (Sahara Español, formerly Rio de Oro)* 1924-1976
34,36 *Spanish West Africa (Africa Occidental Española)* 1949-1951
Spain — POs in other countries:
34,36 *Morocco (Marruecos)* 1903-1914
34 *Tetuan (Morocco)* 1908

34,36 **Spanish Guinea (Guinea Española)**
Spanish Colony 1900. Together with the Atlantic island of Fernando Poo, Rio Muni and other mainland areas, became the independent Republic of Equatorial Guinea in 1968.
Issues, inscr. Guinea Española, or Golfo de Guinea 1902-1959
See Equatorial Guinea for later issues.

34,36 **Spanish Morocco Protectorate**
Spanish Protectorate 1914-1956, part of the independent Kingdom of Morocco, 1956.
Issues 1914-1955

34,36 **Spanish Sahara (Sahara Español)**
Formerly named Rio de Oro, re-named 1924, Spanish sovereignty ended 1976 and territory divided between Morocco and Mauritania, the latter ceding its area to Morocco 1979.
Issues 1924-1976
Joint issues for Spanish Sahara and Ifni, inscr. Africa Occidental Española 1949-1951

42 **Spartanburg (S. Carolina, USA)**
Confederate States of America,
Postmaster's Provisional issues 1861

63 **S.P.M.**
Inscr. for St. Pierre et Miquelon.

13,14,23 **Srbija** — See Serbia.

44 **Sri Lanka**
Former British Colony of Ceylon, independent Commonwealth State 1948, Republic 1972 and re-named Sri Lanka.
Issues — See Ceylon for earlier issues 1972-

22 **Stampalia (Astypalaia)**
Island in the Aegean (Dodecanese) group.
Italian Colonial issues 1912-1932

34 **Stellaland**
African territory annexed by Great Britain 1884, later part of Bechuanaland (now Botswana).
Issues — See Bechuanaland for later issues 1884

14 **Storkow**
Germany (GDR), *local town issues* 1946

42 **Straits** Settlements — See Malaya.

14 **Strausberg**
Germany (GDR), *local town issues* 1945-1946

16 **S.T.T. V.U.J.A. or S.T.Trsta V.U.J.A. (Vojna Uprava Jugoslovenske Armije)**
Inscr. on Yugoslav Military Government issues for Istria 1948-1954

35 **Suaheliland** — See Witu (German Protectorate).

35,37 **Sudan**
Anglo-Egyptian Condominium 1899-1955, self-Government 1954, independent Republic 1956.
Condominium issues 1897-1954
(early issues inscr. in French: Soudan).
Self-Government issues 1954-1956
Republic issues 1956-

14, 16,17 **Sudentenland**
Region of Czechoslovakia annexed by Germany 1938, return to Czech sovereignty 1945. Some local unofficial stamp issues were made in 1938 by the towns of: Asch, Aussig, Karlsbad, Konstantinsbad, Niklasdorf, Reichenberg-Maffersdorf, Rumburg.
Regular stamps of Germany otherwise used 1938-1945.

34 **Südwestafrika** — See South West Africa.

23 **Suez Canal Company (Canal Maritime de Suez)**
Issues 1868

34 **Suid-Afrika** — See South Africa.

34 **Suidwes Afrika** — See South West Africa.

12 **Suisse** — French form for Switzerland. See Switzerland.

42 **Sungei Ujong**
Territory in Malaya incorporated in the State of Negri Sembilan 1895, now part of Malaysia.
Issues 1876-1895
See Negri Sembilan, and Malaya for later issues.

13 **Suomi** — See Finland.

33 **Surinam (Suriname)**
Former Colony of Dutch Guiana and part of the Netherlands West Indies. Independent State 1975.
Issues, inscr. Suriname 1873-

12 **Sverige** — See Sweden.

34 **S.W.A.** — See South West Africa.

34,36 **Swaziland**
Territory under joint protection of Great Britain and the South African Republic (Transvaal), became a British Protectorate 1906. Independent Kingdom in the British Commonwealth, 1968.
Issues 1889-

12 **Sweden (Sverige)**
Kingdom, to which the Kingdom of Norway was united till 1905.
Issues 1855-

12 **Switzerland**
Cantonal and local issues:
Basel *1845-1850*
Genève (Geneva) *1843-1850*
Zürich *1843-1850*
Federal Post issues, inscr. Helvetia from 1862, *1850-*
also Confoederatio Helvetica.
See United Nations for Swiss issues of various international offices of the U.N.

46,48, 50 **Syria (Syrie)**
Formerly a Province in the Ottoman Empire, occupied and under French Mandate 1919, Republic under French Mandate 1926, and an independent Republic 1942. Merged with Egypt 1958 to form the United Arab Republic (UAR), which was dissolved Dec. 1961.
French occupation issues, *1919-1923*
inscr. T.E.O., and O.M.F.
Arab Kingdom issues *1920*
French Mandate issues, *1923-1933*
some inscr. Syrie Grand Liban.
Issues of Republic under French Mandate *1934-1942*
Independent Republic issues *1942-1958*
Issues when part of the UAR *1958-1961*
Syrian Arab issues *1961-*

41 **Szechwan**
China, *regional issues* *1933-1934*

14 **Szegedin**
Town in Hungary and seat of the National Government established during the temporary Bolshevist regime after the 1914-1918 war. The National Government took over central Government later in 1919.
"Szegedin" issues *1919-1921*

57 **Tahiti**
Principal island of the Établissements Français de l'Océanie (French Pacific Settlements, now French Polynesia).
Issues *1882-1915*
See also Océanie, Établissements Français.

39,41 **Taiwan**
Previously named Formosa.
Issues inscr. Republic of China *1945-*
See also Formosa.

35,37 **Tanganyika**
Formerly German East Africa (Deutsch-Ostafrika), British occupation 1915 and Mandate 1920. Independent Commonwealth Republic Dec. 1962, united with Zanzibar Dec. 1963 and State re-named Tanzania.
Issues *1915-1931*
Independent States issues *1961-1964*
See Deutsch-Ostafrika for earlier issues, and Kenya, Uganda and Tanganyika for later ones, and Tanzania for issues 1965-.

34 **Tanger**
First part of composite name inscr. for local issues of Maroc (Morocco):
Arzila, Elksar, Fez, Laraiche *1891-1912*

36 **Tanger (Tangier)**
International Zone of Tangier set up 1923, occupied by Spain 1940-1945, International Zone 1945-1956.
British issues, inscr. Tanger *1927-1957*

39,40 **Tannu Tuva (Touva)**
Part of Outer Mongolia, Russian occupation 1914-1919, independent Republic 1928-1944, now part of the USSR.
Issues *1926-1944*

37 **Tanzania**
Independent Commonwealth Republic of Tanganyika 1962, united with Zanzibar 1964 and country re-named Tanzania.
Issues — See Tanganyika for earlier issues *1965-*

52 **Tasmania**
Formerly named Van Diemen's Land and a British Colony in Australia 1825, a State in the Commonwealth of Australia 1901.
Issues *1853-1913*
(early issues inscr. Van Diemen's Land).

34,36 **Tchad (Chad)**
French military territory of Africa, attached to Oubangui-Chari 1905 (to become Oubangui-Chari-Tchad), autonomous 1920 within French Equatorial Africa (AEF), independent Republic 1960.
Issues *1922-1937*
(Stamps of AEF used 1937-1958).
Republic issues, inscr. République du Tchad *1959-*

39 **Tchong-King**
Issues of French PO in China *1903-1922*

25 **Tellico Plains (Tennessee, USA)**
Confederate States of America,
Postmaster's Provisional issues *1861*

22 **Telos (Episkopi)**— See Piscopi (Aegean Islands).

60 **Terres Australes et Antarctiques Françaises**
French Antarctic Territory (Adélie Land)
Issues *1955-*

62 **Territoire des Comores** — See Comoros.

35,37 **Territoire Français des Afars et Issas**
Formerly French Somaliland (Côte Française des Somalis) and re-named 1967, independent Republic of Djibouti in 1977.
Issues *1967-1977*
See Côte Française des Somalis for earlier issues, and Djibouti for later ones.

34 **Territoire du Niger** — See Niger.

35 **Tete**
Portuguese possession and district of Mozambique.
Separate stamp issues *1913-1920*

34 **Tetouan-Chechouan (or Sheshuan)** and **Tetouan a El'Ksar**
Morocco (Maroc), *local issues* *1891-1912*

34 **Tetuan**
Issues of Spanish PO in Morocco *1908*

42,44 **Thailand (Siam)**
Kingdom of Siam, re-named Thailand in 1939, reverting to the name of Siam during the period 1945-1949.
Issues *1883-*
Issues of Japanese occupation of Malaya *1943*
(used in the Malay States of Kedah, Kelantan, Perlis and Trengganu which were ceded to Thailand by Japan in 1943, these reverting to British rule 1945).

17 **Theresienstadt**
Town of Terezin in Czechoslovakia, in the then German "Protectorate" of Bohemia and Moravia, with German war-time prison camp.
Local German issues for ingoing parcel mail only *1943*

23 **Thessaly**
Region of Thessalia, Greece, occupied by Turkey during the Greek-Turkish war of 1898.
Turkish occupation issues *1898*

23 **Thrace**
Region part of Bulgaria 1913, with temporary autonomous Government of Western Thrace, annexed to Greece 1919/1920.
Issues of autonomous Government of Western Thrace *1913*
Greek occupation issues *1920*

12 **Thurn und Taxis**
German Principality made responsible at the Congress of Vienna in 1815 for the conveyance of mail in many of the smaller German States, a traditional duty already existing in the old German Reich. The Thurn und Taxis postal rights were sold to Prussia in 1867.
Issues *1852-1867*

38,40 **Tibet**
Previously under Chinese rule, autonomous Theocracy 1912, re-occupied by China 1950.
Issues *1912-1950*
Issues of Chinese POs in Tibet, with POs at Lhasa, Gyantse, Phari Jong Shigatse, Yatung *1911*

39 **Tientsin**
Issues of Italian PO at Tientsin, China *1918*

32 **Tierra del Fuego**
Chile, *special local issue* *1891*

43,45 **Timor**
Eastern part of the island of Timor a Portuguese Colony 1586, later an Overseas Territory of Portugal till 1975. Part of Indonesia 1976, re-named Loro Sae.
Issues *1885-1975*

31 **Tobago**
British Caribbean possession 1814 and with the island of Trinidad came under one administration in 1889.
Issues *1879-1896*
(Stamps of Trinidad used 1896-1913).
See Trinidad and Tobago for later issues.

56,58 **Toga** — See Tonga.

34,36 **Togo**
German Colony 1884-1914, Anglo-French occupation and administration 1914-1922. The western (British) part was attached to the Gold Coast (now Ghana). The French sector became autonomous 1956, and an independent Republic 1960.
German Colonial issues *1897-1914*
British-French occupation issues *1914-1921*
French Mandate issues *1921-1956*
Republic issues *1957-*
(République du Togo, or Togolaise)

58,59 **Tokelau Islands**
Also known as the Union Islands, formerly part of the Gilbert and Ellice Islands, and part of New Zealand 1949.
Issues *1948-*

32 **Tolima**
Colombia, *States issues* *1870-1903*

56,58 **Tonga (Toga)**
Group of Pacific islands forming a Kingdom, under British protection 1900, autonomous Kingdom in the British Commonwealth 1970.
Issues *1886-*

20 **Toscana** — See Tuscany (Italy).

39,40 **Touva** — See Tannu Tuva.

38 **Transcaucasian Federation**
Federation of the Soviet Republics of Armenia, Azerbaidzhan and Georgia established 1922, and later absorbed in the USSR 1923.
Issues, inscr. E.S.F.S.R. (Cyrillic) *1923*

48 **Transjordan** — See Jordan.

36 **Transkei**
"Homeland" Republic formed 1976 within the Republic of South Africa.
Issues *1977-*

34 **Transvaal**
Former Boer South African Republic, annexed by Great Britain 1877, reverted to the Boers 1881, annexed again by Great Britain 1900/1902, a Province of the Union of South Africa 1910.
First (Boer) Republic issues, inscr. Z. Afr. Republiek. *1869-1877*
Issues of first British occupation, inscr. Transvaal. *1877-1882*
Second (Boer) Republic (Z. Afr. Republiek) *1882-1900*
Second British occupation, issues, inscr. Transvaal. *1900-1909*
Local unofficial issues were current 1901-1902.

42 **Travancore**
Indian State issues *1888-1949*

42 **Travancore-Cochin**
Indian State issues *1949-1950*

42 **Trengganu**
Former Sultanate tributary to Siam till 1909, a State of the Federation of Malaya, and part of Malaysia 1963.
Issues *1910-*

16,17 **Trieste**
Part of Austria up to 1918, to Italy 1919/1920, Free Territory under Allied Military Government 1947-1954, city reverted to Italy 1954.
Italian issues, some inscr. Venezia Giulia. *1918-1919*
Provisional Yugoslav occupation issues, some inscr. Trst,Istra. *1945*
Issues of Free Territory, Zone A, Allied Military Government, inscr. AMG FTT (Allied Military Govt., Free Territory of Trieste) — comprising the city and the Istrian Peninsula. *1947-1954*
Issues of Yugoslav Military Government, 1948-1954 Zone B, inscr. STT VUJA, or ST Trsta VUJA (Vojna Uprava Jugoslovenske Armije).
For earlier issues of this region, see Venezia Giulia and Istria (1945-1947).

31 **Trinidad**
Former Spanish possession, British in 1802.
Issues *1847-1913*
(first issue inscr. "L.Mc.L"=Lady Mc.Leod).
See Trinidad and Tobago for later issues.

31 **Trinidad and Tobago**
The islands came under one administration in 1889. Part of the British Caribbean Federation 1958 to 1962, when it became independent in the British Commonwealth, and a Republic in 1976.
Issues of Trinidad and Tobago *1913-*

35 **Tripoli di Barberia**
Issues of Italian PO at Tripoli (Libya) *1910*

37 **Tripolitania**
Part of the Ottoman Empire till 1912, Italian possession 1912-1943/1947, incorporated in Libya 1951.
Italian Colonial issues *1923-1935*
British Military and Civil Administration issues *1948-1951*

63 **Tristan da Cunha**
Part of island group in the Atlantic, British Colony 1816, a Dependency of St. Helena 1938.
Issues *1952-1961*
1963-

16,17 **Trst** — See Trieste.

39 **Tsingtau** — See Kiautschou (China).

13,23 **Tsrna Gora** — See Montenegro.

34,36 **Tunisie (Tunisia)**
French Protectorate 1881-1955, independent Kingdom 1956, Republic in 1957.
French Protectorate issues *1888-1957*
Kingdom issues *1957*
Republic issues — (République Tunisienne) *1957-*

12,22, 23,35 **Turkey**
Ottoman Empire issues, some with French inscr. Empire Ottoman, or Postes Ottomanes *1863-1921*
Issues of Turkish Nationalist Government at Angora (now Ankara) *1920-1923*
Republic issues, inscr. Turkiye Cumhuriyeti *1923-*

Turkey — Foreign POs in the Ottoman Empire:
See details under: Austria, France, Germany, Great Britain, Italy, Poland, Romania, Russia.

23 **Turkey**
Issues of Turkish occupation of Thessaly (Greece) during the Greek-Turkish war of 1898. *1898*

30 **Turks and Caicos Islands**
British Colony, now a Dependent Territory.
Issues of Turks Islands *1867-1900*
Issues of Turks and Caicos Islands *1900-*

20 **Tuscany (Toscana)**
Grand Duchy in Italy, later incorporated in the kingdom of Italy.
Grand Duchy issues *1851-1860*
Provisional Government issues *1860-1861*
Superseded 1861 by stamps of the Kingdom of Sardinia, and those of Italy in 1962.

58 **Tuvalu**
Formerly the Ellice group of the British Protectorate of the Gilbert and Ellice Islands, separated from the Gilberts in 1975, and independent Commonwealth State 1978, re-named Tuvalu.
Issues *1976-*
See Gilbert and Ellice Islands for earlier issues.

51 **U.A.E.** — See United Arab Emirates.

37,50 **U.A.R.** — See United Arab Republic; also Egypt, and Syria.

35,37 **Uganda**
British Protectorate 1894/1896, independent 1962, and Republic in the British Commonwealth 1967.
Issues of Uganda Protectorate *1895-1902*
(Issues of Kenya, Uganda and Tanganyika used 1903-1962)
Independent States issues *1962*

38 **Ukraine**
Formed a separate (temporary) Republic after the Russian Revolution of 1917.
Issues, inscr. Ukrains'ka Narodnya Respublika (in Cyrillic) *1918-1923*
Several local and regional stamps were issued in that period, variously inscr.

14 **Ukraine**
German occupation issues *1941-1943*
Local German issues were also made:
BALEX (abbreviation for region of Bolshaya Alexandrovka), Sarny, Wosnessensk — among many others, some being hand-stamped.

51 **Umm al Qaiwain (Umm al Qiwain)**
Formerly one of the Trucial States in Arabia, formed part of the United Arab Emirates (UAE) in 1971.
Issues, inscr. Umm al Qiwain *1964-1967*

42,43 **Union of Burma** — See Burma.

34,36 **Union of South Africa** — See Cape of Good Hope, and South Africa, Republic.

25 **Uniontown (Alabama, USA)**
Confederate States of America,
Postmaster's Provisional issues *1861*

25 **Unionville (S. Carolina, USA)**
Confederate States of America,
Postmaster's Provisional issues *1861*

51 **United Arab Emirates (UAE)**
A State, being a union of the former Trucial States of: Abu Dhabi, Ajman, Dubai, Fujairah, Ras al Khaimah, Sharjah, and Umm al Qaiwain (Umm al Qiwain), formed 1971/1972.
Issues *1973-*
Issues of Manama, Dependent Territory of the State of Ajman *1966-1972*

37,50 **United Arab Republic (UAR)**
Union of the States of Egypt and Syria, 1958, the union dissolved Dec. 1961.
See Egypt and Syria for issues during that period.

14 **United Nations**
Stamps were issued by the Postal authorities of Switzerland for the former League of Nations offices located at Geneva from 1922 to 1944 and cancelled for collectors only. Valid postal issues were made 1944-1946, and inscr. Helvetia, plus Société des Nations (abbreviated S.d.N.) and later Courrier de la Société des Nations (League of Nations Mail).

15 **United Nations**
Issues of the U.N. offices at Geneva for numerous United Nations' Organizations, variously inscr. *1969-*

15 **United Nations**
Issues of the U.N. offices at Vienna, inscr. Vereinte Nationen *1979-*

27 **United Nations Postal Administration**
Established at New York 1950 for mail posted at the U.N. Headquarters at New York.
Issues, variously inscr.: *1951-*
Naciones Unidas (Spanish).
Nations Unies (French).
Ob'edinennye Natsii (Russian) (Cyrillic).
United Nations.

24,25 **United States of America**
26,27 *Postmaster's Provisional issues at the following towns:* *1845-1847*
Alexandria (Va), Annapolis (Md), Boscawen (N.H.), Brattleboro (Vt), Lockport (N.Y.), Millbury (Mass), New Haven (Ct), New York (N.Y.), Providence (R.I.), St. Louis (Miss), Tuscumbia (Ala).
General issues, inscr. US Post Office or US Postage *1847-*
Issues of the Confederate States of America (Civil War 1861-1865) *1861*
See Confederate States of America.
Confederate States, general issues *1861-1865*
Superseded after 1865 by general issues of the USA.

United States of America — POs in other countries and areas of USA administration:

27,30 *Canal Zone (Panama Canal Zone)* *1904-1979*
43 *China (Shanghai)* *1919-1922*
30 *Cuba* *1899-1902*
56,58 *Guam (USA stamps current)* *1899*
Local postal service *1930*
26,57,58 *Hawaii (USA stamps current 1899-)*
43,45 *Philippines — USA administration issues* *1899-1935*
USA Commonwealth issues *1935-1946*
27,30 *Puerto Rico (USA stamps current)* *1899-1900*

54 **U.N.T.E.A.** — *Inscr. on stamps of the UN Administration of West New Guinea. See Netherlands New Guinea.*

19 **Upper Silesia** — See Oberschlesien.

34,36 **Upper Volta** — See Haute-Volta (now Burkina).

51 **Upper Yafa**
Sultanate formerly part of the West Aden Protectorate, independent for a short time in 1967, incorporated in the Republic of Yemen (South) (PDRY) in 1967.
Issues, inscr. State of Upper Yafa *1967*

33 **Uruguay**
Formerly known as Banda Oriental, Republic 1825.
Issues *1856-*

14,38, 39,40 **U.S.S.R.** — See Russia.

14 **Vallées d'Andorre** — See Andorra.

22 **Valona**
Issues of Italian PO in Vlora, Albania *1915*

28 **Vancouver Island**
Became a part of British Columbia, Canada, in 1866, itself part of the Dominion of Canada, 1871.
Issues of British Columbia and Vancouver Island *1860-1865*
Issues of Vancouver Island *1865*

52 **Van Diemen's Land**
Inscr. on early issues of Tasmania, Australia. See Australia.

56,58 **Vanuatu**
Formerly the Anglo-French Condominium of the New Hebrides (Nouvelles Hébrides), now an independent Republic in the British Commonwealth since 1980.
Issues *1980-*
See New Hebrides for earlier issues.

22 **Vathy**
Chief locality on the Aegean island of Samos.
Issues of French PO *1893-1914*

14 **Vatican City**
20 *Issues, inscr. Poste Vaticane* *1929-*
For issues 1852-1870, see Roman (Papal) States, and Italy for issues 1870-1929.

17 **Veglia**
Inscr. on some issues of Fiume (Free City). See Fiume.

36 **Venda**
"Homeland" Republic formed 1979 within the Republic of South Africa.
Issues *1979-*

16,17 **Venezia Giulia**
21 Formerly part of Austria (Julische Venetien), to Italy 1919/1920.
Italian issues for areas acquired from Austria, some inscr. Trieste *1918-1919*

16,17 **Venetia Giulia and Istria**
21 Italian Province of Istria ceded to Yugoslavia in 1947.
Allied Military Government issues, inscr. AMG VG. *1945-1947*
Yugoslav provisional issues, some inscr. Istra, or Trst, among others. *1945*
Yugoslav Military Government issues, some inscr. Istria, or VUJA. *1945-1947*
Yugoslav issues, inscr. STT VUJA, or ST Trsta VUJA. *1948-1954*

21 **Venezia Tridentina (South Tyrol)**
Part of Austria (Südtirol) till 1919/1920, when it was annexed to Italy.
Issues, some inscr. Trentino *1918*

32 **Venezuela**
Independent Republic 1830.
Issues *1859-*

Vereinte Nationen — German form for United Nations.

52 **Victoria**
British Colony in Australia 1851, and part of the Commonwealth of Australia, 1901
Issues *1850-1912*

25 **Victoria (Texas, USA)**
Confederate States of America,
Postmaster's Provisional issues *1861*

60 **Victoria Land**
In the New Zealand Antarctic Ross Dependency.
Special issues for Capt. Scott's expedition to the South Pole, 1910-1913 *1911*

45 **Vietnam**
Comprising the former Indochinese States of Tonkin, Annam and Cochinchina, it became the State of Viet-Nam within the French Community in 1946.
Following years of conflict, was divided into North and South Vietnam in 1954, and after the 1961-1973 war involving the USA, became united as one Republic in 1975/1978.
Issues inscr. Viet-Nam *1945-1959*
Issues of South Vietnam *1955-1975*
Issues of North Vietnam *1946-*
Special issues of the National Front for the Liberation of South Vietnam *1963-1976*

14 **Vilnius**
Inscr. on German occupation issues of Lithuania *1941*

31 **Virgin Islands, British** — See British Virgin Islands.

31 **Virgin Islands, USA**
Formerly the Danish West Indies (Dansk-Vestindien), purchased by the USA in 1917.
Stamps of the USA current since then. See Danish West Indies for pre-1917 issues.

16,17 **Vojna Uprava Jugoslovenske Armije (V.U.J.A.)**
Inscr. on issues of the Yugoslav Military Administration in Venezia Giulia and Istria *1945-1947*

34 **Volta, Haute** — See Haute-Volta.

34 **Vryburg**
Issues of temporary Boer occupation, Cape of Good Hope. See Cape of Good Hope. *1899*

42 **Wadhwan**
Part of the Union of Saurashtra, 1948.
Indian State issues *1888-1892*

11 **Wales and Monmouthshire**
Regional issues of Great Britain (no inscr.) *1958-*

56,58 **Wallis et Futuna**
Part of the French islands group of New Caledonia (Nouvelle Calédonie) in the Pacific. Wallis et Futuna became an Overseas Territory of France, 1961.
Issues — See also New Caledonia *1920-*

13 **Warschau, Gen.-Gouv.**
Inscr. on German occupation issues of Poland (Warsaw) *1916*

12,14 **Wenden**
District of Wenden in the Province of Livonia, later Latvia.
Russian issues *1863-1901*

52 **Western Australia**
British Settlement 1829, a State of the Commonwealth of Australia, 1901.
Issues *1854-1912*

57,59 **Western Samoa**
Inscr. on New Zealand occupation and Mandate of West Samoa — See also Samoa *1935-1961*

35 **Witu-Schutzgebiet (Suaheliland Protectorate)**
Sultanate of Suaheli, a German Protectorate 1885-1890.
Issues *1889*

12 **Württemberg**
German Kingdom, part of the Kingdom of Germany, 1871.
Württemberg maintained its own Postal Administration till 1920.
Kingdom issues *1851-1918*
Republic issues (Volksstaat) *1919-1923*
French occupation issues *1947-1949*

32 **Yca**
Peru, *local provisional issues* *1884*

49,50 **Yemen (North)**
Kingdom till 1967, became the Yemen Arab Republic (YAR).
Kingdom issues *1926-1962*
Royalist issues ("Free Yemen") *1962-1967*
Republic issues *1963-*

49,50 **Yemen (South)**
Independent State 1967, consisting of the former British Colony of Aden and Aden Protectorate States. First named People's Republic of Southern Yemen, re-named People's Democratic Republic (PDRY) in 1970.
Issues *1968-*

13,14, 23 **Yugoslavia**
Kingdom of the Serbs, Croats and Slovenes established 1918 by the union of Serbia, Croatia, Slovenia, Bosnia-Herzegovina and Montenegro. Re-named Yugoslavia, 1929. Became a Republic in 1945.
Independent Kingdom issues *1918-1941*
(early issues with a variety of inscr., including Kraljestvo S.H.S., Kraljevina Jugoslavija, some in Latin and others in Cyrillic).
Issues of Royal Government in Exile during occupation by Germany and Italy *1941-1945*
Republic issues *1945-*
For earlier issues, see Bosnia-Herzegovina, Montenegro, and Serbia.
Yugoslavia — Regional and special issues:
Croatia, inscr. N.D.Hrvatska, with variants *1941-1945*
Montenegro, Italian and German occupation *1941-1945*
(some inscr. Tsrna Gora).
Serbia, German occupation issues *1941-1943*
(inscr. Serbien, or Srbiya).
Slovenia, Italian occupation issues *1941*
(annexed to Italy 1941, stamps of Italy used 1941-1943).
German occupation issues *1944-1945*
(inscr. Provinz Laibach, or Ljubljanska Pokrajina).

39 **Yunnan Province**
China, *regional issues* *1926-1934*

39 **Yunnanfou**
China, *French PO issues, some inscr. Yunnansen* *1903-1922*

13,23 **Yuzhna Bulgariya** — See South Bulgaria.

34 **Z. Afr. Republiek (South African Republic)**
— See Transvaal.

36 **Zaïre**
Former Belgian Congo, independent Republic 1960, country re-named Zaïre 1971.
Issues *1971-*
See Congo (Léopoldville, or Kinshasa) for earlier issues.

35 **Zambezia**
Territory of former Portuguese East Africa and later known as Quelimane, now in Mozambique.
Issues *1894-1914*

37 **Zambia**
Formerly Northern Rhodesia, independent Commonwealth State 1964.
Issues *1964-*
For earlier issues, see Northern Rhodesia, also Rhodesia, and Nyasaland.

14,23 **Zante (Zakynthos)**
Island in the Ionian Sea (Greece).
Italian occupation issues *1941-1943*
German occupation 1943, Italian stamps still used).

35,37 **Zanzibar**
British Protectorate 1890 following a territorial exchange with Germany for the British island of Heligoland, North Sea. Independent within the British Commonwealth and united to Tanganyika, 1963, forming the new State of Tanzania.
Issues *1895-1963*

35 **Zanzibar**
Issues of French PO at Zanzibar *1894-1904*

17,21 **Zara (Zadar)**
Town on Adriatic, formerly Austrian, to Italy 1919-1920, and again 1943-1947, ceded to Yugoslavia 1947 and town re-named Zadar.
German occupation issues *1943-1944*

62 **Zil Eloigne Sesel**
Group of islands part of the Seychelles (Indian Ocean), with separate stamp issues.
Issues, also inscr. Zil Elwannyen Sesel, or other spellings *1980-*

37 **Zimbabwe**
Independent Commonwealth State, previously Rhodesia (UDI) and Southern Rhodesia.
Issues *1980-*
For earlier issues, see Rhodesia (UDI), and Southern Rhodesia.

15 **Zone Française (French Zone)** — See Germany.

34 **Zululand**
Annexed to Natal 1897, and later part of the Union of South Africa 1910.
Issues *1888-1898*

12 **Zürich**
Local Swiss city and Canton issues *1843-1850*
Superseded by Swiss Federal Post stamps, 1850.

UNITED NATI

COLLECT

SERVICES

NATIONS UNIES

7c

ОБЪЕДИНЕН

OCT 10

11 AM